上海高水平地方高校创新团队“一带一路建设的法律保障机制研究”项目

Landmark Cases
on EU Competition Law Vol.4

欧盟竞争法经典案例（第4辑）

（中英对照）

林燕萍 编译

法律出版社
LAW PRESS·CHINA

案例中涉及的欧盟法律法规中英文对照表

序号	中文简称	中文全称	英文全称
1	《欧共体条约》	《关于建立欧洲共同体的条约》	Treaty establishing the European Community
2	《欧盟运行条约》	《欧洲联盟运行条约》	Treaty on the Functioning of the European Union
3	《欧盟基本权利宪章》	《欧洲联盟基本权利宪章》	The Charter of Fundamental Rights of The European Union
4	《消费者健康保护法》	《关于食品和其他商品的消费者健康保护法》	Law on the protection of consumer health in relation to foodstuffs and other goods
5	《欧盟法院规约》	《欧洲联盟法院规约》	Statute of the Court of Justice of the European Union
6	《欧盟法院程序规则》	《欧盟联盟法院程序规则》	Rules of Procedure of the Court
7	《第2011/64/EU号指令》	《关于烟草制品的消费税结构和税率的第2011/64/EU号指令》	Council Directive 2011/64/EU of 21 June 2011 on the structure and rates of excise duty applied to manufactured tobacco
8	《欧盟条约》	《欧洲联盟条约》	the Treaty on European Union

续表

序号	中文简称	中文全称	英文全称
9	《第1/2003号条例》	《关于实施〈欧共体条约〉第81条、第82条的第1/2003号条例》	Council Regulation No 1/2003 of 16 December 2002 on the implementation of the rules on competition laid down in Articles 81 [EC] and 82 [EC]
10	《2006年罚款指南》	《关于依据〈第1/2003号条例〉第23条第2款a项设定罚款方法的指南》	Guidelines on the method of setting fines imposed pursuant to Article 23 (2)(a) of Regulation (EC) No 1/2003
11	《欧共体初审法院司法常务官工作指南》	《欧洲共同体初审法院司法常务官工作指南》	the Instructions to the Registrar of the Court of First Instance of the European Communities
12	《指南文件》	《关于适用〈欧共体条约〉第82条查处占有支配地位企业滥用行为的执法重点指南》	Guidance on the Commission's enforcement priorities in applying Article 82 of the EC Treaty to abusive exclusionary conduct by dominant undertakings
13	《合作公告》	《关于与成员国竞争主管机构合作的公告》	Commission Notice on Cooperation with the Network of Competition Authorities
14	《宽恕公告》	《关于卡特尔案件罚款免除和减轻公告》	Notice on Immunity from fines and reduction of fines in cartel cases

主要专业名词中英文对照表

序号	英文	中文
1	a preliminary ruling	先行裁决
2	Model Leniency Programme	宽恕政策范本
3	unlimited jurisdiction	罚款数额自由裁量权① （罚款数额决定权、改判罚款数额裁量权）
4	Summary application for immunity	简易豁免申请
5	the main application for immunity	主豁免申请
6	the cooperation mechanism	合作机制
7	the relevant market	相关市场
8	shares of the relevant market	市场份额
9	dissuasive effect	劝诫效果
10	'driving forces' of the cartel	卡特尔推动者（卡特尔领头羊）
11	the principles of proportionality and equal treatment	比例原则和平等待遇原则
12	counterclaim	反诉
13	commercial autonomy	商业自主性
14	a failure to provide reasons	未尽说理义务

① 欧盟法赋予欧盟各级法院对罚款数额享有自由裁量权（unlimited jurisdiction），初审法院和欧盟法院都有权改变欧盟委员会的罚款决定，但这种权限是有严格限制的。尽管初审法院和欧盟法院的这种罚款裁量权在欧盟法上都称为"unlimited jurisdiction"，但权限是有一些区别的，所以本书将两者区别开来，初审法院享有的是"罚款数额决定权"，而欧盟法院享有的是"改判罚款数额裁量权"，这种权利统称为"罚款数额自由裁量权"。——译者注

续表

序号	英文	中文
15	a double error of law	法律适用上的双重错误
16	unfounded	毫无依据
17	decisive influence	决定性影响
18	to be reversed	推翻（既定推论）
19	assessments of a factual nature	事实评估
20	a single economic entity	单一经济体
21	total turnover in the preceding business year	年度营业总额
22	monetary fluctuations	汇率波动
23	ceiling of the fine	罚款上限
24	a statement of objections	异议声明
25	the General Court	初审法院
26	European Economic Area（EEA）	欧洲经济区
27	time-barred	丧失时效
28	personal responsibility	个人责任原则
29	interveners	介入诉讼人
30	National competition authorities	成员国竞争主管机构

目录
CONTENTS

1

意大利敦豪快递有限责任公司等诉意大利竞争与市场管理局等

[DHL Express (Italy) S.r.l. and Others v Autorità Garante della Concorrenza e del Mercato and Others]

(*C-428/14, 2016*)

案例导读*

一、案例基本信息

法院	欧盟法院		
提请法院	意大利国务委员会	判决时间	2016年1月20日
案号	Case C-428/14		
关键词	先行裁决;竞争政策;欧洲竞争合作网络(ECN)的文件;成员国竞争主管机构;宽恕政策范本;豁免申请		
当事人	上诉人:意大利敦豪快递有限责任公司[DHL Express(Italy)Srl][①] 意大利敦豪全球货运股份有限公司(DHL Global Forwarding(Italy)SpA)[②] 被上诉人:意大利竞争与市场管理局(Autorità Garante della Concorrenza e del Mercato) 参与人:意大利辛克物流股份有限公司(Schenker Italiana SpA) 敏捷物流有限责任公司(Agility Logistics Srl)		

* 作者:游昕雨。

① SRL为意大利语Società a responsabilità limitata的简称,指有限责任公司。——译者注

② SPA为意大利语Società per azioni的简称,指股份有限公司。——译者注

二、案例涉及的欧盟法规

（一）《欧盟运行条约》第101条[①]规定：

“1.下列行为因与内部市场相冲突而应予以禁止：一切可能影响成员国间的贸易且其目标或结果会阻碍、限制或扭曲内部市场竞争的企业之间的协定、企业联合组织的决定和协同行为，特别是：

（1）以直接或间接方式规定收购或销售价格或其他交易条件；

（2）限制或控制生产、市场、技术发展或投资；

（3）分配市场或供货渠道；

（4）对与其他商业伙伴的同等交易适用不同的条件，从而使之在竞争中处于不利地位；

（5）以其他缔约方接受附加义务为条件缔结合同，这些条件从其本质上说或者根据商业惯例与此等合同的主题无关。

2.本条所禁止的任何协议或决定应自动无效。

3.但在下列情形下可宣告本条第1款不适用：

——企业之间的任何协议或任何类型的协议；

——企业联合组织的任何决定或任何类型的决定；

——任何协同行为或任何类型的协同行为。

上述措施应有助于改善商品的生产或销售，或有助于推动技术或经济进步，同时保证消费者公平分享由此带来的收益，并且做到：

（1）不对有关企业施加并非为达到这些目标所必不可少的限制；

（2）不为有关企业提供在相关产品的实质部分消除竞争的可能性。”

（二）《第1/2003号条例》第15条规定：

“欧盟委员会和成员国的竞争主管机构应当共同组成一个公共管理合作网络，紧密合作，以共同遵守欧共体竞争法。为达到此目的，有必要建立一个各方信息交换及磋商机制。欧盟委员会与成员国密切合作，制

① 程卫东、李靖堃：《欧洲联盟基础条约》，社会科学文献出版社2010年版，第86页。

定和完善在该网络平台内加强合作的具体形式。”

(三)《第1/2003号条例》第11条规定：

“1.欧盟委员会与成员国竞争主管机构之间应当密切合作，以适用共同体竞争规则。

2.为适用第7条、第8条、第9条、第10条和第29条第1款，欧盟委员会应将其收集到的最重要的文件的副本移交给成员国竞争主管机构。应成员国竞争主管机构的要求，欧盟委员会应当向其提供一份现有文件的副本，以供其评估案件。

3.当成员国竞争主管机构根据《欧盟运行条约》第101条、第102条采取行动时，应当在事前或是采取第一次正式调查措施之后及时书面告知欧盟委员会。该信息也应向其他成员国竞争主管机构提供。

4.成员国竞争主管机构应当在作出相关决定前的30天时间内，将有关终止违法行为、接受承诺或撤销集体豁免条例待遇的决定告知欧盟委员会。成员国竞争主管机构应当向欧盟委员会提供相关案件的概述，并告知欧盟委员会其预计作出的决定；如果没有上述决定，则应当提供预计采取行动的其他文件。该信息也应当向其他成员国竞争主管机构提供。根据欧盟委员会的要求，正在采取行动的竞争主管机构也应当向欧盟委员会提供其他已有的、评估案件所必需的文件。提供给欧盟委员会的信息也可以向其他成员国的竞争主管机构披露。对于正在处理的《欧盟运行条约》第101条、第102条项下的案件，成员国竞争主管机构之间也可以交换对案件进行评估的必要信息。

5.成员国竞争主管机构可以就任何涉及共同体法律的案件向欧盟委员会咨询。

6.欧盟委员会根据第三章项下的规定而启动的程序，应当解除成员国竞争主管机构适用《欧盟运行条约》第101条、第102条的权力。如果某成员国竞争主管机构已经对某个案件启动了程序并采取措施，则欧盟委员会只能在与该成员国竞争主管机构进行磋商后再启动程序。”

（四）《第1/2003号条例》第35条第1款：

“成员国应当指定一个或几个竞争主管机构来负责具体实施《欧盟运行条约》第101条、第102条的规定，从而使本条例的规定得到有效遵守……指定的机构可以包括法院。”

（五）《欧盟委员会关于与成员国竞争主管机构合作的公告》（以下简称《合作公告》）第1段规定：

“《第1/2003号条例》创建了一个平行的权力架构，其中欧盟委员会和成员国的竞争主管机构均可平等适用《欧盟运行条约》第101条、第102条对违法者采取措施。成员国竞争主管机构和欧盟委员会共同构建了一个公共执法的合作平台‘网络’，他们在此代表公共利益行使权力并密切合作以保护共同体市场的竞争。该合作平台‘网络’提供了一个场所，对欧共体竞争政策的适用和执行展开讨论并加强合作。它也为欧洲的竞争管理机构提供了适用《欧盟运行条约》第101条、第102条分析、查处案件的合作框架，并且是欧洲营造和保持共同体竞争文化的基础。该合作平台‘网络’被称为‘欧洲竞争合作网络’（European Competition Network，ECN）。”

（六）《合作公告》第14段规定：

“如果一项或多项卡特尔协议或行为……对3个以上成员国的竞争产生影响……则在查处该协议或行为之时，欧盟委员会较其他成员国竞争主管机构具有优先地位。”

（七）《合作公告》第38段规定：

“在欧盟范围内没有统一的豁免制度情况下，向某一成员国机构申请豁免并不意味向任何其他成员国的竞争主管机构申请豁免。因此，当申请人选择要向哪一个竞争主管机构提出豁免申请之时，就会权衡利弊得失，即考虑其违法行为在某一成员国内可能被适用《欧盟运行条约》

第101条并受到处罚的可能性。给予申请人这种申请豁免的选择权，是符合申请人利益的。鉴于各成员国现有豁免制度中对申请时间先后安排的重要性，申请人还需要考虑是否同时向某些竞争主管机构递交豁免申请。申请人需自行考虑各竞争管理机构可能对其采取的措施，从而采取其认为最合适的步骤来保护自己。”

（八）《ECN宽恕政策范本》第3段规定：

“ECN试图构建一个模范［豁免］制度的框架，用以鼓励参与卡特尔协议或其他卡特尔行为的一方（企业或个人）在符合一定条件下积极配合，根据模范［豁免］制度规定主动披露违法行为。参与ECN的成员国承诺，将尽可能的、以最大的努力使其国内的宽恕政策与ECN模范［豁免］制度保持一致。但是ECN模范［豁免］制度并不妨碍成员国的竞争主管机构在其制度框架内对申请人采取更有利的做法。”

（九）《ECN宽恕政策范本》第5段规定：

“竞争主管机构将豁免涉案企业的全部罚款，如果该企业满足以下条件：

（a）该企业经竞争主管机构确认为‘第一个’提供证据的卡特尔成员，且提交的证据使得竞争主管机构能够对涉嫌卡特尔的行为开展针对性调查。

（b）在该企业申请提供证据之前，竞争主管机构本身尚无充足的证据来作出调查决定、申请法院调查令或尚未开展针对被控卡特尔行为的调查；并且

（c）符合获得豁免的其他条件。”

（十）《ECN宽恕政策范本》第22段规定：

“在欧盟委员会根据《合作公告》第14段具有‘优先地位’的情况下，已经或正在向欧盟委员会提交豁免申请的申请人，也可以向其自认为处于《合作公告》规定之‘优先地位’的任何其他成员国竞争主管机构提交

简易豁免申请。简易豁免申请应包含以下简短说明：

……

——被控卡特尔行为的性质；

——……和

——关于被控卡特尔行为的之前行为或未来可能的豁免申请的信息。”

（十一）《ECN宽恕政策范本》第24段规定：

“如果成员国竞争主管机构收到简易申请后要求申请人提供进一步的具体信息，申请人应及时提供相关材料。如果成员国竞争主管机构决定对该案件采取行动，申请人必须在其规定的期限内提交所需的全部相关证据和信息以满足这些调查机构的要求。申请人在规定期限内提交这些信息，则所提供的信息将被视为在提出简易申请之日时提交的。”

（十二）《ECN宽恕政策范本》注释第7条说明：

“ECN宽恕政策范本的目的是为了解决多个平行提出申请的问题，并为潜在的申请人提供了可预见性方法……它创设了统一规范的简易申请模式（简易申请），旨在同时减轻企业和竞争主管机构在大型跨境卡特尔案件中重复申请豁免的负担。”

三、案件事实和审理过程

2007年6月5日，意大利敦豪快递有限责任公司［DHL Express（Italy）Srl］和意大利敦豪全球货运股份有限公司［DHL Global Forwarding（Italy）SpA］（两者合并简称DHL）就其在国际货运代理行业中违反欧盟竞争法的卡特尔行为，向欧盟委员会提交了一份罚款豁免申请。

2007年7月12日，DHL基于意大利国内豁免制度，向意大利竞争与市场管理局（负责制定竞争标准和执行市场规则的竞争主管机构，以下简称AGCM）提交了一份简易豁免申请。根据AGCM的说法，该申请仅涉及国际货物海运和空运部分的卡特尔，不包括陆运；而DHL则认为，该简易豁免申请提及的违法行为涵盖了整个国际货运代理和运输市场。DHL称，尽管其在2007年7月12日提交的豁免申请未能就陆运代理违法行为给出明确而具体的事例，但那是因为实际违法事实在那时尚未被发现。

2007年9月24日，欧盟委员会给予了DHL有条件的豁免，豁免范围涵盖其在整个国际货运代理行业中所参与的卡特尔，包括海运、空运和陆运。

2007年11月5日，意大利辛克物流股份有限公司（以下简称辛克物流）向欧盟委员会提交了一份关于国际货物海运代理卡特尔行为的豁免申请。

2007年11月19日，辛克物流向欧盟委员会提交了第二份关于国际货物陆运代理卡特尔行为的豁免申请。

2007年12月12日，辛克物流向AGCM提交了一份简易豁免申请，提供了意大利货物陆运代理行业卡特尔的有关违法信息。

2008年6月，欧盟委员会决定仅追究在国际货物空运代理服务行业发生的部分卡特尔，从而使国内竞争主管机构有可能追究海运和陆运代理服务的违法行为。

2008年6月23日，为了将申请豁免的范围明确拓展至国际货物陆运代理卡特尔，DHL向AGCM提交了一个附加的简易豁免申请，作为最初于2007年7月12日提交的豁免申请的补充。在附加申请中，DHL称“该申请仅仅是为了补充2007年7月12日提交的豁免申请，因为附加申请豁免之行为并非独立于原申请中请求豁免的违法行为，而仅仅是一个已向AGCM披露之违法行为的新表现形式。同样，欧盟委员会已经将其纳入企业可以获得豁免的考虑范围之内”。

2011年6月15日，AGCM就争议问题作出决定，认定包括DHL、辛克物流和敏捷物流在内的一些企业，参与了在意大利的国际货物陆运代理行业的卡特尔。在该决定中，AGCM认定辛克物流是第一个在意大利国内就货物陆运代理卡特尔申请罚款豁免的公司，辛克物流将免于罚款。AGCM同时认为，DHL在2007年7月12日提交的国内豁免申请中，只要求了空运和海运卡特尔的罚款豁免，而关于陆运卡特尔的豁免申请是在2008年6月23日才提出的。

DHL向意大利拉齐奥地区行政法院（Tribunale amministrativo regionale per il

Lazio）提起了诉讼，主张其根据国内豁免制度应当被列为申请豁免的第一位，从而免于罚款。DHL认为，根据欧盟法原则，国内竞争主管机构在评估其收到的简易豁免申请时，要参考该卡特尔成员提交给欧盟委员会的主豁免申请。

意大利拉齐奥地区行政法院驳回了DHL的起诉，因为原则上不同的豁免制度和申请都是独立和自主的。DHL不服初审判决，向意大利国务委员会提起了上诉。意大利国务委员会决定中止诉讼程序，将案件相关问题提交给欧盟法院，请求欧盟法院作出先行裁决。

欧盟法院于2014年9月18日收到申请，并于2016年1月20日作出判决。

四、争议焦点和主要法律观点

本案的争议焦点有三，围绕着欧洲竞争合作网络（European Competition Network，ECN）内欧盟委员会与各成员国竞争管理机构权力行使，以及相应的豁免制度之间的关系展开，意大利国务委员会要求欧盟法院解释欧盟法，尤其是在本案所示情况下《欧盟运行条约》第101条、《欧盟条约》第4条第3款和《第1/2003号条例》第11条作何解释。提请法院要求欧盟法院对以下两个问题作出解释：

第一，成员国竞争主管机构是否要遵守ECN制定的规范，即本案中的《ECN宽恕政策范本》对于成员国竞争主管机构是否有拘束力？

第二，一家卡特尔成员企业向欧盟委员会提交的豁免申请与其向成员国竞争主管机构提交的简易申请，这两者之间是否存在一种法律联系：如果简易申请准确地反映了提交给欧盟委员会的豁免申请中的内容，则成员国竞争主管机构应当根据提交给欧盟委员会的豁免申请来评估简易申请？如果简易申请请求豁免之行为的范围在实质上比提交给欧盟委员会的豁免申请更窄，则成员国竞争主管机构是否需要主动联系欧盟委员会或该申请企业，以查明：这些企业在简易豁免申请中没有提到，而在提交给欧盟委员会的豁免申请中已经提到的那些违法行为是否真实存在？

就第一个问题，欧盟法院明确说明，《ECN宽恕政策范本》对成员国的法院、仲裁庭均没有任何拘束力。ECN旨在鼓励欧盟委员会和成员国竞争主管机构在执行竞争政策时进行讨论合作，而ECN本身无权制定具有法律约束力的规则。在ECN背景下分别于2004年和2006年通过的《合作公告》和《宽恕公告》都被公布在《欧盟官方公报》的“C”系列中。与“L”系列不同的是，“C”系列不是为了公布有法律约束力的措施，而仅仅是提供有关欧盟的信息、建议和意见。所以，ECN无权为成员国创设任何义务。

就第二个问题，欧盟法院在回答时反复强调了豁免制度的自主性。欧盟法院判决认为：欧盟豁免制度和成员国国内豁免制度同时共存但各自具有自主性。企业可以自由选择向所有有权适用《欧盟运行条约》第101条查处违法行为的竞争主管机构之中的哪一个申请豁免。国内竞争主管机构也可以自由地选择适用国内或欧盟豁免制度来评估豁免申请。如果提交给欧盟委员会的豁免申请与提交给成员国竞争管理机构的简易申请之间存在所谓的法律联系，这种法律联系迫使成员国竞争主管机构必须根据申请人提交给欧盟委员会的豁免申请来评估简易申请，这会动摇申请人享有的自主选择权。豁免制度的一个基本原则是，欧盟层面没有统一的豁免申请制度，也没有“主”申请与“次”申请之说，而只有提交给欧盟委员会的豁免申请和提交给国内竞争管理机构的简易豁免申请，且任何接受豁免申请的竞争主管机构的唯一责任就是自主评估该申请。

所以，对于同一个卡特尔，参与该卡特尔的企业向欧盟委员会提交的豁免申请与向成员国竞争主管机构提交的简易豁免申请之间没有任何法律联系。因此，成员国竞争主管机构无须根据申请人向欧盟委员会提交的豁免申请来评估简易豁免申请，无论申请人提交的简易豁免申请是否准确地反映了其向欧盟委员会提交的豁免申请的内容。如果申请人提交给成员国竞争主管机构的简易豁免申请在实质范围上比提交给欧盟委员会的豁免申请更窄，则成员国竞争主管机构并不需要联系欧盟委员会或该申请企业，以查明：这些企业在简易豁免申请中没有提到，而在提交给欧盟委员会的豁免申请中已经提到的那些违法行为是否真实存在？

五、本案的意义及其启示

本案争议的核心是，如何理解欧盟层面的豁免政策和成员国国内的豁免政策之间的关系，或者说欧盟委员会和成员国竞争主管机构在行使权力上的相互关系。我们知道，宽恕政策的设计源于"囚徒困境"理论，即在卡特尔内部设立这样一个"困境"，以鼓励其参与者主动揭发卡特尔违法行为，以便获得豁免或减轻处罚。

在欧盟竞争法领域，欧盟层面的宽恕政策和成员国国内的宽恕政策是共存并行的两套独立的制度。这是因为在欧洲一体化进程中，各国在经济领域的合作比在政治领域的合作更早更有效。在这种情况下各国在打击跨境卡特尔行为时就显得措手无措，因为成员国各自的竞争主管机构无法进行有效的沟通和合作。欧盟委员会也难以在欧盟层面对垄断行为实施有效的打击，况且，各成员国各自复杂不统一的豁免申请制度也使卡特尔参与企业在提出豁免申请过程中增加很多成本。

为此，在欧盟层面成立了一个欧洲竞争合作网络（ECN）平台，通过这个平台使欧盟委员会与成员国之间构建一个合作与沟通机制，确保欧盟法与成员国竞争法规则的一致性。这是一个独立的、平行于欧盟委员会和成员国国内竞争主管机构的一个体系，它为欧盟层面和成员国之间提供了适用和理解《欧盟运行条约》第101条、第102条的合作框架，并且也宣传了欧盟竞争法的理念和竞争文化。

2006年，ECN通过了《宽恕政策范本》。2007年，意大利国内竞争主管机构AGCM在国内采用了类似的模式——简易豁免申请制度。这些导向具有良好的效果，使更多的卡特尔参与者积极举报各种隐蔽的卡特尔行为。竞争法领域的宽恕政策可以起到事半功倍的效果。合理合法地运用这一政策可以达到良好的警示作用。

本案不仅体现了欧盟竞争法中的宽恕政策，还梳理了欧盟层面、成员国层面，以及欧洲竞争网络机制各自独立、平行的法律关系和职责范围。这三套平行独立的体系，既有法律上的联系，又各有特色。如何处理好这三者关系，也是欧盟法院作出先行裁决的难点所在。通过这个案件我们可以看到欧盟法院的基本态度和最新观点。它再次重申了ECN仅仅是成员国竞争主管机构与欧盟委员会的一个合作和交流平台，ECN出台的相关政策对成员国竞争主管机构没有相关的法律约束力。此外，欧盟委员会与各成员国的竞争主管机构也不存在等级关系，他们是两套独立、平行的运作体系，各自享有充分的自主性；为了更好地发挥ECN的合作宗旨，应该在欧盟层面简化豁免程序，以激励更多的卡特尔参与者主动揭露其违法行为，以便从程序上提高竞争法执法机构的工作效率。

表1-1 C-428/14（2016）涉及的法律

序号	原文	中文名称	所在段落
1	Treaty on the Functioning of the European Union（TFEU）	《欧盟运行条约》	1、2、4、5、6、7、8、22、23、28、29、36、44、45、48、54、56、59、60、67、68、71、77、78、79、80、81、84
2	Treaty on European Union（TEU）	《欧盟条约》	1、28
3	Council Regulation（EC）No 1/2003 of 16 December 2002 on the implementation of the rules on competition laid down in Articles 101［TFEU］and 102［TFEU］	《关于实施〈欧盟运行条约〉第101条、第102条的第1/2003号条例》	1、3、4、5、6、28、29、30、31、36、41、44、45、58、66、67、68、71、77、78、84
4	Commission Notice on Cooperation with the Network of Competition Authorities	《欧盟委员会关于与成员国国内竞争主管机构合作的公告》	6、7、12、16、27、31、33、34、43、55
5	ECN Model Leniency Programme	《ECN宽恕政策范本》	9、10、11、12、13、14、27、28、29、38、41、42、43、44、56、74、75、76、77

续表

序号	原文	中文名称	所在段落
6	Communicazione sulla non imposizione e sulla riduzione delle sanzioni ai sensi dell' articolo 15 della legge 10 ottobre 1990, n. 287	《关于根据第287/90号法律第15条免除或减轻处罚的通知》	15、16、18、24、25、69、71、83
7	Notice on Immunity from fines and reduction of fines in cartel cases	《关于卡特尔案件罚款豁免和减轻公告》	33、34、37、42、82

表1-2　C-428/14（2016）涉及的判例

序号	判例名称	案号	所在段落
1	Pfleiderer	EU:C:2011:389	28、33、36、37、38、39、78、79
2	X	EU:C:2009:359	30
3	Tele2 Polska	EU:C:2011:270	30
4	Polska Telefonia Cyfrowa	EU:C:2011:294	34
5	Expedia	EU:C:2012:795	34
6	Kone and Others	EU:C:2014:1317	42、78
7	Kamberaj	EU:C:2012:233	48、49

续表

序号	判例名称	案号	所在段落
8	Banco Privado Português and Massa Insolvente do Banco Privado Português	EU: C: 2015: 151	48、49
9	Jaeger	EU: C: 2003: 437	70
10	Consorci Sanitari del Maresme	EU: C: 2015: 664	70
11	LG Display and LG Display Taiwan v Commission	EU: C: 2015: 258	82

JUDGMENT OF THE COURT（Second Chamber）

20 January 2016

（Reference for a preliminary ruling—Competition policy—Article 101 TFEU—Regulation（EC）No 1/2003—International freight forwarding sector—National competition authorities—Legal status of instruments of the European Competition Network—Model Leniency Programme of that network—Application for immunity submitted to the Commission—Summary application for immunity submitted to national competition authorities—Relationship between those two applications）

In Case C-428/14,

REQUEST for a preliminary ruling under Article 267 TFEU from the Consiglio di Stato（Council of State, Italy）, made by decision of 1 April 2014, received at the Court on 18 September 2014, in the proceedings

DHL Express（Italy）Srl,

DHL Global Forwarding（Italy）SpA

v

Autorità Garante della Concorrenza e del Mercato,

interveners:

Schenker Italiana SpA,

Agility Logistics Srl,

判例正文*

欧盟法院判决（第二法庭）
2016年1月20日

（申请先行裁决—竞争政策—《欧盟运行条约》第101条—《第1/2003号条例》—国际货运代理行业—成员国国内竞争主管机构—欧洲竞争合作网络通过文件的法律地位—宽恕政策范本—提交给欧盟委员会的豁免申请—提交给成员国国内竞争主管机构的简易豁免申请—这两种豁免申请的关系）

案号：C-428/14

意大利国务委员会于2014年4月1日根据《欧盟运行条约》第267条向欧盟法院提出先行裁决申请，本法院于2014年9月18日收到该申请。

意大利敦豪快递有限责任公司；

意大利敦豪全球货运股份有限公司；

诉

意大利竞争与市场管理局；

介入诉讼人：①

意大利辛克物流股份有限公司；

敏捷物流有限责任公司。

---

* 初译者：游昕雨；校对：林燕萍、戴娜。

① 介入诉讼人（interveners）指的是自愿并经法庭许可而加入到某一诉讼中来，并成为该诉讼的一方当事人，以维护自己的权利或利益的人。——译者注

THE COURT (Second Chamber),

composed of R. Silva de Lapuerta, President of the First Chamber, acting as President of the Second Chamber, J.L. da Cruz Vilaça (Rapporteur), A. Arabadjiev, C. Lycourgos and J.–C. Bonichot, Judges,

Advocate General: M. Wathelet,

Registrar: V. Giacobbo–Peyronnel, Administrator,

having regard to the written procedure and further to the hearing on 9 July 2015,

after considering the observations submitted on behalf of:

–DHL Express (Italy) Srl and DHL Global Forwarding (Italy) SpA, by M. Siragusa and G. Rizza, avvocati,

–Schenker Italiana SpA, by G.L. Zampa, G. Barone et A. Di Giò, avvocati,

–Agility Logistics Srl, by A. Lirosi, M. Padellaro and A. Pera, avvocati,

–the Italian Government, by G. Palmieri, acting as Agent, assisted by S. Fiorentino and P. Gentili, avvocati dello Stato,

–the German Government, by T. Henze and A. Lippstreu, acting as Agents,

–the French Government, by D. Colas and J. Bousin, acting as Agents,

–the Austrian Government, by C. Pesendorfer, acting as Agent,

–the United Kingdom Government, by V. Kaye, acting as Agent, assisted by D. Beard QC, and V. Wakefield, Barrister,

–the European Commission, by L. Malferrari, G. Meeßen and T. Vecchi, acting as Agents,

after hearing the Opinion of the Advocate General at the sitting on 10 September 2015,

gives the following

欧盟法院（第二法庭）

由审判长R.西尔瓦·德拉普塔（第一法庭审判长兼任）、法官J.L.克鲁兹维拉萨（判决书起草人）、A.阿拉巴吉耶夫、C.卢卡斯和J.-C.伯尼丘特组成；

佐审官：M.瓦特莱特；

书记官：V.贾科布·皮龙（首席行政官）。

本院进行了所有书面程序后，于2015年7月9日开庭审理了本案，听取了下列各方代表的意见：

——意大利敦豪快递有限责任公司和意大利敦豪全球货运股份有限公司，代理律师为M.西拉古萨和G.里扎；

——意大利辛克物流股份有限公司，代理律师为G.L.赞巴和G.巴罗；

——意大利政府，由G.帕尔米里担任代理人，S.菲奥伦蒂诺和P.根蒂利两位国家律师协助；

——德国政府，由T.亨泽和A.利普斯担任代理人；

——法国政府，由D.可拉斯和J.布森担任代理人；

——奥地利政府，由C.佩森多夫担任代理人；

——英国政府，由V.凯尔担任代理人，D.伯德和V.韦克菲尔德两位律师协助；

——欧盟委员会，由L.麦尔菲瑞、G.麦芬和T.惟奇担任代理人；

在听取了2015年9月10日庭审中的佐审官意见后，本院作出如下判决：

Judgment

1 This request for a preliminary ruling concerns the interpretation of Articles 101 TFEU, Article 4(3) TEU and Article 11 of Council Regulation (EC) No 1/2003 of 16 December 2002 on the implementation of the rules on competition laid down in Articles 101 [TFEU] and 102 [TFEU] (OJ 2003 L 1, p. 1).

2 The request has been made in proceedings between DHL Express (Italy) Srl and DHL Global Forwarding (Italy) SpA (together, 'DHL'), on the one hand, and the Autorità Garante della Concorrenza e del Mercato (Authority responsible for competition compliance and enforcement of market rules, 'the AGCM'), on the other, concerning the AGCM's decision to impose fines on DHL for participating in a cartel in the sector of international road freight forwarding to and from Italy, in breach of Article 101 TFEU ('the decision at issue').

The legal framework

EU law

3 Recital 15 of Regulation No 1/2003 reads:

'The Commission and the competition authorities of the Member States should form together a network of public authorities applying the Community competition rules in close cooperation. For that purpose it is necessary to set up arrangements for information and consultation. Further modalities for the cooperation within the network will be laid down and revised by the Commission, in close cooperation with the Member States.'

4 Article 11 of Regulation No 1/2003, headed 'Cooperation between the Commission and the competition authorities of the Member States', provides:

'1. The Commission and the competition authorities of the Member States shall apply the Community competition rules in close cooperation.

判　决

1 该先行裁决申请涉及对《欧盟运行条约》第101条、《欧共体条约》第4条第3款和《关于实施〈欧盟运行条约〉第101条、第102条的第1/2003号条例》[①]（OJ 2003 L 1, p. 1，以下简称《第1/2003号条例》）第11条的解释。

2 该申请所涉及的争议已经进入了诉讼程序。当事人一方是意大利敦豪快递有限责任公司和意大利敦豪全球货运股份有限公司（两者合并简称DHL）；另一方是意大利竞争与市场管理局（负责制定竞争标准和执行市场规则的机构，以下简称AGCM）。双方争议源于AGCM作出的对DHL处以罚款的决定。因DHL参与了一个在意大利进出口的国际货物陆运代理卡特尔，违反了《欧盟运行条约》第101条（以下简称AGCM的决定）。

法律背景

欧盟法

3 《第1/2003号条例》第15条规定：

“欧盟委员会和成员国的竞争主管机构应当共同组成一个公共管理合作网络，紧密合作，以共同遵守欧共体竞争法。为达到此目的，有必要建立一个各方信息交换及磋商机制。欧盟委员会与成员国密切合作，制定和完善在该网络平台内加强合作的具体形式。”

4 《第1/2003号条例》第11条规定了“欧盟委员会与成员国竞争主管机构之间的合作”：

“1.欧盟委员会与成员国竞争主管机构之间应当密切合作，以适用共同体竞争规则。

① 《第1/2003号条例》的全称是《关于实施〈欧共体条约〉第81条、第82条的第1/2003号条例》。在某些法官看来，既然《欧共体条约》被《欧盟运行条约》取代，则可以将《第1/2003号条例》看成《关于实施〈欧盟运行条约〉第101条、第102条的第1/2003号条例》。法官在援引时作了调整，以免援引被误解。——译者注

2. The Commission shall transmit to the competition authorities of the Member States copies of the most important documents it has collected with a view to applying Articles 7, 8, 9, 10 and Article 29(1). At the request of the competition authority of a Member State, the Commission shall provide it with a copy of other existing documents necessary for the assessment of the case.

3. The competition authorities of the Member States shall, when acting under Article [101 TFEU] or Article [102 TFEU], inform the Commission in writing before or without delay after commencing the first formal investigative measure. This information may also be made available to the competition authorities of the other Member States.

4. No later than 30 days before the adoption of a decision requiring that an infringement be brought to an end, accepting commitments or withdrawing the benefit of a block exemption Regulation, the competition authorities of the Member States shall inform the Commission. To that effect, they shall provide the Commission with a summary of the case, the envisaged decision or, in the absence thereof, any other document indicating the proposed course of action. This information may also be made available to the competition authorities of the other Member States. At the request of the Commission, the acting competition authority shall make available to the Commission other documents it holds which are necessary for the assessment of the case. The information supplied to the Commission may be made available to the competition authorities of the other Member States. National competition authorities may also exchange between themselves information necessary for the assessment of a case that they are dealing with under Article [101 TFEU] or Article [102 TFEU].

5. The competition authorities of the Member States may consult the Commission on any case involving the application of Community law.

6. The initiation by the Commission of proceedings for the adoption of a decision under Chapter Ⅲ shall relieve the competition authorities of the Member States of their competence to apply Articles [101 TFEU] and [102 TFEU]. If a competition authority of a Member State is already acting on a case, the Commission shall only initiate proceedings after consulting with that national competition authority.'

5 Article 35(1) of Regulation No 1/2003 provides:

'The Member States shall designate the competition authority or authorities responsible for the application of Articles [101 TFEU] and [102 TFEU] in such a way that the provisions of this regulation are effectively complied with. ... The authorities designated may include courts.'

2.为适用该条例第7条、第8条、第9条、第10条和第29条第1款，欧盟委员会应将其收集到的最重要的文件的副本移交给成员国竞争主管机构。应成员国竞争主管机构的要求，欧盟委员会应当向其提供一份现有文件的副本，以供其评估案件。

3.当成员国竞争主管机构根据《欧盟运行条约》第101条、第102条采取行动时，应当在事前或是采取第一次正式调查措施之后及时书面告知欧盟委员会。该信息也应向其他成员国竞争主管机构提供。

4.成员国竞争主管机构应当在作出相关决定前的30天时间内，将有关终止违法行为、接受承诺或撤销集体豁免条例待遇的决定告知欧盟委员会。成员国竞争主管机构应当向欧盟委员会提供相关案件的概述，并告知欧盟委员会其预计作出的决定；如果没有上述决定，则应当提供预计采取行动的其他文件。该信息也应当向其他成员国竞争主管机构提供。根据欧盟委员会的要求，正在采取行动的竞争主管机构也应当向欧盟委员会提供其他已有的、评估案件所必需的文件。提供给欧盟委员会的信息也可以向其他成员国的竞争主管机构披露。对于正在处理的《欧盟运行条约》第101条、第102条项下的案件，成员国竞争主管机构之间也可以交换对案件进行评估的必要信息。

5.成员国竞争主管机构可以就任何涉及共同体法律的案件向欧盟委员会咨询。

6.欧盟委员会根据第3章项下的规定而启动的程序，应当解除成员国竞争主管机构适用《欧盟运行条约》第101条、第102条的权力。如果某成员国竞争主管机构已经对某个案件启动了程序并采取措施，则欧盟委员会只能在与该成员国竞争主管机构进行磋商后再启动程序。”

5 《第1/2003号条例》第35条第1款规定：

“成员国应当指定一个或几个竞争主管机构来负责具体实施《欧盟运行条约》第101条、第102条的规定，从而使本条例的规定得到有效遵守……指定的机构可以包括法院。”

6 Paragraph 1 of the Commission Notice on Cooperation with the Network of Competition Authorities (OJ 2004, C 101, p. 43, 'the Notice on Cooperation') states:

'... Regulation ... No 1/2003 ... creates a system of parallel competences in which the Commission and the Member States' competition authorities ... can apply Article [101 TFEU] and Article [102 TFEU]. Together the [national competition authorities] and the Commission form a network of public authorities: they act in the public interest and cooperate closely in order to protect competition. The network is a forum for discussion and cooperation in the application and enforcement of EC competition policy. It provides a framework for the cooperation of European competition authorities in cases where Articles [101 TFEU] and [102 TFEU] are applied and is the basis for the creation and maintenance of a common competition culture in Europe. The network is called "European Competition Network" (ECN).'

7 In view of this system of parallel competences, in which all the competition authorities have the power to apply Article 101 TFEU, paragraphs 8 to 15 of the Notice on Cooperation set out the criteria for determining which authorities are 'well placed' to deal with a case. Thus, in accordance with paragraph 14 of that notice, 'the Commission is particularly well placed if one or several agreement (s) or practice (s)... have effects on competition in more than three Member States ...'

8 According to paragraph 38 of that notice:

'In the absence of a European Union-wide system of fully harmonised leniency programmes, an application for leniency to a given authority is not to be considered as an application for leniency to any other authority. It is therefore in the interest of the applicant to apply for leniency to all competition authorities which have competence to apply Article [101 TFEU] in the territory which is affected by the infringement and which may be considered well placed to act against the infringement in question. In view of the importance of timing in most existing leniency programmes, applicants will also need to consider whether it would be appropriate to file leniency applications with the relevant authorities simultaneously. It is for the applicant to take the steps which it considers appropriate to protect its position with respect to possible proceedings by these authorities.'

6 《关于与成员国竞争主管机构合作的公告》(OJ 2004, C 101, p. 43, 以下简称《合作公告》)第一段规定:

"《第1/2003号条例》创建了一个平行的权力架构,其中欧盟委员会和成员国的竞争主管机构均可平等适用《欧盟运行条约》第101条、第102条对违法者采取措施。成员国竞争主管机构和欧盟委员会共同构建了一个公共执法的合作平台'网络',他们在此代表公共利益行使权力并密切合作以保护共同体市场的竞争。该合作平台'网络'提供了一个场所,对欧共体竞争政策的适用和执行展开讨论并加强合作。它也为欧洲的竞争管理机构提供了适用《欧盟运行条约》第101条、第102条分析、查处案件的合作框架,并且是欧洲营造和保持共同体竞争文化的基础。该合作平台'网络'被称为'欧洲竞争合作网络'(European Competition Network, ECN)。"

7 考虑到在这种平行的权力架构中,欧盟委员会与成员国竞争主管机构都有权适用《欧盟运行条约》第101条对违法行为采取措施,各机构权力产生竞合,所以《合作公告》第8段至第15段明确了一个标准,以确定哪个机构在解决案件上具有"优先地位"。因此,依据《合作公告》第14段,"如果一项或多项卡特尔协议或行为……对3个以上成员国的竞争产生影响……则在查处该协议或行为之时,欧盟委员会较其他成员国竞争主管机构具有优先地位。"

8 《合作公告》第38段规定:

"在欧盟范围内没有统一的豁免制度情况下,向某一成员国机构申请豁免并不意味向任何其他成员国的竞争主管机构申请豁免。因此,当申请人选择要向哪一个竞争主管机构提出豁免申请之时,就会权衡利弊得失,即考虑其违法行为在某一成员国内可能被适用《欧盟运行条约》第101条并受到处罚的可能性。给予申请人这种申请豁免的选择权,是符合申请人利益的。鉴于各成员国现有豁免制度中对申请时间先后安排的重要性,申请人还需要考虑是否同时向某些竞争主管机构递交豁免申请。申请人需自行考虑各竞争主管机构可能对其采取的措施,从而采取其认为最合适的步骤来保护自己。"

9 In the context of the ECN, a Model Leniency Programme was adopted in 2006 ('the ECN Model Leniency Programme'). That programme, which was not published in the *Official Journal of the European Union*, is available only on the Commission's website. It was revised in November 2012, after the events at issue in the main proceedings and, consequently, after the decision of the AGCM which is the subject–matter of the action before referring court.

10 Paragraph 3 of the ECN Model Leniency Programme states:

'The ECN Model [Leniency] Programme sets out a framework for rewarding the cooperation of undertakings which are party to agreements and practices falling within its scope. The ECN members commit to using their best efforts, within the limits of their competence, to align their respective programmes with the ECN Model [Leniency] Programme. The ECN Model [Leniency] Programme does not prevent a CA from adopting a more favourable approach towards applicants within its programme.'

11 According to Paragraph 5 of that programme, concerning 'Type 1A' immunity from fines:

'The [competition authority] will grant an undertaking immunity from any fine which would otherwise have been imposed provided:

(a) The undertaking is the first to submit evidence which in the [competition authority]'s view, at the time it evaluates the application, will enable the [competition authority] to carry out targeted inspections in connection with an alleged cartel.

(b) The [competition authority] did not, at the time of the application, already have sufficient evidence to adopt an inspection decision/seek a court warrant for an inspection or had not already carried out an inspection in connection with the alleged cartel arrangement; and

(c) The conditions attached to leniency are met.'

12 Paragraph 22 of the ECN Model Leniency Programme provides that, '[i]n cases where the Commission is "particularly well placed" to deal with a case in accordance with paragraph 14 of the ... Notice [on Cooperation], the applicant that has or is in the process of filing an application for immunity with the Commission may file summary applications with any [national competition authorities] which the applicant considers might be "well placed" to act under the ... Notice [on Cooperation]. Summary applications should include a short description of the following:

...

–The nature of the alleged cartel conduct;

9 在“欧洲竞争合作网络”实施的背景下，2006年通过了《欧洲竞争合作网络宽恕政策范本》（以下简称《ECN宽恕政策范本》）。该范本未在《欧盟官方公报》上公布，仅在欧盟委员会网站上公示。《ECN宽恕政策范本》于2012年11月进行了修订，本案主诉讼程序中的案件事实在此之前就已经发生，所以本案争议问题——AGCM的处罚决定——是在范本修订之前就已经作出。

10 《ECN宽恕政策范本》第3段规定：

“ECN试图构建一个模范［豁免］制度的框架，用以鼓励参与卡特尔协议或其他卡特尔行为的一方（企业或个人）在符合一定条件下积极配合，根据模范［豁免］制度规定主动披露违法行为。参与ECN的成员国承诺，将尽可能的、以最大的努力使其国内的宽恕政策与ECN模范［豁免］制度保持一致。但是ECN模范［豁免］制度并不妨碍成员国的竞争主管机构在其制度框架内对申请人采取更有利的做法。”

11 《ECN宽恕政策范本》第5段是关于“1A型”罚款豁免的规定：

“竞争主管机构将豁免涉案企业的全部罚款，如果该企业满足以下条件：

（a）该企业经竞争主管机构确认是第一个提供证据的卡特尔成员，且提交的证据使得竞争主管机构能够对涉嫌卡特尔的行为开展针对性调查。

（b）该企业申请提供证据之前，竞争主管机构本身尚无充足的证据来作出调查决定、申请法院调查令或尚未开展针对被控卡特尔行为的调查；并且

（c）符合获得豁免的其他条件。”

12 《ECN宽恕政策范本》第22段规定：“在欧盟委员会根据《合作公告》第14段具有‘优先地位’的情况下，已经或正在向欧盟委员会提交豁免申请的申请人，也可以向其自认为处于《合作公告》规定之‘优先地位’的任何其他成员国竞争主管机构提交简易豁免申请。简易豁免申请应包含以下简短说明：

……

——被控卡特尔行为的性质；

–..., and

–Information on its other past or possible future leniency applications in relation to the alleged cartel.'

13 Paragraph 24 of the ECN Model Leniency Programme states:

'Should [a national competition authority] having received a summary application decide to request specific further information, the applicant should provide such information promptly. Should [a national competition authority] decide to act upon the case, it will determine a period of time within which the applicant must make a full submission of all relevant evidence and information required to meet the threshold. If the applicant submits such information within the set period, the information provided will be deemed to have been submitted on the date when the summary application was made.'

14 Explanatory Note 7 to the ECN Mode Leniency Programme states:

'The purpose of the ECN Model [Leniency] Programme is to address the issue of multiple parallel applications and to provide a greater degree of predictability for potential applicants. ... [I] t sets out the features of a uniform type of short form applications (so–called summary applications) designed to alleviate the burden on both undertakings and [competition authorities] associated with multiple filing in large, cross–border cartel cases.'

Italian law

15 On 15 February 2007, the AGCM adopted a Notice on the non–imposition or reduction of penalties under Article 15 of Law No 287/90 (Communicazione sulla non imposizione e sulla riduzione delle sanzioni ai sensi dell' articolo 15 della legge 10 ottobre 1990, n. 287), which incorporates the Italian leniency programme ('the national leniency programme').

16 Article 16 of the national leniency programme, entitled 'Summary application', provides as follows:

'In cases where the Commission is best placed to deal with a case and conduct the procedure, an undertaking which has submitted or is preparing to submit to the Commission an application for non–imposition of penalties may submit to the [AGCM] a similar application for leniency, drafted in "summary" form, where it considers that the [AGCM] is also in a position to take action in the matter. Pursuant to [paragraph] 14 of the [Notice on Cooperation], the Commission is best placed where one or more agreements or practices, including networks of agreements or of similar practices, have an impact on competition in more than three Member States.'

——……和

——关于被控卡特尔行为的之前行为或未来可能的豁免申请的信息。”

13 《ECN宽恕政策范本》第24段规定：

“如果成员国竞争主管机构收到简易申请后要求申请人提供进一步的具体信息，申请人应及时提供相关材料。如果成员国竞争主管机构决定对该案件采取行动，申请人必须在其规定的期限内提交所需的全部相关证据和信息以满足这些调查机构的要求。申请人在规定期限内提交这些信息，则所提供的信息将被视为在提出简易申请之日时提交的。”

14 《ECN宽恕政策范本》注释第7条说明：

“ECN宽恕政策范本的目的是为了解决多个平行提出申请的问题，并为潜在的申请人提供了可预见性方法……它创设了统一规范的简易的申请模式（简易申请），旨在同时减轻企业和竞争主管机构在大型跨境卡特尔案件中重复申请豁免的负担。”

意大利法律

15 2007年2月15日，AGCM通过了《关于根据第287/90号法律第15条免除或减轻处罚的通知》（Communicazione sulla non imposizione e sulla riduzione delle sanzioni ai sensi dell'articolo 15 della legge 10 ottobre 1990, n. 287），其中规定了意大利的宽恕政策（以下简称《意大利宽恕政策》）。

16 《意大利宽恕政策》第16条是关于“简易豁免申请”的规定：

“根据《合作公告》第14段的规定，如果一项或多项卡特尔协议或行为……对3个以上成员国的竞争产生影响……则在查处该协议或行为之时，欧盟委员会较其他成员国竞争主管机构具有优先地位。当欧盟委员会根据此条规定在某一案件的处理和启动程序上具有优先地位时，已经或将要向欧盟委员会申请罚款豁免的企业如果认为意大利竞争主管机构AGCM也可以就此案采取行动，那么该企业也可以向AGCM提交类似的、以‘简易’形式起草的豁免申请。”

The dispute in the main proceedings and the questions referred for a preliminary ruling

17 On 5 June 2007, DHL submitted to the European Commission an application for immunity from fines concerning several infringements of EU competition law in the sector of international freight forwarding. On 24 September 2007, the Commission granted DHL conditional immunity for the entire international forwarding sector, that is to say, as regards maritime, air and road transit. On 20 December 2007, DHL brought to the attention of the Commission certain information concerning the conduct of undertakings in the international road freight forwarding sector in Italy. In June 2008, the Commission decided to pursue only the part of the cartel concerning international air freight forwarding services, leaving the national competition authorities the possibility of pursuing the infringements in relation to the sea and road freight forwarding services.

18 In parallel, on 12 July 2007, DHL submitted to the AGCM a summary application for immunity under the national leniency programme. In that application, DHL provided information concerning unlawful conduct in the international freight forwarding and transport market. According to the AGCM, that application concerned only the international sea and air freight transport sectors, and did not concern the road transport sector. However, according to DHL, that summary application concerned illegal conduct observed throughout the international freight forwarding and transport market. DHL stated that, whilst its application of 12 July 2007 did not give concrete and specific examples of conduct observed in relation to road freight forwarding, that was merely because such conduct had not yet been discovered.

19 On 23 June 2008, DHL submitted an additional summary application for immunity to the AGCM, supplementing the application initially submitted on 12 July 2007, in order to expressly extend that application to the international road freight forwarding sector. In that additional application, DHL stated that ‘the present declaration merely constitutes, for all purposes and effects, a supplement to the application submitted on 12 July 2007, in so far as the additional conduct to which it relates does not amount to a separate infringement not covered by the original declaration and is nothing more than a new manifestation of infringements already reported and, as such, the Commission took account of them for the purposes of the leniency granted to the undertaking’.

在主诉讼程序中的争议和提请先行裁决的问题

17 2007年6月5日，DHL就一些在国际货运代理行业中违反欧盟竞争法的卡特尔行为，向欧盟委员会提交了一份罚款豁免申请。2007年9月24日，欧盟委员会给予了DHL有条件的豁免，豁免范围涵盖其在整个国际货运代理行业中所参与的卡特尔，也就是包括海运、空运和陆运货物代理的卡特尔。2007年12月20日，DHL向欧盟委员会提供线索，提醒欧盟委员会关注意大利国际货物陆运代理行业中某些企业的行为。2008年6月，欧盟委员会决定仅追究在国际货物空运代理服务行业发生的部分卡特尔，从而使国内竞争主管机构有可能追究海运和陆运代理服务的违法行为。

18 同时，2007年7月12日，DHL基于国内豁免制度，向意大利国内竞争主管机构——AGCM提交了一份简易豁免申请。在该申请中，DHL提供了某些企业在国际货运代理和货物运输市场中实施违法行为的信息。根据AGCM的说法，该申请仅涉及国际货物海运和空运部分的卡特尔，不包括陆运；而DHL则认为该简易豁免申请提及的违法行为涵盖了整个国际货运代理和运输市场。DHL称，尽管其在2007年7月12日提交的豁免申请未能就陆运代理违法行为给出明确而具体的事例，但那只是因为实际违法事实在那时尚未被发现。

19 2008年6月23日，为了将申请豁免的范围明确拓展至国际货物陆运代理卡特尔，DHL向AGCM提交了一个附加的简易豁免申请，作为最初于2007年7月12日提交的豁免申请的补充。在附加申请中，DHL称“该申请仅仅是为了补充2007年7月12日提交的豁免申请，因为附加申请豁免之行为并非独立于原申请中请求豁免的违法行为，而仅仅是一个已向AGCM披露之违法行为的新表现形式。同样地，欧盟委员会已经将其纳入企业获得豁免的考虑范围之内”。

20 In the meantime, on 5 November 2007, Deutsche Bahn AG submitted to the Commission—on its own behalf and on behalf, in particular, of Schenker Italiana SpA ('Schenker')—a first leniency application concerning sea freight forwarding and, a second application, on 19 November 2007, concerning road freight forwarding. In addition, on 12 December 2007, Schenker submitted a summary application for leniency to the AGCM, providing information on road freight forwarding in Italy.

21 On 20 November 2007, Agility Logistics Srl ('Agility') submitted to the Commission a summary application for reduction of the fine, in relation to infringements on the international freight forwarding and transport market. On 12 May 2008, Agility Logistics International submitted a summary application for leniency to the AGCM, on its own behalf and on behalf of its subsidiary Agility, concerning the Italian cartel in relation to road freight forwarding.

22 On 18 November 2009, the AGCM opened a procedure concerning possible infringements of Article 101 TFEU in the international freight transport sector.

23 In the decision at issue, adopted on 15 June 2011, the AGCM concluded that several undertakings, including DHL, Schenker and Agility had, in breach of Article 101 TFEU, taken part in a cartel in the international road freight forwarding sector affecting operations to and from Italy.

24 In that decision, the AGCM recognised that Schenker was the first company to have applied for immunity from fines in Italy for road freight forwarding. Under the national leniency programme, no fine was imposed on that company. DHL and Agility, however, were ordered to pay fines, which were subsequently reduced to 49% and 50%, respectively, of the initial amounts. The AGCM also considered that, in its application of 12 July 2007, DHL had requested immunity from fines only for air freight and sea freight forwarding, the application in respect of road freight forwarding having been filed by DHL only on 23 June 2008.

20 同时，2007年11月5日，德国联邦铁路公司（Deutsche Bahn AG）——代表自己，并同时特别代表意大利辛克物流股份有限公司（以下简称辛克物流）——向欧盟委员会提交了一份关于国际货物海运代理卡特尔行为的豁免申请，并于2007年11月19日提交了第二份关于国际货物陆运代理卡特尔行为的豁免申请。另外，2007年12月12日，辛克物流又向AGCM提交了一份简易豁免申请，提供了意大利货物陆运代理行业卡特尔的有关违法信息。

21 2007年11月20日，敏捷物流有限责任公司（以下简称敏捷物流）就其在国际货运代理和运输市场中实施的违法行为向欧盟委员会提交了一份减轻罚款的简易豁免申请。2008年5月12日，敏捷国际物流公司代表自己与其子公司敏捷物流，就它们参与意大利国际货物陆运代理卡特尔的行为向AGCM提交了一份简易豁免申请。

22 2009年11月18日，AGCM对涉嫌在国际货物运输行业违反《欧盟运行条约》第101条的行为启动调查程序。

23 2011年6月15日，AGCM就争议问题作出决定，认定包括DHL、辛克物流和敏捷物流在内的一些企业，参与了在意大利的国际货物陆运代理行业（此类货物皆在意大利进出口）发生的卡特尔，违反了《欧盟运行条约》第101条。

24 在该决定中，AGCM认定辛克物流是第一个在意大利国内就货物陆运代理卡特尔申请罚款豁免的公司。根据其国内豁免制度，辛克物流将免于罚款。相对的，DHL和敏捷物流就需要支付罚款，但随后也分别减轻了处罚，即减少至原罚款数额的49%和50%。AGCM同时认为，DHL在2007年7月12日提交的国内豁免申请中，只要求了国际货物空运和海运代理卡特尔的罚款豁免，而关于陆运代理卡特尔的豁免申请是DHL在2008年6月23日才提出的。

25 DHL brought an action for partial annulment of the decision at issue before the Tribunale amministrativo regionale per il Lazio (Regional Administrative Court for Lazio, Italy) on the ground that it should have been accorded the first place in the queue for the national leniency programme and therefore immunity from fines. According to DHL, the principles of EU law require a national authority which receives a summary leniency application to assess it taking into account the main application for immunity which that company submitted to the Commission. Moreover, DHL submitted that the summary applications submitted by Schenker and Agility to the AGCM were inadmissible.

26 The Tribunale amministrativo regionale per il Lazio (Regional Administrative Court for Lazio, Italy) rejected the action brought by DHL on the basis that, as a matter of principle, the different leniency programmes and the applications in relation to those programmes were autonomous and independent.

27 DHL lodged an appeal before the referring court against the judgment at first instance. That company submits that the decision at issue does not respect the principles set out, inter alia, in the Notice on Cooperation and in the ECN Model Leniency Programme. According to DHL, the rules and instruments of the ECN are binding on the AGCM, since it is a national competition authority which forms part of that network.

28 In those circumstances, the Consiglio di Stato (Council of State) decided to stay the proceedings and to refer the following question to the Court of Justice for a preliminary ruling:

'On a proper construction of Article 101 TFEU, Article 4(3) TEU and Article 11 of Regulation (EC) No 1/2003, does it follow that:

(i) national competition authorities may not, in their own implementation practices, deviate from the instruments defined and adopted by the ECN and, in particular, from the ECN Model Leniency Programme, in a case such as that at issue before the referring court, without running counter to the findings of the Court of Justice of the European Union in paragraphs 21 and 22 of the judgment of 14 June 2011 in *Pfleiderer* (Case C-360/09, EU: C: 2011: 389)?

25 DHL向意大利拉齐奥地区行政法院提起了诉讼，主张其根据国内豁免制度应当被列为申请豁免的第一位，从而免于罚款。DHL认为，根据欧盟法原则，国内竞争主管机构在评估其收到的简易豁免申请时，要参考该卡特尔成员提交给欧盟委员会的主豁免申请。[①]此外，DHL还认为辛克物流和敏捷物流向AGCM提交的简易豁免申请是不可采纳的。

26 意大利拉齐奥地区行政法院驳回了DHL的起诉，因为原则上不同的豁免制度是自主且独立的，相应地，依据各豁免制度提起的豁免申请也是自主且独立的。

27 DHL不服初审判决，向意大利国务委员会[②]提起了上诉。DHL认为AGCM的决定没有遵守在《合作公告》和《ECN宽恕政策范本》中确立的欧盟法原则。DHL认为，AGCM应当遵守ECN的规则和文件，因为其作为国内竞争主管机构是ECN的一部分。

28 在这种情况下，意大利国务委员会决定中止诉讼程序，将以下问题提交给欧盟法院，请求欧盟法院作出先行裁决：

“《欧盟运行条约》第101条、《欧盟条约》第4条第3款和《第1/2003号条例》第11条作如下解释是否合理：

(i)在处理如本案所涉争议之时，成员国竞争主管机构在实践中不能违背由ECN规定并通过的规范，尤其是《ECN宽恕政策范本》，也不得与欧盟法院在2011年6月14日作出的‘Pfleiderer’案(C-360/09, EU: C: 2011: 389)判决第21段和第22段中的观点背道而驰；

① 所谓的“主豁免申请”只是上诉人DHL的一面之词，因为DHL试图说服法院要求成员国竞争主管机构参考提交给欧盟委员会的豁免申请，所以DHL将提交给欧盟委员会的豁免申请自称为“主豁免”，将提交给成员国国内竞争主管机构的豁免申请称为“次豁免”。DHL这样做是因为其提交欧盟委员会的豁免申请中是包括“陆运”卡特尔的，如果意大利竞争主管机构参考提交给欧盟委员会的豁免申请，则DHL就可以获得海陆空全面的豁免。所以“主豁免申请”这个词只能出现在DHL的个人意见叙述中，和提请法院的提请问题中(提请法院也被误导使用了这个词)。判决主文部分，欧盟法院否决了这个词的使用不当，强调不存在“主”“次”之分，提交给欧盟委员会的和提交给成员国的是“平行”的豁免申请。——译者注

② 本案中，意大利国务委员会是意大利最高行政法院，也是向欧盟法院提请先行裁决的法院，故亦称“提请法院”。——译者注

(ii) a legal link exists between the main application for immunity that an undertaking has submitted or is about to submit to the Commission and the summary application for immunity submitted by that undertaking to a national competition authority in respect of the same cartel, with the effect that—notwithstanding the provision made under paragraph 38 of the Commission Notice on Cooperation within the Network of Competition Authorities—the national competition authority is obliged, under paragraph 22 of the 2006 ECN Model Leniency Programme (now paragraph 24 according to the numbering of the 2012 ECN Model Leniency Programme) and the related Explanatory Note 45 (now Explanatory Note 49 according to the numbering of the 2012 Model Leniency Programme), to take the following steps:

-to assess the summary application in the light of the main application for immunity, examining whether the summary application accurately reflects the content of the main application; and

-failing which—if the national competition authority believes that the summary application received is narrower in material scope than the main application submitted by the same undertaking, on the basis of which the Commission has granted conditional immunity to that undertaking—to contact the Commission, or that undertaking, in order to ascertain whether, following the submission of the summary application, that undertaking has identified, through its internal investigations, actual and specific examples of conduct in the sector purportedly covered by the main application for immunity but not by the summary application?

(iii) pursuant to paragraph 3 and paragraphs 22 to 24 of the 2006 ECN Model Leniency Programme and Explanatory Notes 8, 41, 45 and 46 and taking account of the amendment introduced by paragraphs 24 to 26 of the 2012 ECN Model Leniency Programme and Explanatory Notes 44 and 49, a national competition authority which at the material time applied a leniency programme as described in the main proceedings could, with regard to a given secret cartel in respect of which the first undertaking has submitted or was about to submit to the Commission a main application for immunity, legitimately take receipt of:

-only a summary application for immunity from that undertaking; or

-also additional summary applications for immunity from various undertakings that had initially submitted to the Commission 'unacceptable' applications for immunity or applications for a reduction in the fine, in particular where the main applications submitted by the latter undertakings were made after the first undertaking was granted conditional immunity?'

(ii)尽管有《欧盟委员会关于与成员国竞争主管机构合作的公告》第38段‘在欧盟范围内没有统一的豁免制度情况下，向某一成员国机构申请豁免并不意味向任何其他成员国的竞争主管机构申请豁免’的规定，但是对于同一个卡特尔，企业已经或将要向欧盟委员会提交的主豁免申请与其向国内竞争主管机构提交的简易豁免申请存在法律上的联系，所以国内竞争主管机构有义务根据2006年《ECN宽恕政策范本》第22段（2012年《ECN宽恕政策范本》第24段）和相关的注释第45条（2012年《ECN宽恕政策范本》注释第49条），按照如下步骤采取措施：

——根据主豁免申请评估简易豁免申请，检验简易豁免申请是否准确地反映了主豁免申请的内容；并且

——若简易豁免申请并未准确反映主豁免申请的内容，并且国内竞争主管机构基于欧盟委员会已授予该企业有条件的豁免，确信其收到的简易申请在请求豁免的实质范围上比提交给欧盟委员会的主豁免申请范围更窄——则国内竞争主管机构应主动联系欧盟委员会或该申请企业，以查明：这些企业在简易豁免申请中没有提到，而在提交给欧盟委员会的豁免申请中已经提到的那些违法行为是否真实存在？

(iii)根据2006年《ECN宽恕政策范本》第3段、第22段至第24段，以及注释第8条、第41条、第45条、第46条，并考虑到2012年修订后的《ECN宽恕政策范本》第24段至第26段和注释第44条、第49条，在同一个尚未查明的隐蔽卡特尔中，若第一家卡特尔成员企业已经或将要向欧盟委员会提交主豁免申请，则国内竞争主管机构应当适时地根据如本案所述之豁免制度合法接收：

——仅限该第一家申请豁免之卡特尔成员企业提交的简易豁免申请；或

——也可以接受最初向欧盟委员会提交豁免申请或减轻罚款申请但被欧盟委员会否决的其他企业的简易豁免申请，尤其是那些在第一家企业已被授予有条件豁免以后再向欧盟委员会申请豁免的卡特尔成员的简易豁免申请。”

Consideration of the questions referred

The first question

29 By its first question, the referring court asks, in essence, whether EU law, in particular Article 101 TFEU and Regulation No 1/2003, must be interpreted as meaning that the instruments adopted in the context of the ECN, in particular the ECN Model Leniency Programme, are binding on national competition authorities.

30 It is settled case–law that the cooperation mechanism between the Commission and the national competition authorities which was set up in Chapter IV of Regulation No 1/2003 is intended to ensure the coherent application of the competition rules in the Member States (see, to that effect, judgments in X, C–429/07, EU: C: 2009: 359, paragraph 20, and in Tele2 Polska, C–375/09, EU: C: 2011: 270, paragraph 26).

31 According to recital 15 of Regulation No 1/2003, the Commission and the competition authorities of the Member States should form together a network of public authorities applying the EU competition rules in close cooperation. In that respect, paragraph 1 of the Notice on Cooperation states that that network is a forum for discussion and cooperation in the application and enforcement of EU competition policy.

32 It follows that the ECN, being intended to encourage discussion and cooperation in the implementation of competition policy, does not have the power to adopt legally binding rules.

33 In that respect, the Court has already held that neither the Commission Notice on Cooperation, nor the Commission Notice on immunity from fines and reduction of fines in cartel cases (OJ 2006 C 298, p. 17; 'the Leniency Notice') is binding on Member States (see judgment in *Pfleiderer*, C–360/09, EU: C: 2011: 389, paragraph 21).

34 Moreover, the Notice on Cooperation and the Leniency Notice, adopted in the context of the ECN, were published in 2004 and 2006, respectively, in the 'C' series of the *Official Journal of the European Union*, which, by contrast with the 'L' series of the Official Journal, is not intended for the publication of legally binding measures, but only of information, recommendations and opinions concerning the European Union (judgments in *Polska Telefonia Cyfrowa*, C–410/09, EU: C: 2011: 294, paragraph 35, and *Expedia*, C–226/11, EU: C: 2012: 795, paragraph 30).

35 It follows that those notices are not capable of creating obligations on Member States.

欧盟法院对提请法院所提问题的分析

第一个问题

29 第一个问题中，提请法院实质上是在问：欧盟法，尤其是《欧盟运行条约》第101条和《第1/2003号条例》，是否应当被解释为：ECN通过的文件，尤其是《ECN宽恕政策范本》，对成员国竞争主管机构有拘束力？

30 根据欧盟法院的以往判例，《第1/2003号条例》第4章在欧盟委员会和成员国国内竞争主管机构之间建立合作机制，旨在确保共同体竞争规则在成员国中的统一适用（参见判例：X，C 429/07，EU：C：2009：359，第20段；Tele2 Polska，C 375/09，EU：C：2011：270，第26段）。

31 根据《第1/2003号条例》第15条，欧盟委员会和成员国竞争主管机构应共同建成一个公共管理合作网络平台，加强合作，以共同适用欧盟竞争规则查处违法行为。对此，《合作公告》第1段指出，该"网络"是各竞争主管机构就欧盟竞争政策的适用和执行展开讨论并加强合作的平台。

32 因此，ECN旨在鼓励欧盟委员会和成员国竞争主管机构在执行竞争政策时进行讨论和合作，而ECN本身无权制定具有法律约束力的规则。

33 关于这一点，欧盟法院已有判例佐证。例如，在"Pfleiderer"案中，欧盟法院认为，《合作公告》和《关于卡特尔案件罚款豁免和减轻公告》（OJ 2006 C 298，p. 17，简称《2006年宽恕公告》）都不对成员国具有约束力。（参见判例：Pfleiderer，C 360/09，EU：C：2011：389，第21段）

34 此外，在ECN背景下分别于2004年和2006年通过的《合作公告》和《宽恕公告》都被公布在《欧盟官方公报》的"C"系列中。与"L"系列不同的是，"C"系列不是为了公布有法律约束力的措施，而仅提供有关欧盟的相关信息、建议和意见（参见判例：Polska Telefonia Cyfrowa，C 410/09，EU：C：2011：294，第35段；Expedia，C 226/11，EU：C：2012：795，第30段）。

35 因此，这些公告不能为成员国创设义务。

36 As regards, in particular, the leniency programme applicable, within the European Union, to undertakings that cooperate with the Commission or with the national competition authorities in order to uncover unlawful cartels, it must be noted that neither the provisions of the FEU Treaty on competition nor Regulation No 1/2003 lay down common rules on leniency (judgment in *Pfleiderer*, C-360/09, EU: C: 2011: 389, paragraph 20). Thus, in the absence of a centralised system, at the EU level, for the receipt and assessment of leniency applications in relation to infringements of Article 101 TFEU, the treatment of such applications sent to a national competition authority is determined by that authority under the national law of the Member State in question.

37 In that respect, it should be pointed out that the Leniency Notice relates only to leniency programmes implemented by the Commission itself (judgment in *Pfleiderer*, C-360/09, EU: C: 2011: 389, paragraph 21).

38 In that context, it must be recalled that the Court has already held that the ECN Model Leniency Programme has no binding effect on the courts and tribunals of the Member States (judgment in *Pfleiderer*, C-360/09, EU: C: 2011: 389, paragraph 22).

39 DHL submits, however, that that case-law concerns only national courts and tribunals and not national competition authorities. According to DHL, the Court's conclusion in *Pfleiderer* (C-360/09, EU: C: 2011: 389) was solely justified by the fact that the provisions in question did not have direct effect and that, accordingly, national courts could not apply them in civil or administrative disputes.

40 That argument cannot be accepted.

41 First, given that, in accordance with Article 35(1) of Regulation No 1/2003, the Member States may designate courts as national competition authorities, the uniform application of EU law in the Member States would be undermined. The binding effect of the ECN Model Leniency Programme would vary depending on the nature, judicial or administrative, of the national competition authorities of the various Member States.

36 至于成员国国内豁免制度，可以适用于主动与欧盟委员会或成员国竞争主管机构合作来揭露非法卡特尔的企业。必须强调的是，《欧盟运行条约》关于竞争部分的规定和《第1/2003号条例》都没有明确关于豁免程序的一般规则（参见判例：Pfleiderer，C 360/09，EU：C：2011：389，第20段）。因此，在欧盟层面缺乏统一豁免制度的情况下，成员国竞争主管机构收到关于违反《欧盟运行条约》第101条行为的豁免申请后，如何处理此等申请、是否接受申请以及怎样评估，皆应由成员国竞争主管机构根据其国内法决定。

37 应当指出，《宽恕公告》只针对欧盟委员会本身实施的豁免制度生效。（参见判例：Pfleiderer，C 360/09，EU：C：2011：389，第21段）

38 在这种情况下，必须再次强调欧盟法院以往判例的观点：《ECN宽恕政策范本》对成员国的法院、仲裁庭均没有任何拘束力。（参见判例：Pfleiderer，C 360/09，EU：C：2011：389，第22段）

39 然而，DHL表示，上述"Pfleiderer"案判决所指的"无拘束力"仅针对成员国国内法院和仲裁庭而言，而无关乎成员国竞争主管机构。也就是说，所述规范文件对国内法院和仲裁庭没有拘束力，但对竞争主管机构有拘束力。如果根据DHL的推论，那么欧盟法院在"Pfleiderer"案（C 360/09，EU：C：2011：389）中的结论也表明，《ECN宽恕政策范本》对成员国的法院、仲裁庭均没有直接拘束力。可见，成员国国内法院不能在民事或行政争议中适用这些规则。

40 因此，本院不能采纳DHL的观点。

41 首先，根据《第1/2003号条例》第35条第1款，成员国可以将法院指定为国内竞争主管机构。若DHL的观点成立，则欧盟法在成员国之间的适用将无法统一。因为《ECN宽恕政策范本》的拘束力将因各成员国国内竞争主管机构的性质不同（司法性或行政性）而有差异，即如果是司法机构则对其没有拘束力；反之，如果是行政机构则对其有拘束力。

42 Secondly, the Court has already held that the leniency programme established by the Commission, through its Leniency Notice, is not binding on Member States (judgment in *Kone and Others*, C-557/12, EU: C: 2014: 1317, paragraph 36). That conclusion also applies to the ECN Model Leniency Programme.

43 Furthermore, DHL's argument that the national competition authorities have formally undertaken to respect the principles set out in the Notice on Cooperation does not change the legal status, under EU law, of that notice, nor that of the ENC Model Leniency Programme.

44 In the light of the foregoing, the answer to the first question is that EU law, in particular Article 101 TFEU and Regulation No 1/2003, must be interpreted as meaning that the instruments adopted in the context of the ECN, in particular the ECN Model Leniency Programme, are not binding on national competition authorities.

The second question

45 By its second question, the referring court asks, in the first place, whether EU law, in particular Article 101 TFEU and Regulation No 1/2003, must be interpreted as meaning that there is a legal link between the application for immunity which an undertaking submits or is preparing to submit to the Commission and the summary application submitted to a national competition authority in respect of the same cartel which requires that authority to assess the summary application in the light of the application for immunity, where the summary application accurately reflects the content of the application for immunity submitted to the Commission. In the second place, the referring court asks whether, in the event that the summary application has a more limited material scope than the application for immunity, the national competition authority is required to contact the Commission or the undertaking itself, in order to establish whether that undertaking has found specific examples of unlawful conduct in the sector allegedly covered by the application for immunity, but which is not covered by the summary application.

Admissibility

46 Agility and the French Government argue that the first part of the second question is inadmissible, on the ground, respectively, that it is irrelevant and that it is hypothetical.

42 其次，欧盟法院以往判例表明，欧盟委员会通过《宽恕公告》设立的豁免制度对成员国没有拘束力（参见判例：Kone and Others，C-557/12，EU：C：2014：1317，第36段）。同样地，《ECN宽恕政策范本》对成员国也没有拘束力。

43 最后，虽然DHL称成员国竞争主管机构已经正式承诺遵守《合作公告》中规定的原则，但这种承诺并不能改变ENC作出的公告在欧盟法中的法律地位，也不会改变《ECN宽恕政策范本》在欧盟法中的法律地位。

44 鉴于上述理由，欧盟法院认为，根据欧盟法的原则，尤其是《欧盟运行条约》第101条和《第1/2003号条例》的规定，ECN通过的文件，尤其是《ECN宽恕政策范本》，对成员国竞争主管机构没有拘束力。

第二个问题

45 第二个问题中，提请法院的问题是：第一，欧盟法，尤其是《欧盟运行条约》第101条和《第1/2003号条例》是否应当被解释为：企业已经或将要向欧盟委员会提交的豁免申请与其向成员国竞争主管机构提交的简易申请，这两者之间存在一种法律联系：如果简易申请中准确地反映了提交给欧盟委员会的豁免申请中的内容，则成员国竞争主管机构应当根据提交给欧盟委员会的豁免申请来评估简易申请。第二，如果简易申请请求豁免的范围在实质上比提交给欧盟委员会的豁免申请更窄，则成员国竞争主管机构是否还需要主动联系欧盟委员会或该申请企业，以查明：这些企业在简易豁免申请中没有提到、而在提交给欧盟委员会的豁免申请中已经提到的那些违法行为是否真实存在？

可采纳性问题

46 敏捷物流和法国政府都主张，第二个问题的第一部分是不可采纳的，因为敏捷物流认为其与本案争议无关，而法国政府认为那是假设性的问题。

47 According to Agility and the French Government, the question that arises in the main proceedings is whether a summary application must be interpreted in the light of the application for immunity submitted to the Commission where those applications do not have the same material scope. By contrast, by the first part of the second question, the referring court asks whether, in the event that the summary application accurately reflects the content of the application for immunity submitted to the Commission, the summary application must be interpreted in the light of that application for immunity.

48 It must be borne in mind in this regard that, according to the Court' s settled case-law, in the context of the cooperation between the Court and the national courts provided for in Article 267 TFEU, it is solely for the national court before which a dispute has been brought, and which must assume responsibility for the subsequent judicial decision, to determine, in the light of the particular circumstances of the case, both the need for a preliminary ruling to enable it to deliver judgment and the relevance of the questions which it submits to the Court. Consequently, where the questions submitted concern the interpretation of EU law, the Court is in principle bound to give a ruling (see, inter alia, judgments in *Kamberaj*, C-571/10, EU: C: 2012: 233, paragraph 40, and in *Banco Privado Português and Massa Insolvente do Banco Privado Português*, C-667/13, EU: C: 2015: 151, paragraph 34).

49 In those circumstances, the Court may refuse to rule on a question referred by a national court only where it is quite obvious that the interpretation of EU law that is sought bears no relation to the actual facts of the main action or its purpose, where the problem is hypothetical, or where the Court does not have before it the factual or legal material necessary to give a useful answer to the questions submitted to it (see, inter alia, judgments in Kamberaj, C-571/10, EU: C: 2012: 233, paragraph 42, and in Banco Privado Português and Massa Insolvente do Banco Privado Português, C-667/13, EU: C: 2015: 151, paragraph 36).

50 That is not the case here.

51 First, it can be seen from the order for reference that, on 5 June 2007, DHL submitted an application for immunity to the Commission concerning several infringements of EU competition law in the international freight forwarding services sector. Secondly, on 12 July 2007, DHL submitted a summary application to the AGCM in relation to unlawful conduct in the market for international road freight forwarding to and from Italy.

47 敏捷物流和法国政府认为，在本案主诉讼程序中出现的问题实际上是：如果卡特尔成员向欧盟委员会提出的豁免申请与向成员国竞争主管机构提出的简易申请实质范围不同，成员国是否必须根据提交给欧盟委员会的豁免申请来评估简易申请？提请法院提出的第二个问题的第一部分则与之完全相反，提请法院问欧盟法院的问题是：如果简易申请能够准确地反映了提交给欧盟委员会的豁免申请的全部内容，则国内竞争主管机构是否必须根据提交给欧盟委员会的豁免申请来评估简易豁免申请？

48 本院认为，根据欧盟法院的以往判例，在《欧盟运行条约》第267条规定的欧盟法院与国内法院合作的基础上，只能由处理争议且必须对最终司法判决承担责任的国内法院来根据案件具体情况决定，是否需要提请欧盟法院作出先行裁决，以及提交给欧盟法院的相关问题是什么。因此，只要提请法院提出的问题涉及欧盟法的解释，欧盟法院原则上必须作出裁决（参见判例：Kamberaj，C 571/10，EU：C：2012：233，第40段；以及判例：Banco Privado Português and Massa Insolvente do Banco Privado Português，C 667/13，EU：C：2015：151，第34段）。

49 只有当国内法院要求欧盟法院对欧盟法的解释与案件争议本质或判决目的毫无关系时，或当国内法院提出的问题是假设性的，或当欧盟法院获得的案件材料或法律材料不充分，导致欧盟法院无法就提交的问题作出明确的答复时，欧盟法院才可以拒绝对提请法院提出的问题作出答复（参见判例：Kamberaj，C 571/10，EU：C：2012：233，第42段；以及判例：Banco Privado Português and Massa Insolvente do Banco Privado Português，C 667/13，EU：C：2015：151，第36段）。

50 在本案中，上述情况都不在可以拒绝答复的理由之列。

51 首先，从先行裁决的申请中可以看出，DHL于2007年6月5日向欧盟委员会提交了关于在国际货运代理服务行业中发生的一些违反欧盟竞争法行为的豁免申请；其次，DHL于2007年7月12日向AGCM提交了关于在意大利进出口的国际货物陆运行业发生的违法行为的简易豁免申请。

52 Since there is disagreement between the AGCM and DHL concerning the material content of the summary application and, consequently, concerning the possible similarities or differences as regards the scope of the applications at issue in the main proceedings, it is not obvious that the response to the first part of the second question would be of no use to the referring court.

53 In those circumstances, the first part of the second question referred must be regarded as admissible.

Substance

54 The leniency system is based on the principle that the competition authorities are to grant immunity from fines to the undertaking that reports its participation in a cartel if it is the first to submit evidence, inter alia, enabling the Commission to find an infringement of Article 101 TFEU.

55 In accordance with paragraph 38 of the Notice on Cooperation, in the absence of a European Union-wide system of fully harmonised leniency programmes, an application for leniency to a given authority is not to be considered as an application for leniency to any other authority. As noted in paragraph 36 above, the treatment of a leniency application is determined by the law of each Member State.

56 In that respect, paragraph 1 of the ECN Model Leniency Programme states that it is in the interest of undertakings to apply for leniency to all competition authorities which have competence to apply Article 101 of the FEU Treaty in the territory which is affected by the infringement in question and which may be considered well placed to act against that infringement.

57 It should also be pointed out that the national competition authorities are free to adopt leniency programmes and each of those programmes is autonomous, not only in respect of other national programmes, but also in respect of the EU leniency programme.

58 The coexistence and autonomy that thus characterise the relationships between the EU leniency programme and those of the Member States are a reflection of the system of parallel competence between the Commission and national competition authorities established by Regulation No 1/2003.

52 最后，由于AGCM与DHL对简易豁免申请的实质内容存在分歧，因此他们对DHL提交给欧盟委员会的豁免申请和提交给AGCM的简易豁免申请之间可能存在的差异存在分歧。但是这并不影响欧盟法院对第二个问题第一部分的答复，也不是说对提请法院毫无用处。

53 为此，欧盟法院对第二个问题的第一部分内容可以接受并作出答复。

实质性问题

54 豁免制度的基本原则是：在所有主动向竞争主管机构报告自己参与卡特尔的企业中，如果一家企业首先提交证据，使欧盟委员会能够发现违反《欧盟运行条约》第101条的隐蔽卡特尔，那么竞争主管机构将给予该第一家报告的企业罚款豁免。

55 根据《合作公告》第38段，由于欧盟范围内缺乏全面统一的豁免制度，向某一成员国机构申请豁免并不意味向任何其他成员国的竞争主管机构申请豁免。如前文第36段所述，对豁免申请的处理由竞争主管机构根据各成员国的国内法决定。

56 为此，《ECN宽恕政策范本》第1条指出，企业可以从其自身利益考虑向受到违犯行为影响的某一国的竞争主管机构提出豁免申请，这一竞争主管机构具有查处违法行为的“优先地位”，有权适用《欧盟运行条约》第101条的规定。

57 还应指出的是，成员国国内竞争主管机构可以自由地选择适用国内法或欧盟法中的豁免制度。因为无论是国内豁免制度还是欧盟豁免制度都是独立、自主的。

58 欧盟豁免制度和成员国国内豁免制度同时共存但各自具有自主性，这两者之间的关系正如《第1/2003号条例》所规定的，即在欧盟委员会与成员国竞争主管机构之间建立一个平行的权力架构机制。

59 It follows that, in the case of a cartel the anticompetitive effects of which are liable to manifest themselves in several Member States and, consequently, may give rise to the intervention of various national competition authorities, as well as the Commission, it is in the interest of an undertaking which wishes to benefit from the leniency system in respect of its participation in the cartel in question to submit applications for immunity, not only to the Commission, but also to the national authorities potentially competent to apply Article 101 TFEU.

60 The autonomy of leniency programmes must necessarily extend to the various applications for immunity submitted to the Commission and to the national competition authorities, given that they constitute an integral part of those programmes. In that respect, it must be noted that the autonomy of those applications follows directly from the fact that there is, at the EU level, no single system of self-reporting for undertakings that participate in cartels in breach of Article 101 TFEU. That autonomy cannot, moreover, be affected by the fact that the various applications concern the same infringement of competition law.

61 The existence, as alleged, of a legal link between the application for immunity submitted to the Commission and the summary application submitted to the national competition authorities, obliging those authorities to assess the summary application in the light of the application for immunity, would call into question the autonomy of the various applications and, consequently, the rationale behind the system of summary applications. That system is based on the principle that there is not, at the EU level, a single leniency application or a 'main' application submitted in parallel to 'secondary' applications, but rather applications for immunity submitted to the Commission and summary applications submitted to the national competition authorities, the assessment of which is the exclusive responsibility of the authority to which the application in question is addressed.

62 In any event, no provision of EU law in relation to cartels requires national competition authorities to interpret a summary application in the light of an application for immunity submitted to the Commission, irrespective of whether or not that summary application accurately reflects the content of the application submitted to the Commission.

63 As regards any obligation for the national competition authority to contact the Commission or the undertaking which submitted a summary application to it, where the material scope of that summary application is more limited than that of the application for immunity, it must be noted, as the Advocate General pointed out in point 78 of his Opinion, that such an obligation would be liable to attenuate the duty of cooperation of leniency applicants, which is one of the pillars of any leniency programme.

59 因此，如果一个卡特尔行为可能在数个成员国内产生反竞争的影响，并且可能导致各国竞争主管机构和欧盟委员会都有权进行查处，则该卡特尔成员想通过豁免制度获取利益，可以从其自身利益考虑，不仅要向欧盟委员会提交豁免申请，也要向有权适用《欧盟运行条约》第101条查处卡特尔行为的成员国竞争主管机构提交豁免申请。

60 豁免制度的这种自主选择权必须扩大到提交给欧盟委员会或成员国竞争主管机构的各种豁免申请，因为这些豁免申请都是豁免制度不可或缺的组成部分。必须强调的是，所有申请人都有权自主选择的直接原因是：因为在欧盟层面没有一个单独的专门豁免制度针对违反《欧盟运行条约》第101条而进入“自首”程序。此外，尽管多个豁免申请都是针对同一个违反竞争法的卡特尔行为，这种自主选择权仍然不受影响。

61 如果提交给欧盟委员会的豁免申请与提交给成员国竞争主管机构的简易申请之间存在所谓的法律联系，这种法律联系迫使成员国竞争主管机构必须根据申请人提交给欧盟委员会的豁免申请来评估简易申请，这会动摇申请人享有的自主选择权，并且也将动摇简易豁免申请制度之所以存在的合理性。豁免制度的一个基本原则是，欧盟层面没有统一的豁免申请制度，也没有“主”申请与“次”申请之说，而只有提交给欧盟委员会的豁免申请和提交给国内竞争管理机构的简易豁免申请，且任何接受豁免申请的竞争主管机构的唯一责任就是自主评估该申请。

62 由此可见，欧盟法中任何有关卡特尔的规定，都没有要求成员国竞争主管机构需要根据申请人向欧盟委员会提交的豁免申请来评估简易豁免申请，无论简易豁免申请是否准确地反映了向欧盟委员会提交的豁免申请的全部内容。

63 至于当简易豁免申请在实质范围上比提交给欧盟委员会的豁免申请更窄时，成员国竞争主管机构是否有义务联系欧盟委员会或提交简易申请的企业，对于这一问题，正如佐审官在其意见书第78点中指出的，应该注意到，如果成员国竞争主管机构承担这样的义务，将减轻提出该项豁免申请的企业的责任，而事实上他们才应该承担主要责任。

64 In those circumstances, it is for the undertaking applying to national competition authorities for leniency to ensure that any application which it submits is devoid of ambiguities as to its scope, all the more so since, as noted in paragraph 62 above, there is no obligation on the national competition authorities to assess a summary application in the light of an application for immunity submitted to the Commission.

65 That interpretation, based on the obligation of the undertaking to inform the national competition authorities if it becomes apparent that the actual scope of the cartel is different from that which it had declared to those authorities, or from that which it had submitted to the Commission, is the only interpretation capable of ensuring respect for the autonomy of the various leniency systems.

66 If the mere possibility, for the national competition authorities, to contact undertakings from which they have received summary applications in order to obtain further information were replaced with an obligation to contact those undertakings or the Commission where the material scope of those applications is more limited than that of the applications for immunity submitted to the Commission, it would create a hierarchy among the applications concerned, in breach of the decentralised system laid down by Regulation No 1/2003.

67 The answer to the second question must therefore be as follows:

–EU law, in particular Article 101 TFEU and Regulation No 1/2003, must be interpreted as meaning that there is no legal link between the application for immunity which an undertaking submits or is preparing to submit to the Commission and the summary application submitted to a national competition authority in respect of the same cartel, requiring that authority to assess the summary application in the light of the application for immunity. Whether or not the summary application accurately reflects the content of the application for immunity submitted to the Commission is, in that respect, irrelevant.

–Where the summary application submitted to a national competition authority has a more limited material scope than the application for immunity submitted to the Commission, that national authority is not required to contact the Commission or the undertaking itself, in order to establish whether that undertaking has found specific examples of unlawful conduct in the sector allegedly covered by the application for immunity, but which is not covered by the summary application.

64 因此，正如前文第62段所述，既然成员国竞争主管机构没有义务根据申请人向欧盟委员会提交的豁免申请来评估简易豁免申请，就应该由提出豁免申请的卡特尔企业向竞争主管机构保证其提交的所有申请材料是完整的，不存在范围大小的模糊性。

65 当卡特尔成员企业向成员国竞争主管机构提交申请豁免时，如果其在豁免申请中所提及的卡特尔违反范围明显不同于先前已经提交给其他机构或欧盟委员会的申请豁免的范围，则该卡特尔成员就有义务把这种差异告知该成员国竞争主管机构。由申请豁免的卡特尔成员承担这种告知义务，才能保证在所有豁免制度中各层面都享有自主选择权。这样的解释是唯一恰当的。

66 当然，当卡特尔成员企业向成员国竞争主管机构提交的简易豁免申请范围比向欧盟委员会提交的豁免申请范围更窄时，成员国竞争主管机构确实有可能为了获得更多的信息而联系该提交简易豁免申请的企业，但这并不是强加给成员国竞争主管机构的一项义务。如果理解为这是一项义务，则会导致在不同的豁免制度机制下形成一种层次等级关系，这也违背了《第1/2003号条例》所确立的独立、平行的制度架构。

67 综上，对第二个问题的答复如下：

——欧盟法，尤其是《欧盟运行条约》第101条和《第1/2003号条例》，应当被解释为：对于同一个卡特尔，卡特尔成员企业已经或将要向欧盟委员会提交的豁免申请与向成员国竞争主管机构提交的简易豁免申请之间没有任何法律联系。因此，成员国竞争主管机构无须根据申请人向欧盟委员会提交的豁免申请来评估简易豁免申请，无论申请人提交的简易豁免申请是否准确地反映了其向欧盟委员会提交的豁免申请的全部内容。

——如果申请人提交给成员国竞争主管机构的简易豁免申请在实质范围上比提交给欧盟委员会的豁免申请更窄，则成员国竞争主管机构没有必要联系欧盟委员会或该申请企业，没有义务去查明这些企业在简易豁免申请中没有提到，而在提交给欧盟委员会的豁免申请中已经提到的那些违法行为是否真实存在。

The third question

68 By its third question, the referring court asks, in essence, whether EU law, in particular Article 101 TFEU and Regulation No 1/2003, must be interpreted as meaning that, where a first undertaking has submitted an application for immunity to the Commission, only that undertaking may submit a summary application to a national competition authority or if other undertakings, which had submitted an application for a reduction of the fine to the Commission, are also entitled to do so.

Admissibility

69 The Italian and Austrian Governments submit that the third question referred is inadmissible in that, by that question, the referring court asks the Court to interpret national law, in particular the national leniency programme.

70 According to settled case law, it is not for the Court, in preliminary ruling proceedings, to rule upon the compatibility of provisions of national law with EU law or to interpret national legislation or regulations (see, inter alia, judgments in *Jaeger*, C-151/02, EU:C:2003:437, paragraph 43, and in *Consorci Sanitari del Maresme*, C-203/14, EU:C:2015:664, paragraph 43).

71 However, in the present case, it can be seen from the third question that the referring court essentially seeks guidance from the Court as to the interpretation of EU law, in particular, Article 101 TFEU and Regulation No 1/2003, in the context of the operation of the system of parallel competences between the Commission and the national competition authorities, in order to determine whether, under the national leniency programme, the AGCM 'could lawfully' accept certain applications for immunity.

72 Accordingly, it is necessary to give an answer that will be of use to the referring court by providing the latter with guidance as to the interpretation of EU law, which will enable that court to rule itself on the lawfulness of the decision at issue.

73 It follows that the third question referred must be considered admissible.

第三个问题

68 提请法院提出的第三个问题是：欧盟法，尤其是《欧盟运行条约》第101条和《第1/2003号条例》是否应当被解释为：如果第一家卡特尔成员企业向欧盟委员会提交了豁免申请，是否意味着只有这家企业可以向成员国竞争主管机构提交简易豁免申请；或者说，其他向欧盟委员会提交了减轻罚款申请的卡特尔成员企业也有权向成员国竞争主管机构提交简易豁免申请。

可采纳性问题

69 意大利政府和奥地利政府认为第三个问题是不可采纳的，因为该问题实际上是提请法院要求欧盟法院解释国内法，尤其是成员国国内的豁免制度。

70 根据欧盟法院以往判例，在先行裁决程序中不应由欧盟法院裁决成员国国内法与欧盟法条款的一致性，或解释成员国国内法律或规则。（参见判例：Jaeger，C-151/02，EU：C：2003：437，第43段；以及判例：Consorci Sanitari del Maresme，C-203/14，EU：C：2015：664，第43段）

71 但就本案来说，提请法院提出的第三个问题实际上是希望能在欧盟委员会和成员国竞争主管机构之间构成的平行权力体系运行中，寻求欧盟法院的指导意见来解释欧盟法，尤其是《欧盟运行条约》第101条和《第1/2003号条例》中的相关规定，从而决定在国内豁免制度下，AGCM是否能“合法地”接受某些豁免申请。

72 所以，欧盟法院有必要解答提请法院的问题，指导提请法院理解欧盟法，使其能合法地对案件作出裁决。

73 因此，提请法院提出的第三个问题是可采纳的。

Substance

74 The doubt on the part of the referring court that gave rise to the third question referred relates to the fact that the ENC Model Leniency Programme indicated that the system of summary applications for immunity at the national level was open to the undertaking that had applied to the Commission for immunity from fines, whereas it was not clear whether that system was also open to undertakings that had applied to the Commission for a mere reduction of fines.

75 The possibility for an undertaking which was not the first to submit an application for immunity to the Commission and which, accordingly, was not eligible for full immunity, but only a reduction of the fine, to submit a summary application for immunity to the national competition authorities was expressly set out in the ENC Model Leniency Programme only after the amendments made to that programme in 2012.

76 In that respect, the fact that the ENC Model Leniency Programme, in the version existing at the material time, did not expressly refer to the possibility for the undertakings that had submitted an application to the Commission for reduction of fines to lodge a summary application for immunity before the national competition authorities cannot be interpreted as precluding those authorities from accepting, in those circumstances, such a summary application.

77 As noted in paragraph 44 above, the instruments adopted in the context of the ECN, in particular the ECN Model Leniency Programme, are not binding on national competition authorities. Given the non-binding nature of that programme, it follows, first, that Member States are not required to incorporate provisions of the ECN Model Leniency Programme in their leniency systems and, secondly, that they are also not precluded from adopting, at the national level, rules which are not present in that model programme or which diverge from it, in so far as that competence is exercised in compliance with EU law, in particular Article 101 TFEU and Regulation No 1/2003.

78 The Member States' competence to determine their leniency programmes must be exercised in accordance with EU law, including Regulation No 1/2003. In particular, the Member States may not render the implementation of EU law impossible or excessively difficult and, specifically, in the area of competition law, they must ensure that the rules which they establish or apply do not jeopardise the effective application of Articles 101 TFEU and 102 TFEU (judgments in *Pfleiderer*, C-360/09, EU: C: 2011: 389, paragraph 24, and in *Kone and Others*, C-557/12, EU: C: 2014: 1317, paragraph 26).

实质性问题

74 提请法院的第三个问题是，根据《ECN宽恕政策范本》的规定，如果允许已经向欧盟委员会提交豁免申请的卡特尔成员企业可以再向成员国竞争主管机构提交简易豁免申请，那么，已向欧盟委员会提交减轻罚款申请的卡特尔成员企业是否也被允许向成员国竞争主管机构提交相应的简易豁免申请？

75 如果一家企业不是第一个向欧盟委员会提交豁免申请的卡特尔成员，因此不具备获得完全豁免的资格，只能获得减轻罚款，其是否可以向成员国竞争主管机构提交简易豁免申请，这种情况只有在2012年修正后的《ECN模范豁免制度》中有明确的阐述。

76 在这方面，旧版本的《ECN宽恕政策范本》并没有明确提到一家已经向欧盟委员会提交减轻罚款申请的卡特尔成员企业，是否也可以再向成员国竞争主管机构提出简易豁免申请。但这一事实不能被理解为其限制了其他成员国竞争主管机构接受这样的简易豁免申请。

77 如前文第44段所提到的，在ECN通过的文件，尤其是《ECN宽恕政策范本》，对成员国竞争主管机构没有拘束力。鉴于该制度不具拘束力的性质，可以作出这样的推论：首先，成员国不需要将《ECN宽恕政策范本》的规定并入其国内豁免制度；其次，只要依照欧盟法，尤其是《欧盟运行条约》第101条和《第1/2003号条例》行使权力，则成员国可以在国内层面采用《ECN宽恕政策范本》中未出现或与其有分歧的规则。

78 成员国有权自行制定其国内豁免制度，但前提是必须遵循欧盟法的规定，包括《第1/2003号条例》。尤其是，成员国不能使欧盟法的适用陷入不可能或极度困难的境地，特别是在竞争法领域，成员国必须确保其建立或适用的国内法规不会危及《欧盟运行条约》第101条、第102条的有效实施。（参见判例：Pfleiderer，C 360/09，EU：C：2011：389，第24段，以及判例：Kone and Others，C 557/12，EU：C：2014：1317，第26段）

79 The Court has already held that leniency programmes are useful tools if efforts to uncover and bring to an end infringements of competition rules are to be effective and serve, therefore, the objective of effective application of Articles 101 TFEU and 102 TFEU (judgment in *Pfleiderer*, C–360/09, EU: C: 2011: 389, paragraph 25).

80 In that respect, it must be pointed out that the effective application of Article 101 TFEU does not preclude a national leniency system which allows the acceptance of a summary leniency application submitted by an undertaking which had not submitted an application for full immunity.

81 On the contrary, that approach is in accordance with the underlying purpose and spirit of the establishment of the system of leniency applications. That system is intended, inter alia, to promote the uncovering of conduct contrary to Article 101 TFEU by encouraging participants in cartels to report them. It is therefore intended to encourage the submission of such applications, not to limit their number.

82 Thus, the Court of Justice has held that the aim of the Leniency Notice is to create a climate of uncertainty within cartels in order to encourage the reporting of them to the Commission (judgment in *LG Display and LG Display Taiwan* v *Commission*, C–227/14 P, EU: C: 2015: 258, paragraph 87). That uncertainty arises, inter alia, from the fact that only one cartel participant can obtain full immunity and that, at any moment, the Commission may, on its own initiative, identify the existence of that cartel.

83 In that context, it is possible that an undertaking which was not the first to submit an application for immunity to the Commission and which, consequently, is eligible only for a reduction of the fine may, by lodging a summary application for immunity, be the first to inform the national competition authority of the existence of the cartel concerned. In such a situation, in the event that the Commission does not pursue its investigation concerning the same matters as were reported to the national authority, the undertaking concerned could be granted full immunity under the national leniency programme.

79 根据欧盟法院以往判例，如果成员国制定的国内豁免制度在揭露和制止违反竞争规则的行为方面是有效的，从而有助于《欧盟运行条约》第101条、第102条的有效实施，那么该国内豁免制度就是有益的措施。（参见判例：Pfleiderer，C 360/09，EU：C：2011：389，第25段）

80 必须强调的是，为了《欧盟运行条约》第101条的有效实施，并不禁止成员国国内豁免制度可以允许其竞争主管机构接受一家卡特尔成员企业提交的简易豁免申请，尽管该企业未向欧盟委员会提交完全的豁免申请。

81 鼓励成员国竞争主管机构接受卡特尔成员提交简易豁免申请，这种做法才更加符合建立豁免制度的根本目的和精神。豁免制度旨在通过鼓励卡特尔参与者主动报告，以揭露违反《欧盟运行条约》第101条的行为。因此其目的是鼓励卡特尔成员主动提交这种豁免申请，而非限制其提交豁免申请的数量。

82 正因如此，欧盟法院以往判例表明，《宽恕公告》的目的是在卡特尔内部营造不稳定的氛围，鼓励卡特尔成员主动向欧盟委员会报告（参见判例：LG Display and LG Display Taiwan v Commission，C 227/14 P，EU：C：2015：258，第87段）。这种不稳定氛围的产生，是由于只有一名卡特尔参与者可以获得完全豁免，而且欧盟委员会可以随时主动确认哪一个卡特尔参与者可以获得完全豁免。

83 在这个基础上，也可能存在这样一种情况：一个卡特尔成员企业虽然不是首先（第一个）向欧盟委员会提交豁免申请的，并因此只能获得减轻罚款的资格，但它却是第一个提出简易豁免申请，向成员国竞争主管机构告发了存在的卡特尔行为。在告发行为发生时，欧盟委员会还没有将同一卡特尔报告给成员国竞争主管机构，也没有就此卡特尔行为展开调查，在这种情况下，向成员国竞争主管机构提出简易豁免申请的这家企业可以基于成员国的国内豁免制度而获得完全豁免。①

① 在成员国国内属于“首位告发者”，基于成员国国内豁免制度获得完全豁免罚款，而不是减轻罚款金额。——译者注

84 Consequently, the answer to the third question is that EU law, in particular Article 101 TFEU and Regulation No 1/2003, must be interpreted as not precluding a national competition authority from accepting, in circumstances such as those at issue in the main proceedings, a summary application for immunity from an undertaking which had not submitted an application for full immunity to the Commission, but rather an application for reduction of the fine.

Costs

85 Since these proceedings are, for the parties to the main proceedings, a step in the action pending before the national court, the decision on costs is a matter for that court. Costs incurred in submitting observations to the Court, other than the costs of those parties, are not recoverable.

On those grounds, the Court (Second Chamber) hereby rules:

1.EU law, in particular Article 101 TFEU and Council Regulation (EC) No 1/2003 of 16 December 2002 on the implementation of the rules on competition laid down in Articles 101 [TFEU] and 102 [TFEU], must be interpreted as meaning that the instruments adopted in the context of the European Competition Network, in particular the Model Leniency Programme of that network, are not binding on national competition authorities.

2.EU law, in particular Article 101 TFEU and Regulation No 1/2003, must be interpreted as meaning that there is no legal link between the application for immunity which an undertaking submits or is preparing to submit to the European Commission and the summary application submitted to a national competition authority in respect of the same cartel, requiring that authority to assess the summary application in the light of the application for immunity. Whether or not the summary application accurately reflects the content of the application for immunity submitted to the Commission is, in that respect, irrelevant.

Where the summary application submitted to a national competition authority has a more limited material scope than the application for immunity submitted to the Commission, that national authority is not required to contact the Commission or the undertaking itself, in order to establish whether that undertaking has found specific examples of unlawful conduct in the sector allegedly covered by the application for immunity, but which is not covered by the summary application.

3.EU law, in particular Article 101 TFEU and Regulation No 1/2003, must be interpreted as not precluding a national competition authority from accepting, in circumstances such as those at issue in the main proceedings, a summary application for immunity from an undertaking which had not submitted an application for full immunity to the Commission, but rather an application for reduction of the fine.

84 因此，对第三个问题的答复是：欧盟法，尤其是《欧盟运行条约》第101条和《第1/2003号条例》应该被解释为：在如本案所示的情况下，如果一家卡特尔成员企业未向欧盟委员会提交完全的豁免申请而仅是申请减轻罚款，那么成员国竞争主管机构也可以接受该卡特尔成员企业提交的简易豁免申请。成员国竞争主管机构的这一自主权利不受限制。

诉讼费用

85 对参加主诉讼程序的当事人来说，先行裁决的程序仅仅是成员国国内法院诉讼期间的一个阶段，有关诉讼费用的决定应由该国内法院作出。对于当事人向本院提出申请时所支出的费用，均不予偿付。

综上，欧盟法院（第二法庭）判决如下：

1.欧盟法，尤其是《欧盟运行条约》第101条和《关于实施〈欧共体条约〉第101条、第102条的第1/2003号条例》，应当被解释为：欧洲竞争网络通过的文件，尤其是《ECN宽恕政策范本》，对成员国竞争主管机构没有拘束力。

2.欧盟法，尤其是《欧盟运行条约》第101条和《第1/2003号条例》，应当被解释为：对于同一卡特尔，卡特尔成员企业已经或将要向欧盟委员会提交的豁免申请与向成员国竞争主管机构提交的简易豁免申请之间没有任何法律联系，从而该成员国竞争主管机构无需根据申请人提交给欧盟委员会的豁免申请来评估简易豁免申请，无论申请人提交的简易申请是否准确地反映了其向欧盟委员会提交的豁免申请的内容。

如果申请人提交给成员国竞争主管机构的简易豁免申请在实质范围上比提交给欧盟委员会的豁免申请更窄，则成员国竞争主管机构没有必要联系欧盟委员会或该申请企业，没有义务去查明这些企业在简易豁免申请中没有提到，而在提交给欧盟委员会的豁免申请中已经提到的那些违法行为是否真实存在。

3.欧盟法，尤其是《欧盟运行条约》第101条和《第1/2003号条例》应该被解释为：在如本案所示的情况下，如果一家卡特尔成员企业未向欧盟委员会提交完全豁免申请而仅是申请减轻罚款，那么成员国竞争主管机构也可以接受该卡特尔成员企业提交的简易豁免申请。成员国竞争主管机构的这一自主权利不受限制。

2

雷普索尔润滑剂公司等
诉
欧盟委员会

（Repsol Lubricantes y Especialidades SA and Others v European Commission）

（*Case C 617/13P*）

案例导读*

一、案例基本信息

法　院	欧盟法院		
提请法院	初审法院	判决时间	2016年6月9日
案　号	Case C-617/13P		
关键词	说明理由的义务、听证权、禁止证据预先评估原则		
当事人	上 诉 人：雷普索尔润滑剂公司（Repsol Lubricantes y Especialidades SA） 雷普索尔石油公司（Repsol Petróleo SA） 雷普索尔公司（Repsol SA） 被上诉人：欧盟委员会（European Commission）		

二、案例涉及的欧盟法规

（一）《第1/2003号条例》

第23条第3款规定："在计算罚款金额时，应当同时考虑违法行为的严重程度和持续时间。"

第31条规定："在审查欧盟委员会作出的罚款决定或者分期罚款决定时，欧盟法院拥有无限管辖权，包括撤销罚款决定，降低或提高罚款或分期罚款的金额。"

---

* 作者：李彦龙。

（二）《关于依据〈第17号条例〉第15条第2款和〈欧洲煤钢共同体条约〉第65条第5款的规定设定罚款方法的指南》（以下简称《1998年罚款指南》）规定：

“罚款基本金额应当依据违法行为的严重程度和持续时间计算。

A.严重性

在认定违法行为的严重程度时，应考虑该行为的性质、可测算出的对市场影响以及相关地区市场的规模。

违法行为分为3类：轻度违法行为，严重违法行为和非常严重违法行为。”

（三）《宽恕公告》

第7条规定：“欧盟委员会可以降低提供合作的卡特尔企业的罚款金额。降低的罚款金额必须反映出该企业在欧盟委员会认定违法行为时所做的实质性贡献，并且应以该证据的质量或时间的形式体现。降低罚款应限于那些向欧盟委员会提供证据的企业，并且该证据对欧盟委员会已经掌握的情况具有明显的附加价值。”

第21条规定：“为计算罚款的减免金额，卡特尔企业向欧盟委员会提供的涉嫌违法行为的证据必须对欧盟委员会已经掌握的情况具有明显附加价值，并且在提供证据之前必须停止参与涉嫌违法行为。”

第23条规定：“欧盟委员会有权在行政程序结束后做出的最终决定中认定：

（a）卡特尔企业提供的证据对于欧盟委员会已经掌握的情况是否具有明显附加价值；

……

此外，如果卡特尔企业提供了欧盟委员会尚未掌握的并且对于认定卡特尔行为严重程度或持续时间具有直接作用的证据，欧盟委员会在认定该企业的罚款金额时将不再考虑严重程度和持续时间这两个因素。”

三、案件事实和审理过程

从1991年起，雷普索尔集团、英国石油集团、CEPSA-PROAS集团、尼纳斯集团和西班牙高浦石油集团等13家公司在西班牙的渗透沥青市场上形成了卡特尔，表现形式为分割市场和对渗透沥青价格的垄断。直至2002年6月20日，英国石油集团根据《宽恕公告》首先向欧盟委员会提交了罚款豁免申请，该违法行为才得以浮出水面。

雷普索尔润滑剂公司（Repsol Lubricantes y Especialidades SA，以下简称润滑剂公司）、雷普索尔石油公司（Repsol Petróleo SA，以下简称石油公司）和雷普索尔公司（Repsol SA）是3家关联公司，具体而言，润滑剂公司是石油公司的子公司，而石油公司又是雷普索尔公司的子公司，3家企业隶属于雷普索尔集团，因参与上述卡特尔行为而被欧盟委员会处以连带罚款80 496 000欧元。欧盟委员会在计算罚款金额时，考虑了以下4个因素：这些公司在相关地区市场上的市场份额、罚款金额能否发挥劝诫效果、这些企业在卡特尔中的重要程度以及是否符合罚款减免的条件。

3家企业不服欧盟委员会的罚款决定，认为其在2004年3月31日依据《宽恕公告》提交的声明对于欧盟委员会调查卡特尔行为的实际存续期间具有重要作用，因而认为欧盟委员会适用法律错误，于是向初审法院起诉撤销欧盟委员会的罚款决定，或者降低罚款金额。初审法院驳回了其诉讼请求，于是3家企业又上诉至欧盟法院。

四、争议焦点和主要法律观点

本案的争议焦点是：如何理解《宽恕公告》第23条b款末段中的“（欧盟委员会）尚未掌握的事实”？具体而言，是否有具体明确的标准以界定“尚未掌握的事实”，从而更准确地适用第23条b款末段所规定的内容？

对于该问题，上诉人主张同时适用两项标准：一是欧盟委员会已经实际获得了相应的文件，二是欧盟委员会已经实际知晓了这些文件所载的事实。具体到本案，上诉人认为，英国石油集团在2002年6月20日提交的豁免申请中隐瞒了该卡特尔行为的实际持续时间，而欧盟委员会在2002年10月1日和2日的调查中已经获得了关于该卡特尔行为实际持续时间的文件，但并未实际知晓其中的具体内容。因此，是上诉人2004年3月31日提交的声明才使欧盟委员会意识到英国石油集团隐瞒了相关事实。根据《宽恕公告》，上诉人提交的声明对于认定卡特尔行为的实际持续时间具有直接作用，因而有权享有一定的罚款减免甚至豁免。

但欧盟法院持有不同的观点，即一旦欧盟委员会获得了相关证据，就应当认定其知晓了这些证据的内容，而无论欧盟委员会实际上是否对这些证据进行了检查分析。换言之，“尚未掌握”只适用一项标准，即是否实际获得了相应的证据。此外，法院对《宽恕公告》第23条b款末段作了新的解释，明确了“尚未掌握的事实”所应具备的标准：只有当卡特尔企业向欧盟委员会提交的证据客观上对于欧盟委员会已经获得的证据具有明显的附加价值时，才可以认定为欧盟委员会尚未掌握的“证据”。本案中，欧盟委员会在2002年10月1日和2日的调查中已经获得了关于该卡特尔行为实际持续时间的文件，所以应当推定其已经知晓了卡特尔行为的实际持续时间。因此，上诉人在2004年3月31日提交的声明并不具有“明显附加价值”，无权获得罚款减免。

五、本案的意义及其启示

本案中，欧盟法院对《宽恕公告》第23条b款段作了新的解释，进一步界定了“(欧盟委员会)尚未掌握的事实”的内涵和标准。

从判例中，我们可以总结出适用该条款应当考虑以下3个方面：

1.证明标准：(1)卡特尔企业应证明欧盟委员会尚未掌握相关事实；(2)这些事实可以使欧盟委员会对相关违法行为作出新的认定。

2.适用范围：卡特尔企业提供的信息应当与卡特尔行为的严重程度和持续时间相关。

3.立法目的：是否有利于快速而彻底地终止违法行为。

本案中，上诉人从主观角度出发提出了“认知”标准，推断欧盟委员会实际知晓相关的事实。但法院拒绝采纳这一标准，理由是这不符合以往判例中已确定的标准。同时，法院对该条款作了体系解释，将第23条b款末段的规定置于整个罚款豁免体系之下，赋予了“欧盟委员会尚未掌握的事实”以新的内涵：卡特尔企业向欧盟委员会提交的证据客观上对于欧盟委员会已经获得的证据应具有明显附加价值。至此，欧盟法院再次明确了判断一项证据是否属于“尚未掌握的事实”应当采取客观标准，只要欧盟委员会实际获得了相关文件即可，无论其是否对这些文件进行了审查。

值得注意的是，法院在本案中并未确立“明显附加价值”的标准，这给欧盟司法机关留下了很大的自由裁量权。而这部分自有裁量权可以根据个案的具体情况来定，没有统一的标准。这也说明了查处反垄断案件的复杂性和不确定性。对于这一点我们应该重点关注。

表2-1　C-617/13P（2016）涉及的法律

序号	原文	中文名称	所在段落
1	Treaty on the Functioning of the European Union（TFEU）	《欧盟运行条约》	79、84、86、99
2	Treaty establishing the European Community（EC）	《欧共体条约》	1、4、22
3	Council Regulation（EC）No 1/2003 of 16 December 2002 on the implementation of the rules on competition laid down in Articles［81 and 82 EC］	《欧盟委员会第1/2003号条例》	84、86
4	Guidelines on the method of setting fines imposed pursuant to Article 15（2）of Regulation No 17 and Article［65（5）CS］	《1998年罚款指南》	5、6、76、78、90
5	Notice on Immunity from fines and reduction of fines in cartel cases	《宽恕公告》	17、19、28、34、53、54、55、62、64、65、67、69、70、71、74
6	Statute of the Court of Justice of the European Union	《欧盟法院规约》	42、47
7	Regulation No 17	《第17号条例》	4、18
8	Rules of Procedure of the Court of Justice	《欧盟法院程序规则》	58、104、105
9	Charter of Fundamental Rights of the European Union	《欧洲联盟基本权利宪章》	86
10	European Convention for the Protection of Human Rights and Fundamental Freedoms	《欧洲保护人权和基本自由公约》	93

表2–2　C–557/12（2014）涉及的判例

序号	判例名称	案号	所在段落
1	MasterCard and Others v Commission	EU：C：2014：2201	47
2	ASPLA v Commission	EU：C：2014：348	58
3	Inuit Tapiriit Kanatami and Others v Commission	EU：C：2015：535	59
4	Toshiba Corporation v Commission	EU：C：2016：26	63
5	LG Display and LG Display Taiwan v Commission	EU：C：2015：258	66、67、68、69
6	E.ON Energie v Commission	EU：C：2012：738	81
7	AC–Treuhand v Commission	EU：C：2015：717	84、86
8	Groupe Gascogne v Commission	EU：C：2013：770	95
9	Telefónica and Telefónica de España v Commission	EU：C：2014：2062	98
10	ICF v Commission	EU：C：2014：2274	98、100
11	Guardian Industries and Guardian Europe v Commission	EU：C：2014：2363	98、100

JUDGMENT OF THE COURT (Fifth Chamber)

9 June 2016 (*)

(Appeal—Article 81 EC—Agreements, decisions and concerted practices—Spanish market for penetration bitumen—Market sharing and price coordination—Notice on immunity from fines and reduction of fines in cartel cases (2002)—Final paragraph of point 23 (b)—Partial immunity from fines—Evidence of facts previously unknown to the Commission)

In Case C-617/13 P,

APPEAL under Article 56 of the Statute of the Court of Justice of the European Union, brought on 27 November 2013,

Repsol Lubricantes y Especialidades SA, formerly Repsol Lubricantes YPF y Especialidades SA, established in Madrid (Spain),

Repsol Petróleo SA, established in Madrid,

Repsol SA, established in Madrid,

represented by L. Ortiz Blanco, J. Buendía Sierra, M. Muñoz de Juan, A. Givaja Sanz and A. Lamadrid de Pablo, abogados,

appellants,

the other party to the proceedings being:

European Commission, represented by C. Urraca Caviedes and F. Castillo de la Torre, acting as Agents,

defendant at first instance,

判例正文*

欧盟法院判决（第五法庭）
2016年6月9日

（上诉—《欧共体条约》第81条—协议、决定以及协同行为—西班牙的渗透沥青市场—市场分割和价格协定—《欧盟委员会关于卡特尔案件罚款豁免和减轻公告》—第23条b款末段—罚款的部分豁免—欧盟委员会尚未获得的证据）

案号：C-617/13P

2013年11月27日，上诉人依据《欧盟法院规约》第56条向本院提起上诉。

上诉人（初审原告）：

雷普索尔润滑剂公司，前身为雷普索尔YPE专业润滑剂公司，成立于马德里（西班牙）；

雷普索尔石油公司，成立于马德里；

雷普索尔公司，成立于马德里。

代理人为L.奥尔蒂斯·布兰科、J.布恩迪亚·塞拉、M.穆尼奥斯·德·胡安、A.吉瓦嘉·桑兹和A.拉马德里德·帕勃罗。

被上诉人（初审被告）：

欧盟委员会，代理人为C. 尤里卡·卡文迪和F. 卡斯迪尔·托里。

---

* 初译者：李彦龙；校对者：林燕萍、戴娜。

THE COURT (Fifth Chamber),

composed of T. von Danwitz, President of the Fourth Chamber, acting as President of the Fifth Chamber, K. Lenaerts, President of the Court, acting as a Judge of the Fifth Chamber, D. Šváby (Rapporteur), A. Rosas and C. Vajda, Judges,

Advocate General: N. Jääskinen,

Registrar: M. Ferreira, principal administrator,

having regard to the written procedure and further to the hearing on 15 April 2015,

after hearing the Advocate General at the sitting on 16 July 2015,

gives the following

欧盟法院(第五法庭)

由审判长T.冯·丹威兹(第四法庭庭长)、法院院长K.莱纳特斯、法官D.斯瓦(判决书起草人)、法官A.罗萨斯和C.瓦杰达组成。

佐审官:N.贾斯金宁;

书记官:M.费雷拉(首席行政官);

在进行了所有书面审理程序之后,本庭于2015年4月15日开庭审理此案,并且于2015年7月16日听取了佐审官的意见。

经审理,本院作出如下判决:

Judgment

1 By their appeal, Repsol Lubricantes y Especialidades SA, formerly Repsol Lubricantes YPF y Especialidades SA ('RPA/Rylesa'), Repsol Petróleo SA ('Repsol Petróleo') and Repsol SA ('Repsol'), ask the Court to set aside the judgment of the General Court of the European Union of 16 September 2013 in Repsol Lubricantes y Especialidades and Others v Commission (T-496/07, 'the judgment under appeal', EU: T: 2013: 4464), which dismissed their action for annulment of Commission Decision C(2007)4441 final of 3 October 2007 relating to a proceeding under Article [81 EC] (Case COMP/38.710—Bitumen (Spain)) ('the decision at issue'), and, in the alternative, the reduction of the amount of the fine imposed on them.

Legal context

Regulation No 1/2003

2 Under the title 'Fines', Article 23 of Council Regulation (EC) No 1/2003 of 16 December 2002 on the implementation of the rules on competition laid down in Articles [81 and 82 EC] (OJ 2003 L 1, p. 1) provides, in paragraph 3, that 'in fixing the amount of the fine, regard shall be had both to the gravity and the duration of the infringement'.

3 Article 31 of that regulation provides:

'The Court of Justice shall have unlimited jurisdiction to review decisions whereby the Commission has fixed a fine or periodic penalty payment. It may cancel, reduce or increase the fine or periodic penalty payment imposed.'

The 1998 Guidelines

4 Under paragraph 1 of the Commission notice entitled 'Guidelines on the method of setting fines imposed pursuant to Article 15(2) of Regulation No 17 and Article [65(5) CS]' (OJ 1998 C 9, p. 3; 'the 1998 Guidelines') 'the basic amount will be determined according to the gravity and duration of the infringement, which are the only criteria referred to in Article 15(2) of [Council] Regulation No 17' of 6 February 1962: first regulation implementing Articles [81 and 82 EC] (OJ, English Special Edition 1959-1962, p. 87).

判 决

1 雷普索尔润滑剂公司（以下简称润滑剂公司）、雷普索尔石油公司（以下简称石油公司）和雷普索尔公司在上诉中请求欧盟法院撤销初审法院作出的“雷普索尔润滑剂公司等诉欧盟委员会案”的判决（T 496/07，EU：T：2013：4464，以下简称初审法院判决）。在该判决中，初审法院驳回了上诉人关于撤销欧盟委员会在2007年8月3日根据《欧共体条约》第81条作出的第4441号决定（COMP/38.710，以下简称欧盟委会员决定）的诉讼请求和上诉人关于降低罚款金额的请求。

法律背景

《第1/2003号条例》

2 《关于实施〈欧共体条约〉第81条和第82条的欧盟委员会第1/2003号条例》（OJ 2003 L 1，第1页）第23条第3段规定：在计算罚款金额时，应当同时考虑违法行为的严重程度和持续时间。

3 该条例第31条规定：“对于欧盟委员会所作的罚款决定或者分期罚款决定，欧盟法院拥有无限审查权，并且欧盟法院可以撤销罚款决定、降低或提高罚款（或分期罚款）金额。”

《1998年罚款指南》

4 《依据〈第17号条例〉第15条第2款和〈欧洲煤钢共同体条约〉第65条第5款规定设定罚款方法的指南》（OJ 1998 C 9，第3页）第1段规定：“罚款基本金额应当依据违法行为的严重程度和持续时间计算，这是《第17号条例》第15条第2款确立的唯一标准。《第17号条例》于1962年2月6日颁布，是第一部关于实施《欧共体条约》第81条和第82条的条例（OJ，英文特殊版1959~1962，第87页）。”

5 As regards the gravity of the infringement, Section 1.A of the 1998 Guidelines provides that in assessing the gravity of the infringement, account must be taken of its nature, its actual impact on the market, where this can be measured, and the size of the relevant geographic market. Under that provision, infringements are put into one of three categories: minor infringements, serious infringements and very serious infringements.

6 According to the 1998 Guidelines, very serious infringements comprise, in particular, horizontal restrictions such as 'price cartels' and market-sharing quotas. For those infringements, the basic amount of the likely fine is 'above [EUR] 20 million'.

2002 Leniency Notice

7 The Commission Notice on immunity from fines and reduction of fines in cartel cases (OJ 2002 C 45, p. 3, 'the 2002 Leniency Notice') sets out the conditions under which undertakings cooperating with the Commission during an investigation it is carrying out into a cartel may be exempted from fines, or may be granted reductions in any fine which would otherwise have been imposed on them.

8 Point 7 of that notice states:

'Cooperation by one or more undertakings may justify a reduction of a fine by the Commission. Any reduction of a fine must reflect an undertaking's actual contribution, in terms of quality and timing, to the Commission's establishment of the infringement. Reductions are to be limited to those undertakings that provide the Commission with evidence that adds significant value to that already in the Commission's possession.'

9 Under Section B of that notice, headed 'Reduction of a fine', points 21 and 23 thereof provide:

'21.In order to qualify, an undertaking must provide the Commission with evidence of the suspected infringement which represents significant added value with respect to the evidence already in the Commission's possession and must terminate its involvement in the suspected infringement no later than the time at which it submits the evidence.

...

23.The Commission will determine in any final decision adopted at the end of the administrative procedure:

(a) whether the evidence provided by an undertaking represented significant added value with respect to the evidence in the Commission's possession at that same time;

5 关于违法行为的严重程度,《1998年罚款指南》第1节A款规定:“在认定违法行为的严重程度时,应考虑该行为的性质、可测算的行为危害程度;该行为对市场的影响以及相关地区市场的规模。本条规定将违法行为分为3类:轻度违法行为,严重违法行为和非常严重违法行为。”

6 依据《1998年罚款指南》,“非常严重违法行为”主要表现为进行横向限制,例如进行价格卡特尔和分割市场份额,对此的罚款金额不低于2000万欧元。

《宽恕公告》

7 《欧盟委员会关于卡特尔案件罚款豁免和减轻的公告》(OJ 2002 C 45,第3页)规定了卡特尔成员企业为欧盟委员会调查卡特尔提供合作时得以免除或减轻罚款的条件。

8 公告第7条规定:

“欧盟委员会可以降低提供合作的卡特尔企业的罚款金额。降低的罚款金额必须反映出该企业在欧盟委员会认定违法行为时所做的实质性贡献,并且应以该证据的质量或时间的形式体现。降低罚款应限于那些向欧盟委员会提供证据的企业,并且该证据对欧盟委员会已经掌握的情况具有明显的附加价值。”

9 公告B节第21条和第23条(标题为“罚款减免”)规定:

“21 为计算罚款的减免金额,卡特尔成员企业向欧盟委员会提供的涉嫌违法行为的证据必须对欧盟委员会已经掌握的情况具有明显的附加价值,并且在提供证据之前必须停止参与涉嫌违法行为。

……

23 欧盟委员会有权在行政程序结束后做出的最终决定中认定:

(a)卡特尔成员企业提供的证据对于欧盟委员会已经掌握的情况是否具有明显的附加价值;

...

In addition, if an undertaking provides evidence relating to facts previously unknown to the Commission which have a direct bearing on the gravity or duration of the suspected cartel, the Commission will not take these elements into account when setting any fine to be imposed on the undertaking which provided this evidence.'

Background to the dispute and the decision at issue

10 The background to the dispute was set out in paragraphs 1 to 91 of the judgment under appeal and may be summarised as follows.

11 The product concerned by the infringement is penetration bitumen, namely a type of bitumen which has not been processed and is used for the construction and maintenance of roads.

12 The Spanish bitumen market comprises, first, three producers, namely the Repsol, CEPSA–PROAS and BP groups, and, second, importers, including the Nynäs and Petróleos de Portugal (Petrogal) groups.

13 During the period corresponding to the years 1991 to 2002, 99.99% of RPA/Rylesa was held by Repsol Petróleo, itself a 99.97% subsidiary of Repsol YPF SA ('Repsol YPF'), now Repsol, the parent company of the Repsol group.

14 RPA/Rylesa produces and markets bitumen products. One of Repsol Petróleo's activities is the production of penetration bitumen and its sale to RPA/Rylesa in order for it to be marketed.

15 Two other companies of the Repsol group, Petróleos del Norte SA and Asfalnor SA carry out, in Spain, an activity related to penetration bitumen.

16 From their sales of penetration bitumen to third parties, RPA/Rylesa and Petróleos del Norte generated, in Spain, turnover of EUR 97 500 000 during the 2001 fiscal year, that is, 34.04% of the relevant market. The total consolidated turnover of the Repsol group was EUR 51 355 000 000 for 2006, which corresponds to the fiscal year prior to the adoption of the decision at issue.

……

此外，如果卡特尔成员企业提供了欧盟委员会尚未获得的并且对于认定卡特尔行为严重程度或持续时间具有直接作用的证据，欧盟委员会在认定该企业的罚款金额时将不再考虑严重程度和持续时间这两个因素。”

争议的背景和欧盟委员会的决定：

10 初审法院判决的第1段至第91段描述了该争议的背景，可以总结出如下内容：

11 该违法行为所涉及的产品是渗透沥青，这是一种未经加工的沥青产品，用于道路建设和维护。

12 西班牙沥青市场参与者分为两类：第一类是3家生产商，即雷普索尔集团，CEPSA-PROAS集团和英国石油集团英国石油集团；第二类是进口商，包括尼纳斯集团和由上诉人组成的西班牙高浦石油集团。

13 1991年至2002年，润滑剂公司99.99%的股份由石油公司持有，石油公司99.97%的股份由雷普索尔YPE公司，即现在的雷普索尔公司持有，而雷普索尔公司是雷普索尔集团的母公司。

14 润滑剂公司生产并销售沥青产品，石油公司的一项业务是生产渗透沥青产品并出售给润滑剂公司，然后由润滑剂公司进行销售。

15 雷普索尔集团的另外两家公司Petróleos del Norte和Asfalnor则在西班牙市场开展了一项与渗透沥青产品有关的业务。

16 在2001财政年度，润滑剂公司和Petróleos del Norte这两家公司在西班牙市场上销售给第三方的渗透沥青产品营业额达9750万欧元，占相关市场份额达34.04%。雷普索尔集团在2006年的总营业额为5，135，500万欧元，这与欧盟委员会决定做出时的前一财政年度营业额相当。

17 Following an application for immunity submitted on 20 June 2002 by BP pursuant to the 2002 Leniency Notice, investigations were carried out on 1 and 2 October 2002 at the premises of the Repsol, CEPSA–PROAS, BP, Nynäs and Petrogal groups.

18 On 6 February 2004, the Commission sent the companies concerned a first round of requests for information pursuant to Article 11(3) of Regulation No 17.

19 By faxes of, respectively, 31 March and 5 April 2004, the appellants and PROAS submitted an application to the Commission pursuant to its 2002 Leniency Notice, together with a corporate statement.

20 After having sent four other requests for information to the undertakings concerned, the Commission formally initiated proceedings and, between 24 and 28 August 2006, notified a statement of objections to the companies concerned in the BP, Repsol, CEPSA–PROAS, Nynäs and Petrogal groups.

21 On 3 October 2007, the Commission adopted the decision at issue by which it found that the 13 companies to which it was addressed had participated in a complex of market–sharing agreements and price coordination of penetration bitumen in Spain (excluding the Canary Islands).

22 The Commission considered that each of the two restrictions of competition established, namely the horizontal market–sharing agreements and the price coordination, was by its nature among the most serious types of infringements of Article 81 EC, which, according to the case–law, are capable of warranting the classification of 'very serious' infringements.

23 The Commission set the 'starting amount' of the fines to be imposed at EUR 40 000 000 by taking into account the seriousness of the infringement, the estimated value of the relevant market, namely EUR 286 400 000 for 2001, the last full year of the infringement, and the fact that the infringement was limited to sales of bitumen in one Member State.

24 The Commission then placed the companies to which the decision at issue was addressed in different categories, defined by reference to their relative importance on the relevant market, for the purposes of applying differential treatment, in order to take account of their effective economic capacity to cause significant damage to competition.

17 英国石油集团于2002年6月20日根据《宽恕公告》(OJ 2002 C 45, p. 3)向欧盟委员会提交了豁免申请，随后，欧盟委员会于2002年10月1日和2日对雷普索尔集团、CEPSA-PROAS集团、英国石油集团和尼纳斯集团以及西班牙高浦石油集团的营业场所展开了调查。

18 欧盟委员会在2004年2月6日，依据《第17号条例》第11条第3款向这些公司发出了第一轮信息披露要求。

19 根据《宽恕公告》，上诉人和CEPSA-PROAS集团分别于2004年3月31日、2004年4月5日分别以传真方式向欧盟委会员提交了豁免申请和公司声明。

20 欧盟委员会向相关企业发出4轮信息披露要求之后，正式启动了调查程序，并在2006年8月24日至28日，向英国石油集团、雷普索尔集团、CEPSA-PROAS集团、尼纳斯集团和西班牙高浦石油集团等公司发出异议声明。

21 2007年10月3日，欧盟委员会作出决定，认定其调查的13家涉案公司以分割市场、价格协定的形式参与了在西班牙领土(不包括加纳利群岛)内渗透沥青市场的卡特尔联合体，企业之间签订卡特尔协议、实施协同行为。

22 欧盟委员会认为这两种限制竞争形式(横向市场分割协议和价格协定)本质上都属于《欧共体条约》第81条所规定的最严重的违法行为，依据以往的判例，这些行为都足以归入“非常严重”的违法行为类别。

23 欧盟委员会将罚款的“起始金额”设定为4000万欧元，这个金额设定考虑到了违法行为的严重程度、对相关市场的预估影响(在2001年为28 640万欧元)、最后一整年的违法行为，并且将违法行为限定在一个成员国之内的沥青销售行为。

24 鉴于涉案企业利用其经济能力对竞争所造成的重大损害程度不同，为了提供不同程度的处罚方式，欧盟委员会将涉案企业划分为不同类别，其划分的依据是它们在相关市场上的相对重要性程度。

25 The Repsol group and PROAS, whose shares of the relevant market amounted, respectively, to 34.04% and 31.67% in 2001, were placed in the first category, the BP group, with a market share of 15.19%, in the second category, and the Nynäs and Petrogal groups, whose market shares varied between 4.54% and 5.24%, in the third category. On that basis, the basic amounts of the fines to be imposed were adjusted as follows:

–category one, for the Repsol group and PROAS: EUR 40 000 000;

–category two, for the BP group: EUR 18 000 000; and

–category three, for the Nynäs and Petrogal groups: EUR 5 500 000.

26 In order to determine the amount of the fines at a level to ensure a sufficiently dissuasive effect, the Commission took the view that it was appropriate to apply a multiplier of 1.2 to the basic amount of the fine to be imposed on the Repsol group.

27 After increasing the basic amount of the fines according to the length of the infringement, namely a period of 11 years and 7 months (from 1 March 1991 to 1 October 2002) as regards the Repsol group, the Commission found that the amount of the fine to be imposed on it had to be increased by 30% on the basis of aggravating circumstances, since that group had been amongst the significant 'driving forces' of the cartel at issue.

28 The Commission also decided that, pursuant to the 2002 Leniency Notice, the Repsol group was entitled to a reduction of 40% of the amount of the fine which should have normally been imposed on it.

29 On the basis of those factors, RPA/Rylesa, Repsol Petróleo and Repsol YPF were fined jointly and severally EUR 80 496 000.

Procedure before the General Court and the judgment under appeal

30 By application lodged at the General Court Registry on 18 December 2007, the appellants applied for annulment of the decision at issue, and, in the alternative, for a reduction of the amount of the fine imposed on them.

31 In support of their action, they raised eight pleas in law of which only the fourth to the sixth and the eighth pleas are relevant to the present appeal.

25 2001年，雷普索尔集团和 PRAOS 集团在相关市场上的占有份额分别为34.04%和31.67%，因此被归为第一类；英国石油集团的市场份额为15.19%，因此被归为第二类；尼纳斯集团和西班牙高浦石油集团的市场份额在4.54%和5.24%之间，因此被归为了第三类。在此基础上，这些涉案企业的罚款基数调整为以下金额：

第一类，雷普索尔集团和PROAS集团：4000万欧元；

第二类，英国石油集团：1800万欧元；

第三类，尼纳斯集团和西班牙高浦石油集团：各550万欧元。

26 为了使罚款金额起到足够的震慑作用，欧盟委员会认为对雷普索尔集团的罚款金额应是其罚款基数的1.2倍。

27 依据违法行为存续时间的长度（总计11年7个月，即1991年3月1日至2002年9月1日）提高了罚款基数之后，欧盟委员会认为雷普索尔集团在该卡特尔组织中扮演了显著的“推动者”角色，因此决定对雷普索尔集团在其已提高的基数上再提高30%。

28 依据《宽恕公告》，欧盟委员会还决定雷普索尔集团在罚款金额的40%内有权得以豁免。

29 基于上述理由，润滑剂公司、石油公司和雷普索尔YPF公司被判令共同承担80 496 000欧元罚款的连带责任。

初审法院的审理程序及判决

30 2007年12月18日，润滑剂公司、石油公司和雷普索尔YPF公司这3家企业共同向初审法院提交起诉状，请求撤销欧盟委员会对该案的罚款决定，或者降低罚款金额。

31 初审中，3家企业提出八项诉讼请求，其中第4项至第6项与第8项与上诉有关。

32 The fourth and fifth pleas in law, which the General Court examined together, alleged, first, an error of fact and law vitiating the examination of the evidence adduced by the appellants in their responses to the statement of objections, in support of the demonstration of the commercial autonomy of RPA/Rylesa in relation to Repsol Petróleo and Repsol YPF, and, second, that the additional evidence relating to the relationships of those three companies were not able to support the presumption of the actual exercise of decisive influence of those two latter companies over the first.

33 The sixth plea alleged that the amount of the fine imposed was set in infringement of the principles of proportionality and equal treatment.

34 By their eighth plea, the appellants challenged, in essence, the Commission's application of the 2002 Leniency Notice and, in particular, of the final paragraph of point 23 (b) thereof.

35 The General Court rejected each of those pleas and dismissed the action in its entirety.

36 The General Court also dismissed the Commission's counterclaim seeking that the amount of the fine imposed on the appellants be increased.

Forms of order sought

37 By their appeal, the appellants claim that the Court of Justice should:

–set aside the judgment under appeal and annul the decision at issue;

–reduce the amount of the fine imposed;

–establish the excessive and unjustified duration of the judicial proceedings before the General Court; and

–order the Commission to pay the costs.

38 The Commission contends that the Court of Justice should:

–dismiss the appeal; and

–order the appellants to pay all the costs.

The appeal

39 The appellants put forward four grounds in support of their appeal.

32 初审法院合并审理的第4项和第5项诉讼请求为：首先，在答复欧盟委员会异议声明的文件中，3家企业引证了“润滑剂公司相对于石油公司和雷普索尔YPF公司具有商业自主权”的证据，但欧盟委员会在事实认定和法律适用方面均存在错误，以致错误地审定了这些证据；其次，关于这3家企业相互关系的补充证据并不足以支持石油公司和雷普索尔YPF公司对润滑剂公司可以实际施加决定性的影响力，这一推定不能够成立。

33 第6项诉讼请求为：罚款金额违反了比例原则和平等待遇原则。

34 3家企业的第8项诉讼请求是在根本上质疑欧盟委员会适用《宽恕公告》，特别是第23条b款末段的正确性。

35 初审法院驳回了3家企业的所有诉请。

36 初审法院同样驳回了欧盟委员会请求提高罚款金额的反诉。

当事人提交到欧盟法院的诉讼请求

37 在上诉程序中，上诉人向欧盟法院提出如下诉讼请求：

——撤销初审法院的判决；

——降低罚款金额；

——认定初审法院的初审程序严重超审限且不公正；

——责令欧盟委员会支付诉讼费用。

38 欧盟委员会认为，欧盟法院应当：

——驳回上诉请求；

——责令上诉人支付诉讼费用。

上诉

39 上诉人提出以下4个理由支持其上诉请求。

The first ground of appeal, alleging an error of law in the assessment of RPA/Rylesa's commercial autonomy or, in the alternative, a failure to provide reasons for that assessment

Arguments of the parties

40 In support of their first ground of appeal, directed against paragraphs 179 to 207 of the judgment under appeal, the appellants claim that the judgment under appeal is vitiated by a double error of law in the assessment of the evidence adduced in support of their arguments designed to demonstrate the commercial autonomy of RPA/Rylesa in relation to Repsol Petróleo and Repsol YPF.

41 They complain that the General Court considered, in particular in paragraphs 202 and 203 of the judgment under appeal, that proof that control of a parent company over its subsidiaries, in which it has a 100%, or almost 100%, holding, was not exercised in practice is insufficient to reverse the presumption of the actual exercise of decisive influence of that parent company over those subsidiaries.

42 The appellants submit, in the alternative, that the General Court failed in its duty to state reasons arising from Article 36 and the first paragraph of Article 53 of the Statute of the Court of Justice of the European Union, by pursuing an excessively individualised assessment of each piece of evidence produced by the appellants, without carrying out an overall assessment of that evidence, except that contained in laconic wording in paragraph 207 of the judgment under appeal.

43 The Commission contends that the first ground of appeal is unfounded.

Findings of the Court

44 With regard to the main part of that ground of appeal, suffice it to state that it is based on a misreading of the judgment under appeal.

45 It is not apparent from any of the points raised by the appellants that the General Court held that the proof that control of a parent company over its subsidiaries, in which it has a 100%, or almost 100%, holding, was not exercised in practice is insufficient to reverse the presumption of the actual exercise of decisive influence of that parent company over those subsidiaries.

46 It follows from the judgment under appeal and, in particular, paragraphs 207 and 211 thereof, solely that the General Court held that the evidence provided by the appellants was not such as to demonstrate the autonomy of RPA/Rylesa's conduct in relation to Repsol Petróleo and to Repsol YPF and, therefore, did not allow the presumption of the latters' actual exercise of decisive influence over the former to be reversed.

第一个上诉理由：在认定润滑剂公司的商业自主性时，初审法院适用法律错误，或者，未尽说理义务。

争议双方的观点

40 为支持其第一个上诉理由，针对初审法院判决书第179段至第207段，上诉人认为，初审法院判决在认定其提交的用以证明润滑剂公司相对于石油公司和雷普索尔YPE公司具有商业自主权的证据方面存在法律适用上的双重错误。

41 上诉人认为，初审法院在其判决书第202段和第203段中错误地认为当母公司享有其子公司100%或将近100%的股份时，即使有证据证明母公司并未实际实施控制行为，该证据也不足以推翻母公司对其子公司可以实际施加决定性影响力的结论。

42 上诉人还认为，初审法院并未履行《欧盟法院规约》第36条和第53条第1段所规定的说理义务，除了初审法院判决书第207段的简单阐述外，初审法院对上诉人提交的每项证据只进行了形式上的逐一审查而未进行整体性的评估。

43 欧盟委员会认为这项上诉理由毫无依据。

本院查明的事实及观点

44 对于第一个上诉理由的主要部分，本院认为这是对初审法院判决的误解。

45 从上诉人所提出的各项理由中并不能明显看出初审法院持有这一观点：当母公司享有其子公司100%或将近100%的股份时，即使有证据证明母公司并未实际实施控制行为，该证据也不足以推翻母公司对其子公司可以实际施加决定性影响力的结论。

46 根据初审法院判决，特别是第207段和第211段，初审法院只是认为上诉人提交的证据不能证明润滑剂公司的行为相对于石油公司和雷普索尔YPE公司具有自主性，因而无法推翻石油公司和雷普索尔YPE公司对润滑剂公司可以实际施加决定性影响力的结论。

47 Furthermore, it should be recalled that, according to the first paragraph of Article 58 of the Statute of the Court of Justice of the European Union, assessments of a factual nature fall outside the jurisdiction of the Court of Justice in the context of an appeal (see, to that effect, judgment of 11 September 2014 in MasterCard and Others v Commission, C-382/12 P, EU: C: 2014: 2201, paragraph 113).

48 As regards the alternative part of the first ground of appeal, it should certainly be noted that, in paragraph 207 of the judgment under appeal, the General Court held, without giving prior reasoning, that, taken together, the points developed by the appellants in connection with their application for annulment did not make it possible to reverse the presumption of the actual exercise of decisive influence of Repsol Petróleo and Repsol YPF over RPA/Rylesa.

49 However, it is apparent from the judgment under appeal that, in rejecting, in paragraphs 207 and 211, the appellants' arguments seeking to establish RPA/Rylesa's commercial autonomy in relation to Repsol Petróleo and Repsol YPF, the General Court did not just conduct a decontextualised analysis of each piece of evidence adduced by the appellants.

50 Apart from the fact that, in paragraphs 164 to 206 of the judgment under appeal, the General Court carried out, in the context of its assessment of the facts which is not subject to appeal, a detailed analysis of each of the pieces of evidence adduced by the parties, which cannot be left out of account for the overall assessment thereof, it follows from paragraphs 208 to 210 of that judgment that the General Court also analysed and assessed some additional evidence, which the Commission had used as a basis in the decision at issue, and which the General Court considered supported the fact that the appellants in fact constituted a single economic entity.

51 In doing so, the General Court did not commit an error of law and, in particular, did not infringe its obligation to provide reasons for its decision in finding that the appellants had not demonstrated the autonomy of RPA/Rylesa's conduct in relation to Repsol Petróleo and Repsol YPF.

52 Accordingly, the first ground of appeal must be rejected as being unfounded.

47 此外，值得注意的是，根据《欧盟法院规约》第58条第1段的规定，欧盟法院无权在上诉程序中对案件的事实性质作出评估。（参见判例：2014年9月11日，MasterCard and Others v Commission，C 382/12 P，EU：C：2014：2201，第113段）

48 关于第一点上诉理由中的“未尽说理义务”，应当注意到，在判决书第207段，初审法院只是先从整体上（没有对提供的材料加以说明）认定上诉人提出的所有与申请撤销罚款决定相关的理由均无法推翻“石油公司和雷普索尔YPE公司对润滑剂公司可以实际施加决定性影响力”的结论。

49 然而，从初审法院判决第207段至第211段可以看出，初审法院对上诉人提出的每一项证据逐一分析，其说理部分完整、条理清晰，全面分析并驳回了上诉人提出的润滑剂公司相对于石油公司和雷普索尔YPE公司具有商业自主性的抗辩。

50 此外，在初审法院判决第164段至第206段，初审法院在评估不能上诉的事实时，对上诉人提交的每一项证据均进行了详细的分析，所以不能说在整体评估时初审法院没有对证据逐一分析；另外，在判决书第208段至第210段，初审法院在分析和评估了欧盟委员会据以作出罚款决定的相关补充证据之后，才认定这些证据足以证明3家上诉公司事实上形成了一个单一经济实体。

51 综上，初审法院并未错误地适用法律，尤其是在认定上诉人未提供充分证据来证明润滑剂公司相对于石油公司和雷普索尔YPE公司具有商业自主性方面，并未违背其所承担的说理义务。

52 上诉人的第一个上诉理由缺乏依据，应予驳回。

The second ground of appeal, alleging an error of law in the interpretation of the 2002 Leniency Notice

Arguments of the parties

53 By their second ground of appeal, directed against paragraphs 339 to 349 of the judgment under appeal, the appellants claim that the General Court erred in law in the interpretation of the final paragraph of point 23(b) of the 2002 Leniency Notice by refusing to grant them partial immunity from the fine on the ground that they had incorrectly claimed that it was Repsol which had produced, in its statement under that notice, the information which enabled the Commission to be aware of the fact that the cartel had continued during the period from 1998 to 2002.

54 In the present case, the appellants, while accepting that the Commission had, prior to their statement under the 2002 Leniency Notice, the documents showing the actual duration of the alleged infringement, submit that it is their statement of the facts in that statement which enabled the Commission to find that the BP group had concealed the truth as to the real duration of the cartel in dispute and that that infringement had continued during that period.

55 In that regard, the appellants claim that the wording of the final paragraph of point 23(b) of the 2002 Leniency Notice and, in particular, the use, in the Spanish version, of the words 'hechos de los cuales la Comisión no tenga conocimiento previo', which correspond to the words 'facts previously unknown' and 'faits précédemment ignorés', in particular in the English and French language versions, must be understood as not covering mere physical possession of documents by the Commission, but also as requiring a 'cognitive element', that is, knowledge by the Commission of the infringement which would be shown by those documents.

56 Furthermore and in any event, the appellants are of the view that the ambiguity of that provision should have led the General Court to adopt the interpretation which was most favourable to them.

57 According to the Commission, the second ground of appeal must be categorised as being new, and, therefore, it is inadmissible since the action for annulment brought by the appellants did not contain any argument relating to the requirement for a 'cognitive element', for the purposes of using the provision relied upon. Alternatively, that ground of appeal is unfounded.

第二个上诉理由：初审法院错误地解释了《宽恕公告》。

争议双方的观点

53 上诉人的第二个上诉理由是针对初审法院判决第339段至第349段，上诉人认为，初审法院认定上诉人根据《宽恕公告》作出的声明没有意义（该声明称雷普索尔集团向欧盟委员会提供了信息，才使欧盟委员会意识到1998年至2002年卡特尔行为仍在继续），所以拒绝给予上诉人部分罚款豁免。审法院在此错误地解释了《宽恕公告》第23条b款末段。

54 本案中，虽然上诉人承认在其根据《宽恕公告》提交声明之前，欧盟委员会已经获得了该违法行为实际持续期间的相关文件。但是，上诉人认为正是自己所提交的声明才使欧盟委员会发现英国石油集团故意隐瞒了卡特尔的实际持续期间以及该违法行为在1998年至2002年仍在继续的事实。

55 对于《宽恕公告》第23条b款末段的措辞和应用，上诉人认为西班牙文版本中的‘hechos de los cuales la Comisión no tenga conocimiento previo’，分别与英文版本的‘facts previously unknown’和法文版本的‘faits précédemment ignorés’相对应，可以理解为：欧盟委员会不仅已经实际获得了这些文件，而且这些文件应当具备“认知因素”，即欧盟委员会应当知晓这些文件所显示的违法行为。

56 此外，上诉人还认为，在任何情况下由于该条款的措辞模棱两可，初审法院应该对上诉人提出的问题作出有力的解释。

57 欧盟委员会认为，第二点上诉理由实际上是“新”的理由，因为上诉人在请求撤销欧盟委员会罚款决定的初审程序中并未提出任何与“认知要素”相关的抗辩。对此，为了准确适用该条款，欧盟法院无权审查该“新”的上诉理由。

Findings of the Court

58 At the outset, it should be borne in mind that, under Article 170(1) of the Rules of Procedure of the Court of Justice, the subject matter of the proceedings before the General Court may not be changed in the appeal. In an appeal, the jurisdiction of the Court of Justice is in principle confined to a review of the findings of law on the pleas argued at first instance (see, to that effect, judgment of 22 May 2014 in ASPLA v Commission, C–35/12 P, EU: C: 2014: 348, paragraph 39 and the case–law cited).

59 A party cannot, consequently, put forward for the first time before the Court of Justice a plea in law which it has not raised before the General Court since that would allow that party to bring before the Court of Justice, whose jurisdiction in appeal proceedings is limited, a wider case than that heard by the General Court (judgment of 3 September 2015 in Inuit Tapiriit Kanatami and Others v Commission, C–398/13 P, EU: C: 2015: 535, paragraph 57 and the case–law cited).

60 However, and as the Advocate General pointed out in points 17 and 18 of his Opinion, it must be held that the appellants had raised, in essence, the arguments at issue in their action for annulment brought before the General Court.

61 Contrary to what the Commission argues, the second ground of appeal must therefore be declared admissible.

62 By that ground of appeal, the appellants criticise the General Court for having committed an error of law in paragraphs 339 to 349 of the judgment under appeal in that it validated the interpretation and application by the Commission of the concept of 'facts previously unknown' under the final paragraph of point 23 (b) of the 2002 Leniency Notice. That provision, they claim, does not refer to mere physical possession of documents, but requires a separate criterion which the appellants describe as a 'cognitive criterion' to be taken into account.

63 In that regard, it should, in the first place, be recalled that, according to settled case–law of the Court of Justice, the General Court has exclusive jurisdiction to find and assess the facts and, in principle, to examine the evidence it accepts in support of those facts. Provided that that evidence has been properly obtained and the general principles of law and the rules of procedure in relation to the burden of proof and the taking of evidence have been observed, it is for the General Court alone to assess the value which should be attached to the evidence produced before it. Save where the clear sense of the evidence has been distorted, that assessment does not therefore constitute a point of law which is subject as such to review by the Court of Justice (judgment of 20 January 2016 in Toshiba Corporation v Commission, C–373/14 P, EU: C: 2016: 26, paragraph 40).

本院查明的事实及观点

58 首先应当指出的是，根据《欧盟法院程序规则》第170条第1款，初审程序中的诉讼标的不得在上诉程序中发生改变。在上诉程序中，一般原则上欧盟法院的管辖权仅限于审查初审法院基于上诉人的诉讼请求做出的与法律解释相关的判决。（参见判例：2014年5月22日，ASPLA v Commission，C 35/12 P，EU：C：2014：348，第39段和引用的判例法）

59 因此，当事人不得将未向初审法院提出的与法律解释相关的诉讼请求直接向欧盟法院提出。在上诉程序中欧盟法院的管辖权是有限的，它也无权受理比初审法院审理该案范围更大的案件。（参见判例：2015年9月3日，Inuit Tapiriit Kanatami and Others v Commission，C 398/13 P，EU：C：2015：535，第57段和引用的判例）

60 然而，正如佐审官在其意见第17段和第18段中指出的，应当认定，上诉人在请求撤销欧盟委员会罚款决定的初审程序中实际上已经提出了该项诉讼请求。

61 因此，欧盟法院对于第二点上诉理由有管辖权。

62 在该项上诉理由中，上诉人认为，初审法院在其判决第339段至第349段中存在适用法律错误，即错误地维持了欧盟委员会对《宽恕公告》第23条b款末段中“之前不为所知的事实”的解释和适用。上诉人认为，这一条款不仅是指实际获得相关文件，还要求具备一个独立的判断标准，即还应当考虑到上诉人所阐述的“认知要素”。

63 对此，有必要指出的是，依据欧盟法院以往判例，初审法院在认定事实和评估事实方面拥有专属管辖权，而且原则上有权对其认定的证据进行审查。如果这些证据来源正当，并且符合有关举证责任和取证的一般法律原则和程序规则，那么初审法院就有权独立来评估这些证据的价值。只有在有明显迹象表明这些证据已被扭曲时，这种证据审查才不属于初审法院的范围，而是由欧盟法院来审查。（参见判例：2016年2月20日，Toshiba Corporation v Commission，C 373/14 P，EU：C：2016：26，第40段）

64 Consequently, the findings of fact made by the General Court, which are challenged in the context of the second ground of appeal, and in particular, that in paragraph 341 of the judgment under appeal, namely that the Commission already had in its possession—before even receiving, on 31 March 2004, the appellants' statement attached to Repsol's application under the 2002 Leniency Notice—the relevant information in contemporaneous documents collected during investigations on 1 and 2 October 2002, cannot be called into question. The same is true with regard to the rejection by the General Court, in particular in paragraph 345 of the judgment under appeal, of the argument relating to the alleged added value of the facts related by Repsol as regards the period from 1998 to 2002.

65 In the second place, as regards the error of law alleged by the appellants, it should be noted that, under the final paragraph of point 23(b) of the 2002 Leniency Notice, 'if an undertaking provides evidence relating to facts previously unknown to the Commission which have a direct bearing on the gravity or duration of the suspected cartel, the Commission will not take these elements into account when setting any fine to be imposed on the undertaking which provided this evidence'.

66 It follows from the very wording of that provision that the partial immunity provided for therein requires two conditions to be satisfied: first, the undertaking in question is the first to prove facts previously unknown to the Commission; and, second, those facts, which have a direct bearing on the gravity or the duration of the suspected cartel, enable the Commission to make new findings concerning the infringement (judgment 23 April 2015 in LG Display and LG Display Taiwan v Commission, C-227/14 P, EU: C: 2015: 258, paragraph 78).

67 The Court has held that the wording 'facts ... unknown to the Commission', is unambiguous and allows the adoption of a restrictive interpretation of the final paragraph of point 23(b) of the 2002 Leniency Notice, by limiting that provision to cases in which a company party to a cartel provides the Commission with new information relating to the gravity or the duration of the infringement (see, to that effect, judgment 23 April 2015 in LG Display and LG Display Taiwan v Commission, C-227/14 P, EU: C: 2015: 258, paragraph 79 and the case-law cited).

68 The Court has also held that the meaning to be given to those words must be able to guarantee the objectives of the final paragraph of point 23(b) of that notice and, in particular, the effectiveness of the leniency programme (see, to that effect, judgment 23 April 2015 in LG Display and LG Display Taiwan v Commission, C-227/14 P, EU: C: 2015: 258, paragraph 84 and the case-law cited). In that regard, as noted by the Advocate General in point 22 of his Opinion, the objective of leniency programmes is to obtain the termination of the infringement by those committing it, in order to end it quickly and completely.

64 因此，上诉人的第二个上诉理由是质疑：由初审法院认定的事实（初审法院判决第341段：在2004年3月31日收到上诉人根据《宽恕公告》提交的附在雷普索尔集团申请中的声明之前，欧盟委员会已经在2002年10月1日和2日调查期间收集的同期文件中获得了相关信息）不属于欧盟法院审理事项。同样，在初审法院判决第345段，初审法院驳回了雷普索尔集团主张的1998年至2002年违法行为仍在继续的事实具有所谓的附加价值，这也不属于欧盟法院审理事项。

65 对于上诉人诉称的法律适用错误，应当注意《宽恕公告》第23条b款的规定：如果卡特尔成员企业提供了欧盟委员会尚未获得的并且对于认定卡特尔行为的严重程度或持续时间具有直接作用的证据，欧盟委员会在认定该企业的罚款金额时将不再考虑严重程度和持续时间这两个因素。

66 根据该条的字面含义，若要获得罚款的部分豁免需满足两个条件：第一，卡特尔成员企业是第一个证明尚未被欧盟委员会获悉的相关事实；第二，这些事实直接关系到卡特尔行为的严重程度和持续时间，并且可以使欧盟委员会从相应的违法行为中获得新的发现。（参见判例：2015年4月23日，LG Display和LG Display Taiwan v Commission，C 227/14 P，EU：C：2015：258，第78段）

67 法院认为，"委员会尚未获得的事实"的含义是明确的，也允许对《宽恕公告》第23条b款末段作限制性解释，即将条款的适用范围限定于卡特尔企业向欧盟委员会提供的新信息应当与违法行为的严重程度和持续时间有关。（参见判例：2015年4月23日，LG Display 和LG Display Taiwan v Commission，C 227/14 P，EU：C：2015：258，第79段和引用的判例）

68 法院也进一步明确，这些措辞的含义应体现出第23条b款末段的立法目的，而且应特别体现宽恕政策的有效性（参见判例：2015年4月23日，LG Display 和 LG Display Taiwan v Commission，C 227/14 P，EU：C：2015：258，第84段和引用的判例法）。对此，佐审官在其意见第22段中指出，宽恕政策的目的是让那些违法企业快速而彻底地终止违法行为。

69 It is thus necessary to ensure the effectiveness of that provision, which—where the undertaking which was the first to submit to the Commission, in order to obtain total immunity from a fine under the 2002 Leniency Notice, evidence enabling the Commission to find an infringement of Article 101 TFEU, but has chosen not to disclose information which demonstrates that the duration of the infringement at issue was longer than disclosed by that evidence—seeks to provide an incentive, by means of partial immunity from a fine, to any other undertaking having participated in that infringement to be the first to disclose such information (see, to that effect, judgment 23 April 2015 in LG Display and LG Display Taiwan v Commission, C-227/14 P, EU: C: 2015: 258, paragraph 85).

70 In view of the foregoing, the 'cognitive' criterion referred to by the appellants cannot be accepted. The final paragraph of point 23 (b) of the 2002 Leniency Notice must be interpreted as meaning that evidence provided by an undertaking in the context of its application under that notice may be considered to be evidence relating to 'facts previously unknown to the Commission' only if it objectively presents significant added value with respect to the evidence already in the Commission's possession.

71 That interpretation follows, first, from the general scheme of the 2002 Leniency Notice. In accordance with points 7, 21 and 23 (a) of that notice, a reduction of the fine imposed by the Commission under that notice presupposes that undertakings seeking to benefit from it provide evidence to the Commission which has a significant added value compared to that already in the Commission's possession. The same is also true as regards the partial immunity laid down in the final paragraph of point 23 (b) of that notice.

72 Second, for the purposes of the application of that provision, it must be held that the Commission's possession of evidence amounts to knowledge of its content, regardless of whether that evidence was actually examined and analysed by its services.

73 In the present case, as follows from paragraph 64 of the present judgment, it was definitively found by the General Court, in paragraph 341 of the judgment under appeal, which refers to paragraph 592 of the decision at issue that, prior to the appellants' statement under the 2002 Leniency Notice, the Commission had information relating to the facts which occurred during the period from 1998 to 2002, obtained during the investigations carried out on 1 and 2 October 2002. Furthermore, the General Court definitively rejected the argument concerning the alleged added value of the facts related by Repsol as regards that period.

69 本案中，为了获得《宽恕公告》中规定的罚款可以全部豁免，英国石油集团第一个向欧盟委员会提交了相关证据，这些证据使欧盟委员会发现了《欧盟运行条约》第101条规定的违法行为，但其并未披露违法行为实际持续期间长于上述证据所反映的持续期间。因此，为了确保《宽恕公告》第23条b款末段的有效性，该条款旨在以部分罚款豁免的方式激励参与违法行为的企业第一个向欧盟委员会披露相关信息。（参见判例：2015年4月23日，LG Display and LG Display Taiwan v Commission，C 227/14 P，EU：C：2015：258，第85段）

70 鉴于上述情况，本院不采纳上诉人提出的“认知”标准。《宽恕公告》第23条b款末段应当解释为，当卡特尔成员企业依据公告向欧盟委员会提出罚款豁免申请时，其提交的证据只有在客观上对于欧盟委员会已经获得的证据具有明显的附加价值时，才可以被认定为“欧盟委员会尚未掌握的”证据。

71 首先，这是对《宽恕公告》作出的系统解释，依据公告第7条、第21条和第23条a款，欧盟委员会降低罚款金额的前提是卡特尔企业向欧盟委员会提交的证据对于欧盟委员会已经获得的证据具有明显的附加价值。对于第23条b款末段规定的部分罚款豁免也应当作出同样的解释。

72 其次，为了准确适用该条款，必须认为，欧盟委员会获得了相关证据就等同于其知晓了这些证据的内容，而无论其实际上是否对这些证据进行了检查分析。

73 如本判决书第64段所述，在本案中，初审法院最后在其判决书第341段（与欧盟委员会罚款决定书第592段相对应）认定，在上诉人依据《宽恕公告》提交声明之前，欧盟委员会在2002年10月1日和2日的调查中已经获得了关于1998年至2002年违法事实的信息。因此，初审法院驳回了雷普索尔集团提出的1998年至2002年的违法事实具有附加价值的抗辩。

74 It is therefore without committing an error of law that, in paragraph 344 of the judgment under appeal, the General Court was able to find that the appellants were not entitled to request, on the basis of the final paragraph of point 23(b) of that notice, that account not be taken, in determining the amount of the fine, of the facts relating to that cartel, which occurred during the period from 1998 to 2002.

75 Consequently, the second ground of appeal must be rejected as being unfounded.

The third ground of appeal, alleging infringement of Article 261 TFEU and the principle of proportionality, in that the General Court failed to carry out a full review, exercising its unlimited jurisdiction, of the fines imposed

Arguments of the parties

76 The appellants submit that the General Court infringed Article 261 TFEU and the principle of proportionality by failing to carry out an independent and comprehensive review of the decision at issue as regards the determination of the basic amount of the fine imposed, which was set at an amount of EUR 40 000 000, that is, double the indicative basic amount laid down by the 1998 Guidelines for infringements categorised as ‘very serious’, even though the factors referred to in the decision at issue should have led to setting the basic amount at an amount less than or equal to EUR 20 000 000.

77 In that regard, the appellants claim that, in response to the sixth plea in law of their action for annulment by which they challenged the basic amount of the fine set by the Commission, by alleging, in particular, an infringement of the principle of proportionality, the General Court merely found, first, that the alleged infringement should in fact be categorised as ‘very serious’, and second, that the Commission had stated that it had taken into account the additional factors set out in the decision at issue, without having checked whether the assessment of those factors by that institution had been correctly carried out.

78 In paragraphs 245 to 250 of the judgment under appeal, the General Court accordingly merely recorded the factors taken into account in the decision at issue without itself having carried out a genuine and independent assessment; that did not allow the appellants to understand the reasons why those factors could have led the Commission and, subsequently, the General Court, to adopt a basic amount of the fine corresponding to twice the minimum laid down by the 1998 Guidelines for infringements categorised as ‘very serious’.

74 因此，初审法院在其判决书第344段认定上诉人无权依据《宽恕公告》第23条b款末段要求欧盟委员会在计算罚款金额时不考虑其在1998年至2002年期间的违法事实。对这一判断，初审法院适用法律正确。

75 因此，上诉人的第二点上诉理由依据不足，应予驳回。

第三个上诉理由：初审法院未行使其罚款数额决定权①对欧盟委员会作出的罚款决定进行全面审查，违反了《欧盟运行条约》第261条和比例原则。

争议双方的观点

76 上诉人认为，初审法院未能对欧盟委员会决定的4000万欧元罚款基数进行独立而全面的审查，违反了《欧盟运行条约》第261条和比例原则。尽管与罚款决定相关的事实决定了本案的罚款基数应当少于或等于2000万欧元，但其仍然是《1998年罚款指南》中规定的对“非常严重”违法行为的指导性罚款基数的2倍。

77 对此，上诉人在请求撤销欧盟委员会罚款决定的第6项诉讼请求中称欧盟委员会确立的罚款基数违反了比例原则，而初审法院对此作出了两点认定：首先，本案中的违法行为应当归入“非常严重”的违法行为类别；其次，欧盟委员会声明其已经评估了罚款决定中列明的附加因素，而初审法院并未审查欧盟委员会作出的评估是否正确。

78 初审法院在其判决第245段至第250段仅记录了欧盟委员会在决定罚款基数时所考虑的因素，而未进行真正的且独立的评估，以致上诉人无法理解为什么这些因素会使欧盟委员会决定本案的罚款基数是《1998年罚款指南》中规定的对“非常严重”违法行为的指导性罚款基数的2倍，也无法理解为什么初审法院会对此予以认可。

① 指初审法院对欧盟委员会所处罚款数额予以重新评估的权利。欧盟法院与初审法院皆享有对欧盟委员会罚款决定重新审查评估的“unlimited jurisdiction”，但欧盟法院显然享有更高一级的权限，是不受限制的“unlimited jurisdiction”。为了便于读者理解，我们把这个同一个词条译作两个中文词汇。初审法院享有的unlimited jurisdiction是“罚款决定权”，欧盟法院享有的unlimited jurisdiction是“无限决定权”。——译者注

79 Finally, the appellants claim that, in the context of the exercise of its unlimited jurisdiction under Article 261 TFEU, the General Court should, in order to assess the proportionality of the basic amount of the fine imposed, have taken into consideration the lack of effect of the infringement and the size of that basic amount in relation to their turnover.

80 The Commission submits that the third ground of appeal must be rejected.

Findings of the Court

81 At the outset, it should be borne in mind that it is not for the Court, when ruling on questions of law in the context of an appeal, to substitute, on grounds of fairness, its own assessment for that of the General Court exercising its unlimited jurisdiction to rule on the amount of fines imposed on undertakings for infringements of EU law (see, inter alia, judgment of 22 November 2012 in E.ON Energie v Commission, C-89/11 P, EU: C: 2012: 738, paragraph 125).

82 It is only inasmuch as the Court considers that the level of the penalty is not merely inappropriate, but also excessive to the point of being disproportionate, that it would have to find that the General Court erred in law, on account of the inappropriateness of the amount of a fine (see, inter alia, judgment of 30 May 2013 in Quinn Barlo and Others v Commission, C-70/12 P, EU: C: 2013: 351, paragraph 57 and the case-law cited).

83 It follows that, as by the third ground of appeal, the appellants dispute the General Court's assessment as to the proportionality of the basic amount of the fine in the light of the factual circumstances of the case, without establishing or even arguing that that amount is not only inappropriate but also excessive, to the point of being disproportionate, that ground of appeal must be rejected as being inadmissible.

84 As to the remainder, it must be borne in mind that, with regard to judicial review of decisions whereby the Commission imposes a fine or periodic penalty payment for infringement of the competition rules, in addition to the review of legality provided for in Article 263 TFEU, the European Union judicature has the unlimited jurisdiction which it is afforded by Article 31 of Regulation No 1/2003, in accordance with Article 261 TFEU, and which empowers it to substitute its own appraisal for the Commission's and, consequently, to cancel, reduce or increase the fine or periodic penalty payment imposed (judgment of 22 October 2015 in AC-Treuhand vCommission, C-194/14 P, EU: C: 2015: 717, paragraph 74 and the case-law cited).

79 最后，上诉人认为，初审法院在行使《欧盟运行条约》第261条规定的无限管辖权时评估罚款基数的比例时，应当考虑违法行为的影响程度和罚款基数相对于营业额的比例。

80 欧盟委员会认为应当驳回上诉人的第三点上诉理由。

本院查明的事实及观点

81 应当注意的是，首先在上诉程序中审查法律问题时，欧盟法院不能以公正为由，将初审法院依其罚款数额决定权所作评估和罚款决定再重新进行评估，从而替换为欧盟法院自己的评估，自行决定对违反欧盟法律的企业的罚款金额。（参见判例：2012年11月22日，E.ON Energie v Commission，C 89/11 P，EU：C：2012：738，第125段）

82 只有当欧盟法院认为某项惩罚措施不仅不合理，而且达到了违反比例原则的程度，欧盟法院才有权以罚款金额不合理为由认定初审法院适用法律错误。（参加判例：2013年5月30日，Quinn Barlo and Others v Commission，C 70/12 P，EU：C：2013：351，第57段和引用的判例法）

83 对此，上诉人在第三点上诉理由中只是质疑了初审法院对罚款金额的比例性进行了评估，并未主张该罚款金额不仅不合理而且达到了违反比例原则的程度，因此欧盟法院应以无权管辖为由驳回上诉人的上诉理由。

84 除此之外，针对欧盟委员会以违反竞争法为由作出的罚款（分期罚款）决定的司法审查，欧盟司法机关享有《欧盟运行条约》第263条规定的合法性审查权，还享有《欧盟委员会第1/2003号条例》第31条和《欧盟运行条约》第261条规定的罚款数额自由裁量权。依据罚款数额自由裁量权，欧盟司法机关有权对欧盟委员会的评估决定进行司法审查，从而决定撤销罚款决定、降低或提高罚款（或分期罚款）金额。（参见判例：2015年10月22日，AC-Treuhand v Commission，C 194/14 P，EU：C：2015：717，第74段和引用的判例法）

85 However, it is important to note that the exercise of powers of unlimited jurisdiction provided for in Article 261 TFEU and in Article 31 of Regulation No 1/2003 does not amount to a review of the Court's own motion and that proceedings before the Courts of the European Union are inter partes. With the exception of pleas involving matters of public policy, which the Courts are required to raise of their own motion, it is therefore for the applicant to raise pleas in law against the decision at issue and to adduce evidence in support of those pleas (judgment of 22 October 2015 in AC-Treuhand v Commission, C-194/14 P, EU:C:2015:717, paragraph 75 and the case-law cited).

86 On the other hand, in order to satisfy the requirements of the principle of effective judicial protection enshrined in the first paragraph of Article 47 of the Charter of Fundamental Rights of the European Union ('the Charter') and bearing in mind that Article 23(3) of Regulation No 1/2003 provides that the amount of the fine must be fixed by reference to the gravity and duration of the infringement, the General Court is bound, in the exercise of the powers conferred by Articles 261 and 263 TFEU, to examine all complaints based on issues of fact and law which seek to show that the amount of the fine is not commensurate with the gravity or the duration of the infringement (judgment of 22 October 2015 in AC-Treuhand v Commission, C-194/14 P, EU:C:2015:717, paragraph 76 and the case-law cited).

87 In the present case, it is important to state that the General Court considered, in paragraphs 250 and 258 of the judgment under appeal, that there was no error in the determination, by the Commission, of the amount of EUR 40 000 000 which served as a basis for calculating the fine imposed on the appellants and that it did not appear disproportionate.

88 To that effect, the General Court, first, assessed, in paragraphs 245 to 249 of that judgment, the gravity of the infringement committed, the scope of the geographic market concerned by it and the appellants' market share and, second, in paragraphs 251 to 257 of that judgment, responded to the requisite legal standard and with sufficient reasoning, to the arguments alleging, in particular, the lack of actual impact of the cartel at issue or the fact that the basic amount of the fine imposed on the appellants represented a significant proportion of their turnover.

89 In so doing, the General Court did not err in law in the exercise of its judicial review.

90 It should also be noted that the 1998 Guidelines provide in the third indent of point 1.A that the basic amount of the fine envisaged for very serious infringements is above EUR 20 000 000. Accordingly, the amount of EUR 20 000 000 is only a minimum amount set by those guidelines above which the Commission sets the starting amount for the calculation of fines for such infringements.

85 尤其应当注意的是，法院根据《欧盟委员会第1/2003号条例》第31条和《欧盟运行条约》第261条的规定，行使的无限管辖权并不等同于审查法院自己提出的动议，欧盟各级法院的诉讼程序仅适用于案件当事人。除非该诉讼请求涉及到公共政策，法院应当主动提出动议外，一般情况下申请人应当针对欧盟委员会的罚款决定提出法律请求，并提供相关证据。（2015年10月22日，AC-Treuhand v Commission，C 194/14 P，EU：C：2015：717，第75段和引用的判例）

86 另外，《欧洲联盟基本权利宪章》（以下简称《宪章》）第47条第1段规定了有效司法保护原则，《欧盟委员会第1/2003号条例》第23条第3款规定了罚款金额必须根据违法行为的严重程度和持续时间确定，因而在行使《欧盟运行条约》第261条和第263条规定的审查权时，初审法院应当审查所有建立在事实和法律上的诉讼请求，以证明罚款金额与违法行为的严重程度和持续时间是不相称的。（参见判例：2015年10月22日，in AC-Treuhand v Commission，C 194/14 P，EU：C：2015：717，第76段和引用的判例）

87 应当指出，在本案中，初审法院在其判决书第250段至第258段中认为，欧盟委员会决定以4000万欧元作为计算罚款的基数是正确的，也没有违反比例原则。

88 为此，在判决书第245段至第249段，首先，初审法院审查了本案违法行为的严重性以及相关地区市场的规模；其次，在判决书第251段至第257段，初审法院针对上诉人的抗辩理由提出了必要的法律依据并作了充分的说理，特别是对上诉人提出的卡特尔行为缺乏影响力和罚款金额相对于上诉人营业额所占的比例过大等理由，初审法院也作了充分的说理。

89 因此，初审法院在行使其司法审查权时并未错误地适用法律。

90 应当注意，《1998年罚款指南》第1节A款第3点规定对“非常严重”违法行为罚款的基本金额不低于2000万欧元。因此，这些罚款指南规定的2000万欧元仅是欧盟委员会对此类违法行为设定的最低罚款金额。

91 In so far as the appellants claim that the General Court erred in law in rejecting their argument that the Commission should have taken into consideration the lack of actual impact of the infringement on the market, suffice it to note, as the Commission did, that the appellants did not, on this issue, challenge before the General Court the decision at issue, which, moreover, made no mention of such a lack of impact, nor did they adduce evidence before the General Court that the effects of the infringement were measurable. In those circumstances, the appellants' argument must be rejected as being inadmissible.

92 Consequently, the third ground of appeal must be rejected as being in part inadmissible and in part unfounded.

The fourth ground of appeal, alleging a failure by the General Court to adjudicate within a reasonable period

Arguments of the parties

93 By their fourth ground of appeal, the appellants claim that the General Court infringed Article 47 of the Charter and Article 6(1) of the European Convention for the Protection of Human Rights and Fundamental Freedoms signed in Rome on 4 November 1950, by not adjudicating within a reasonable period, which justifies a reduction of the fine imposed on them or the finding of the existence of that failure.

94 In that regard, they submit that their action for annulment was lodged on 18 December 2007, that the written procedure was closed on 25 September 2008, that their opinion was requested on 11 July 2012 on the possibility of joining the present case with Cases T-462/07, T-482/07, T-495/07 and T-497/07, that the hearing took place on 14 January 2013 and that the judgment under appeal was delivered on 16 September 2013.

95 They also state that the entirety of the proceedings lasted approximately 5 years and 9 months, with a period of inactivity, between the lodging of the application and the request for an opinion on the possibility of joining the present case with the others, of 4.5 years, analogous to that found by the Court of Justice in the judgment of 26 November 2013 in Groupe Gascogne v Commission (C-58/12 P, EU:C:2013:770).

96 In that regard, the appellants claim that there is no exceptional circumstance which may justify the delay accordingly found in the investigation of the case, which is not due either to the interventions or omissions on their part or to the particular complexity of the case.

91 虽然上诉人认为初审法院驳回其主张的“欧盟委员会在作出罚款决定时应考虑违法行为缺乏真正的市场影响”属于适用法律错误，但是应当注意的是，正如欧盟委员会所阐明的，上诉人并未就此问题向初审法院就欧盟委员会的罚款决定提出质疑，也未曾提出该违法行为缺乏影响力，更未曾向初审法院提交相关证据材料来证明违法行为的影响力是可以检测的。因此，欧盟法院应以无权管辖为由驳回上诉人的以上上诉理由。

92 综上，上诉人的第三个上诉理由，一部分依据不足，另一部分欧盟法院无权管辖，应予驳回。

第四个上诉理由：初审法院未在合理期限内作出裁判。

争议双方的观点

93 上诉人的第四点上诉理由认为，初审法院违反了《宪章》第47条和《欧洲保护人权和基本自由公约》(1950年11月4日签署于罗马)第6条第1款，未在合理期间内作出裁判，因此欧盟法院应当降低罚款金额或者认定超期裁判的确存在。

94 就本案而言，上诉人于2007年12月18日提交诉讼请求，要求撤销欧盟委员会的罚款决定，书面程序结束于2008年9月25日；初审法院在2012年7月11日向上诉人征询了关于将本案与T 462/07，T 482/07，T 495/07 和T 497/07号案件合并审理的意见，在2013年1月14日开庭审理了此案并于2013年9月16日作出了判决。

95 上诉人称整个诉讼程序持续了大约5年零9个月，而且从上诉人提起诉讼到初审法院征询上诉人是否同意与其他案件合并审理的4年半时间里，初审法院一直不作为，这与2013年11月26日的“加斯科涅集团诉欧盟委员会案”相似。(参见判例：C 58/12 P，EU：C：2013：770)

96 对此，上诉人认为，没有任何特殊情况可以证明在案件调查过程中发生的程序迟延是合理的，这不是由上诉人的干预或疏忽造成的，也不是因为案件的特殊复杂性。

97 The Commission contends that the fourth ground of appeal must be rejected.

Findings of the Court

98 It should be borne in mind that the sanction for a breach, by a Court of the European Union, of its obligation under the second paragraph of Article 47 of the Charter to adjudicate on the cases before it within a reasonable period must be an action for damages brought before the General Court, since such an action constitutes an effective remedy. It follows that a claim for compensation in respect of the damage caused by the General Court' s failure to adjudicate within a reasonable period may not be made directly to the Court of Justice in the context of an appeal, but must be brought before the General Court itself(see judgments of 10 July 2014 in Telefónica and Telefónica de España v Commission, C-295/12 P, EU: C: 2014: 2062, paragraph 66; of 9 October 2014 inICF v Commission, C-467/13 P, EU: C: 2014: 2274, paragraph 57; and of 12 November 2014 in Guardian Industries and Guardian Europe vCommission, C-580/12 P, EU: C: 2014: 2363, paragraphs 17 and 18).

99 The General Court, which has jurisdiction under Article 256(1) TFEU, hearing a claim for damages, is required to rule on such a claim sitting in a different composition from that which heard the dispute which gave rise to the procedure whose duration is criticised(see, to that effect, judgments of 10 July 2014 in Telefónica and Telefónica de España v Commission, C-295/12 P, EU: C: 2014: 2062, paragraph 67; of 9 October 2014 in ICF v Commission, C-467/13 P, EU: C: 2014: 2274, paragraph 58; and of 12 November 2014 in Guardian Industries and Guardian Europe v Commission, C-580/12 P, EU: C: 2014: 2363, paragraph 19).

100 That said, where it is clear, without any need for the parties to adduce additional evidence in that regard, that the General Court infringed, in a sufficiently serious manner, its obligation to adjudicate on the case within a reasonable time, the Court of Justice may note that fact(see, to that effect, judgments of 9 October 2014 in ICF v Commission, C-467/13 P, EU: C: 2014: 2274, paragraph 59, and of 12 November 2014 in Guardian Industries and Guardian Europe v Commission, C-580/12 P, EU: C: 2014: 2363, paragraph 20).

97 欧盟委员会认为，应当驳回上诉人的第4点上诉理由。

本院查明的事实及观点

98 与上诉人的主张不同，本院认为，对于超期裁判行为，依据《宪章》第47条第2段，唯一的救济方式是向初审法院提起损害赔偿诉讼，这才是有效的救济方式。因此，关于上诉人所主张的初审法院未能在合理期限内判决对其造成了损害，其损害赔偿请求应提交到初审法院，而不应在上诉程序中向欧盟法院提出。（参见判例：2014年7月10日，Telefónica and Telefónica de España v Commission，C 295/12 P，EU：C：2014：2062，第66段；2014年10月9日，ICF v Commission，C 467/13 P，EU：C：2014：2274，第 57段；2014年11月12日，Guardian Industries and Guardian Europe v Commission，C 580/12 P，EU：C：2014：2363，第17段和第18段）

99 依据《欧盟运行条约》第256条第1款，初审法院有权审理此类损害赔偿诉讼案件，但应另行组成法庭，独立于因程序期限问题而被质疑的先前法庭。（参见案例：2014年7月10日，Telefónica and Telefónica de España v Commission，C 295/12 P，EU：C：2014：2062，第67段；2014年10月9日，ICF v Commission，C 467/13 P，EU：C：2014：2274，第58段；2014年11月12日，Guardian Industries and Guardian Europe v. Commission，C 580/12 P，EU：C：2014：2363，第19段）

100 对此，若能判定初审法院明显地、严重地违反了其应在合理期限内裁判案件的职责，则当事人无须提交证据，欧盟法院也有职责关注这些事实。（参见判例：2014年10月9日，ICF v Commission，C 467/13 P，EU：C：2014：2274，第59段；2014年11月12日，Guardian Industries and Guardian Europe v Commission，C 580/12 P，EU：C：2014：2363，第20段）

101 That is the situation here. The duration of the proceedings before the General Court, namely almost 5 years and 9 months, which includes, in particular, a period of almost 4 years and 4 months which elapsed between the end of the written procedure and the hearing, cannot be explained by either the nature or the complexity of the case or by its context. The proceedings brought before the General Court were not particularly complex. Moreover, it is apparent neither from the judgment under appeal nor from the evidence presented by the parties that that period of inactivity could be objectively justified or that the appellants contributed to it. In that regard, the fact that the General Court requested the appellants' opinion on 11 July 2012 on the possibility of joining the present case with Cases T-462/07, T-482/07, T-495/07 and T-497/07 is irrelevant.

102 However, it follows from the considerations set out in paragraph 98 of the present judgment that the fourth ground of appeal must be rejected.

103 Since none of the appellants' grounds of appeal is able to be upheld, the appeal must be dismissed.

Costs

104 In accordance with Article 184(2) of the Rules of Procedure of the Court of Justice, where the appeal is unfounded, the Court shall make a decision as to costs.

105 Under Article 138(1) of those rules, which apply to the procedure on appeal by virtue of Article 184(1) of those rules, the unsuccessful party must be ordered to pay the costs if they have been applied for in the successful party's pleadings.

106 Since the Commission has applied for costs to be awarded against Repsol Lubricantes y Especialidades, Repsol Petróleo and Repsol and the latter have been unsuccessful, they must be ordered to pay the costs relating to the present appeal proceedings.

On those grounds, the Court (Fifth Chamber) hereby:

1.Dismisses the appeal;

2.Orders Repsol Lubricantes y Especialidades SA, Repsol Petróleo SA and Repsol SA to pay the costs.

101 在本案中，初审法院的初审程序持续了5年零9个月，其中包括了书面程序审理和听证程序（4年零2个月）。这个过程并不是案件性质的复杂性或案件内容的复杂性造成的。从初审法院的审理过程和当事人提交的证据材料来看，都不能判断出这段期间内存在法院的不作为或由当事人的干预造成的。事实上，本案在初审法院的诉讼程序并非特别复杂。此外，初审法院在2012年7月11日向上诉人征询是否同意将本案与T 462/07、T 482/07、T 495/07 和T 497/07号案件合并审理，这与超期裁判也没有关联。

102 可见，如本判决书第98段所述，第4项上诉理由也应予驳回。

103 由于没有任何上诉理由能够得到支持，本院驳回所有上诉请求。

诉讼费用

104 由于上诉不成立，本院根据《欧盟法院程序规则》第184条第2款的规定，对诉讼费用作出以下裁决。

105 依据《欧盟法院程序规则》第138条第1款和第184条第1款关于上述程序的规定，当胜诉方在诉讼中请求败诉方承担诉讼费用时，应责令败诉方承担诉讼费用。

106 由于欧盟委员会已经申请由上诉人润滑剂公司、石油公司及雷普索尔公司承担诉讼费用，而且上诉人已经败诉，所以上诉人应当支付该上诉程序的相关费用。

基于以上理由，本庭（第五法庭）判决如下：

1.驳回上诉；

2.由雷普索尔润滑剂公司、雷普索尔石油公司和雷普索尔公司承担诉讼费用。

3

皮尔金顿集团有限公司等
诉
欧盟委员会

（Pilkington Group and Others v European Commission）

（*Case C-101/15 P*）

案例导读*

一、案例基本信息

法　　院	欧盟法院		
提请法院	初审法院	判决时间	2016年9月7日
案　　号	Case C-101/15 P		
关 键 词	欧洲汽车玻璃市场；罚款适用的汇率；比例原则和平等待遇原则		
当 事 人	上 诉 人：皮尔金顿集团有限公司（Pilkington Group Ltd.） 皮尔金顿汽车有限公司（Pilkington Automotive Ltd.） 皮尔金顿汽车（德国）有限公司 （Pilkington Automotive Deutschland GmbH） 皮尔金顿控股有限公司（Pilkington Holding GmbH） 皮尔金顿（意大利）有限公司（Pilkington Italia SpA） 被上诉人：欧盟委员会（European Commission）		

二、案例涉及的欧盟法规

《欧盟运行条约》第101条①规定：

"1.下列行为因与内部市场相冲突而应予以禁止：一切可能影响成员国间的贸易且其目标或结果会阻碍、限制或扭曲内部市场竞争的企业之间的协定、企业联合组织的决定和协同行为，特别是：

（1）以直接或间接方式规定收购或销售价格或其他交易条件；

（2）限制或控制生产、市场、技术发展或投资；

（3）分配市场或供货渠道；

* 作者：郭清宇。

① 程卫东、李靖堃：《欧洲联盟基础条约》，社会科学文献出版社2010年版，第86页。

(4)对与其他商业伙伴的同等交易适用不同的条件，从而使之在竞争中处于不利地位；

(5)以其他缔约方接受附加义务为条件缔结合同，这些条件从其本质上说或者根据商业惯例与此等合同的主题无关。

2.本条所禁止的任何协议或决定应自动无效。

3.但在下列情形下可宣告本条第1款不适用：

——企业之间的任何协议或任何类型的协议；

——企业联合组织的任何决定或任何类型的决定；

——任何协同行为或任何类型的协同行为。

上述措施应有助于改善商品的生产或销售，或有助于推动技术或经济进步，同时保证消费者公平分享由此带来的收益，并且做到：

(1)不对有关企业施加并非为达到这些目标所必不可少的限制；

(2)不为有关企业提供在相关产品的实质部分消除竞争的可能性。”

三、案件事实和审理过程

本案上诉人为英国皮尔金顿集团下属的几家公司，该集团是世界最大的玻璃生产商。宾利、法拉利、奔驰、宝马等世界级名车均采用皮尔金顿集团制造的专业挡风玻璃。欧盟委员会经调查，认为皮尔金顿集团有限公司等(本案上诉人)通过协同行为参与了针对欧洲经济区内汽车玻璃行业的单一、持续的卡特尔行为。上诉人与欧洲经济区内主要汽车制造商达成关于汽车挡风玻璃、侧灯及尾灯的车辆玻璃供应协议，违反了《欧共体条约》第81条第1款的规定。

2008年11月12日，欧盟委员会认定上诉人于1998年3月10日至2002年9月3日实施了非法卡特尔行为，并对其作出了第6815号罚款决定。之后，该决定经过两次修正：第一次于2009年2月11日由欧盟委员会第863号决定作出修正；第二次于2013年2月28日由欧盟委员会第1119号决定作出修正，且第1119号决定是针对上诉人的最终决定。

2009年2月18日，上诉人首次向初审法院提起诉讼。2013年3月15日，上诉人再次向初审法院提交了一份修正后的诉状。上诉人请求初审法院认定欧盟委员会的决定无效，并提出六项上诉理由。其中，第3项、第5项、第6项上诉理由涉及罚款的计算方法。此外，上诉人请求初审法院依法行使其罚款数额决定权，降低针对上诉人的罚款数额。初审法院在其初审判决中驳回了上诉人的全部诉讼请求。

2015年2月27日，上诉人向欧盟法院提起上诉。上诉人的代理律师为史密夫斐尔律师事务所（Herbert Smith Freehills）专注于欧盟竞争法诉讼的S.维斯金（S. Wisking）律师团队。欧盟法院第四法庭于2016年9月7日作出判决，驳回了上诉人的全部诉讼请求。

四、争议焦点和主要法律观点

本案有3个争议焦点。

第一，关于欧盟委员会对《2006年罚款指南》第13条的解释。《2006年罚款指南》第13条规定，罚款基数是所有与卡特尔有直接或间接关系的产品和服务的销售金额。本案中，上诉人在卡特尔行为发生前曾与部分制造商订立了合同，约定了销售金额。但是上诉人在卡特尔行为期间并未改变或重新约定已经确定的销售金额（本案中的“争议销售金额”）。

上诉人认为，其仅是履行卡特尔行为发生前订立的合同。对这部分合同约定的争议销售金额（卡特尔前约定的销售金额）与卡特尔行为并无直接或间接关系，因此欧盟委员会在决定罚金基数时不应将争议销售金额纳入罚款金额范围。上诉人提出，依据《2006年罚款指南》第6条，此类合同金额不属于“合理罚款范围”。若被纳入罚款范围，则会过高认定卡特尔侵权行为对相关行业的经济影响、各涉案企业在侵权行为中的权重，以及该等侵权行为导致的损害结果。

欧盟法院认为，该部分合同虽然是在卡特尔行为之前订立的，但是这一行为为以后的卡特尔行为奠定了一定基础。考虑到上诉人所处的汽车玻璃行业的特殊性，企业之间一般通过订立货物供应或销售合同来实现垄断价格、货物供应和分割市场的卡特尔行为。案涉企业卡特尔的最终目的是通过已订立和尚未订立的合同，在卡特尔企业间约定针对汽车玻璃行业的货物分配和供应方式。因此，若欧盟委员会无权依据《2006年罚款指南》第13条的规定，将争议销售金额纳入罚款基数，那么本案的罚款金额就无法真正反映侵权行为的经济影响。

第二，关于计算罚金时应适用卡特尔期间的平均汇率还是欧盟委员会决定作出之日时的即期汇率。本案的特殊之处在于，上诉人总营业额的计价货币为英镑。计算罚金需要进行汇率换算，而欧盟委员会在汇率换算时使用了欧洲央行（ECB）在2007年4月1日到2008年3月31日期间的平均汇率，而非决定作出时（2008年11月12日）的即期汇率。据此，上诉人科研少缴纳约4000万欧元的罚金。

《第1/2003号条例》第23条第1款规定："欧盟委员会可以作出决定，对企业或企业协会处以罚款，但该罚款额不超过前一营业年度的总营业额的10%。"上诉人认为其在欧盟委员会决定作出前可能面临极大的货币、汇率风险及不利影响，而该法条的立法目的是为涉案企业规避汇率风险提供的保护措施。

欧盟法院同意佐审官对此问题的意见，即所谓的风险规避并非设定罚款上限的法目的，这条规定是为了通过设定罚款上限来规避过分或不合理罚款。平均汇率最基本的属性是可以降低或规避决定作出前汇率波动的风险。反之，使用即期汇率则缺乏确定性和可预期性。

第三，关于比例原则和平等待遇原则。上诉人认为，卡特尔企业依照其营业总额的一定比例缴纳的罚金应当与其因此承担的不利后果相适应。与本案中的其他卡特尔企业相比，上诉人认为其承担的不利后果更严重。因此，欧盟委员会在作出罚款决定时应该遵守比例原则和平等对待原则。欧盟法院认为，欧盟委员会在确定罚款金额时无须考虑涉案企业的经济情况，特别是无须考虑其财务能力和经济情况。若欧盟委员会有考虑上述因素的义务，反而可能让那些市场适应能力较差（或与市场匹配度低）的企业享受不正当的竞争优势。

五、本案的意义及其启示

本案的判决对我国《反垄断法》的适用有两大意义。

其一，关于如何判断卡特尔行为之前订立的合同能否纳入以后的卡特尔协议的范畴。我国《反垄断法》第46条规定："经营者违反本法规定，达成并实施垄断协议的，由反垄断执法机构责令停止违法行为，没收违法所得，并处上一年度销售额百分之一以上百分之十以下的罚款；尚未实施所达成的垄断协议的，可以处五十万元以下的罚款。”但我国法律未对罚款基数的计算和界定垄断协议的范围作出具体规定，也没有规定有关机构是否有权对卡特尔行为直接或间接关联的产品和服务所对应的经济价值进行估算，更没有对汇率兑换的时间先后有具体细则。法律上的缺位导致执行法中乱象和随意性。我们不妨借鉴欧盟《2006年罚款指南》的规定，授权有关执行机关可以适当扩大对垄断协议的界定范围，进一步查明与该卡特尔行为直接或间接关联的产品和服务所对应的经济价值，将其纳入罚款基数，从而加强对垄断行为的惩戒力度，真正体现《反垄断法》的威慑力。

其二，关于计算罚金时如何适用汇率问题。尽管我国国内反垄断法的实施尚不存在具体的汇率计算问题，但我们不能仅局限于国内环境思考问题。本案关于汇率问题的讨论，有利于我们思考中国企业海外投融资活动中可能面临的汇率风险，以及可能涉及的反垄断法的域外适用问题。欧盟法院和欧盟委员会以平均汇率作为依据，并认为这更能反映侵权行为期间的真实金额状况。关于平均汇率和即期汇率的分析表明了欧盟法院和欧盟委员会的基本态度，这也是欧盟竞争法在计算罚款数额方面的典型案例。

表3-1　C 101/15 P（2016）涉及的法律

序号	原文	中文名称	所在段落
1	Treaty on the Functioning of the European Union（TFEU）	《欧盟运行条约》	60、61、70
2	Council Regulation No 1/2003 of 16 December 2002 on the implementation of the rules on competition laid down in Articles 81 [EC] and 82 [EC]	《关于实施〈欧共体条约〉第81条、第82条的第1/2003号条例》	24、25、27、34、35、38
3	Guidelines on the method of setting fines imposed pursuant to Article 23（2）（a）of Regulation（EC）No 1/2003	《关于依据〈第1/2003号条例〉第23条第2款a项设定罚款方法的指南》	10、12、15、18、64

表3-2　C 101/15 P（2016）涉及的判例

序号	判例名称	案号	所在段落
1	InnoLux v Commission	EU：C：2015：451	16、17、37
2	Team Relocations and Others v Commission	EU：C：2013：464	19
3	Guardian Industries and Guardian Europe v Commission	EU：C：2014：2363	19
4	Enso Española v Commission	EU：C：2000：628	28
5	Sarrió v Commission	EU：C：2000：631	28、42
6	Limburgse Vinyl Maatschappij and Others v Commission	EU：C：2002：582	28

续表

序号	判例名称	案号	所在段落
7	YKK and Others v Commission	EU: C: 2014: 2153	28
8	Dansk Rørindustri and Others v Commission	EU: C: 2005: 408	36、45
9	Novácke chemické závody v Commission	EU: T: 2012: 673	57
10	Aalborg Portland and Others v Commission	EU: C: 2004: 6	62
11	LG Display and LG Display Taiwan v Commission	EU: C: 2015: 258	67
12	Galp Energía España and Others v Commission	EU: C: 2016: 38	71
13	Schindler Holding and Others v Commission	EU: C: 2013: 522	72

JUDGMENT OF THE COURT (Fourth Chamber)

7 September 2016 (*)

(Appeal—Agreements, decisions and concerted practices—Article 101 TFEU—Article 53 of the Agreement on the European Economic Area of 2 May 1992—European market for automotive glass—Market-sharing agreements and exchanges of commercially sensitive information—Fines—2006 Guidelines on the method of setting fines—Point 13—Value of sales—Regulation (EC) No 1/2003—Second subparagraph of Article 23 (2)—Statutory ceiling of the fine—Exchange rate for the calculation of the ceiling of the fine—Amount of the fine—Unlimited jurisdiction—Mono-product undertakings—Proportionality—Equal treatment)

In Case C-101/15 P,

APPEAL under Article 56 of the Statute of the Court of Justice of the European Union, brought on 27 February 2015,

Pilkington Group Ltd, established in Lathom (United Kingdom),

Pilkington Automotive Ltd, established in Lathom,

Pilkington Automotive Deutschland GmbH, established in Witten (Germany),

Pilkington Holding GmbH, established in Gelsenkirchen (Germany),

Pilkington Italia SpA, established in San Salvo (Italy),

represented by S. Wisking and K. Fountoukakos-Kyriakakos, Solicitors, and by C. Puech Baron, avocat,

appellants,

the other party to the proceedings being:

European Commission, represented by A. Biolan, M. Kellerbauer and H. Leupold, acting as Agents,

defendant at first instance,

判例正文*

欧盟法院(第四法庭)
2016年9月7日

(上诉—协议、决定和协同行为—《欧盟运行条约》第101条—1992年5月2日《欧洲经济区协议》第53条—欧洲汽车玻璃市场—市场分割协议和商业敏感信息交换—罚款—《2006年罚款指南》第13条—销售金额—第1/2003号条例—第23(2)条第二款—罚款的法定上限—计算罚款上限适用的汇率—罚款金额—罚款数额决定权—单一产品企业—比例原则—平等待遇原则)

案件号:C-101/15 P

2015年2月27日,上诉人依据《欧盟法院规约》第56条,向本院提出上诉。

上诉人:

皮尔金顿集团有限公司,成立于英国拉托姆;

皮尔金顿汽车有限公司,成立于英国拉托姆;

皮尔金顿汽车(德国)有限公司,成立于德国维滕;

皮尔金顿控股有限公司,成立于德国盖尔森基兴;

皮尔金顿(意大利)有限公司,成立于意大利圣萨尔沃;

代理人:史密夫斐尔律师事务所S.维斯金律师,K.方顿图卡司-凯瑞卡尔斯律师和C.普西·拜伦律师。

被上诉人(原审被告):

欧盟委员会,代理人是A.比欧兰、M.凯伦巴尔和H.伦步多。

---

* 初译者:郭清宇;校对者:林燕萍、戴娜。

THE COURT (Fourth Chamber),

composed of T. von Danwitz, President of the Chamber, C. Lycourgos, E. Juhász, C. Vajda and K. Jürimäe (Rapporteur), Judges,

Advocate General: J. Kokott,

Registrar: L. Hewlett, Principal Administrator,

having regard to the written procedure and further to the hearing on 2 March 2016,

after hearing the Opinion of the Advocate General at the sitting on 14 April 2016,

gives the following

欧盟法院（第四法庭）

由T.冯·丹威兹担任第四法庭庭长，法官C.卢克果斯、E.茱赫兹、C.瓦加达和K.尤里迈（判决书起草人）组成。

佐审官：N.加斯克林；

书记官：L.休利特（首席行政官）。

本院进行了所有书面程序后，于2016年3月2日开庭审理了本案，并于2016年4月14日听取了佐审官的意见。

经审理，本院作出如下判决：

Judgment

1 By their appeal, Pilkington Group Ltd, Pilkington Automotive Ltd, Pilkington Automotive Deutschland GmbH, Pilkington Holding GmbH and Pilkington Italia SpA ('the appellants') ask the Court to set aside the judgment of the General Court of the European Union of 17 December 2014, Pilkington Group and Others v Commission (T-72/09, not published, EU: T: 2014: 1094)('the judgment under appeal'), by which the latter dismissed their action, primarily, for annulment of Commission Decision C(2008)6815 final of 12 November 2008 relating to a proceeding pursuant to Article [81 EC] and Article 53 of the EEA Agreement (COMP/39.125—Carglass), as amended by Commission Decision C(2009)863 final of 11 February 2009 and by Commission Decision C(2013)1119 final of 28 February 2013 ('the decision at issue'), in so far as it concerns the appellants, and, in the alternative, for annulment of Article 2 of that decision in that it imposes a fine on the appellants, or, in the further alternative, for a reduction of that fine.

Legal context

Regulation (EC) No 1/2003

2 Under the heading 'Fines', Article 23(2) of Council Regulation (EC) No 1/2003 of 16 December 2002 on the implementation of the rules on competition laid down in Articles [81 EC and 82 EC] (OJ 2003 L 1, p. 1) provides:

'The Commission may by decision impose fines on undertakings and associations of undertakings where, either intentionally or negligently:

(a) they infringe [Articles 81 EC or 82 EC]; ...

For each undertaking and association of undertakings participating in the infringement, the fine shall not exceed 10% of its total turnover in the preceding business year.

...'

判　决

1　皮尔金顿集团有限公司、皮尔金顿汽车有限公司、皮尔金顿汽车（德国）有限公司、皮尔金顿控股有限公司和皮尔金顿（意大利）有限公司（统称为上诉人）请求本院撤销初审法院于2014年12月17日作出的“皮尔金顿集团有限公司等诉欧盟委员会案”判决（T 72/09，未公开，EU：T：2014：1094）（以下简称初审法院判决）。上诉人上请求欧盟法院撤销欧盟委员会依据《欧共体条约》第81条和《欧洲经济区协议》第53条于2008年11月12日对上诉人作出的第6815号罚款决定（COMP/39.125—汽车玻璃），该决定随后经过欧盟委员会的两次修正，第一次是2009年2月11日作出的第863号决定，第二次是2013年2月28日作出的第1119号决定，且第1119号决定为最终决定（以下简称欧盟委员会决定）。上诉人对该决定不服，向初审法院起诉，请求撤销该决定，或撤销该决定的第2项，或降低上诉人承担的罚金。初审法院驳回了上诉人的全部诉讼请求。

法律背景

《第1/2003号条例》

2　《关于实施〈欧共体条约〉第81条、第82条的第1/2003号条例》（OJ 2003 L 1，p. 1，以下简称《第1/2003号条例》）第23条第2款规定：

“对于企业或企业联合组织的下列行为，无论是故意或过失，欧盟委员会均有权对其处以罚款：

（a）违反《欧共体条约》第81条或第82条的规定；

对于存在上述违法行为的企业或企业联合组织，罚款金额不得超过其上一年度销售总额的10%。

……”

The 2006 Guidelines

3 Points 4 to 6, 13 and 35 of the Guidelines on the method of setting fines imposed pursuant to Article 23(2)(a) of Regulation No 1/2003 (OJ 2006 C 210, p. 2) ('the 2006 Guidelines') state as follows:

'4. ... Fines should have a sufficiently deterrent effect, not only in order to sanction the undertakings concerned (specific deterrence) but also in order to deter other undertakings from engaging in, or continuing, behaviour that is contrary to Articles [81 EC and 82 EC] (general deterrence).

5.In order to achieve these objectives, it is appropriate for the Commission to refer to the value of the sales of goods or services to which the infringement relates as a basis for setting the fine. The duration of the infringement should also play a significant role in the setting of the appropriate amount of the fine...

6.The combination of the value of sales to which the infringement relates and of the duration of the infringement is regarded as providing an appropriate proxy to reflect the economic importance of the infringement as well as the relative weight of each undertaking in the infringement.

13.In determining the basic amount of the fine to be imposed, the Commission will take the value of the undertaking's sales of goods or services to which the infringement directly or indirectly relates [such will be the case for instance for horizontal price fixing arrangements on a given product, where the price of that product then serves as a basis for the price of lower or higher quality products)] in the relevant geographic area within the [European Economic Area (EEA)].

...

35.In exceptional cases, the Commission may, upon request, take account of the undertaking's inability to pay in a specific social and economic context. It will not base any reduction granted for this reason in the fine on the mere finding of an adverse or loss-making financial situation. A reduction could be granted solely on the basis of objective evidence that imposition of the fine as provided for in these Guidelines would irretrievably jeopardise the economic viability of the undertaking concerned and cause its assets to lose all their value.'

《2006年罚款指南》

3 《2006年罚款指南》第4条、第5条、第6条、第13条和第35条对《第1/2003号条例》第 23 条第2款的规定作了进一步阐释。

第4条：对于违反欧盟竞争法的卡特尔行为的罚款应具有特殊威慑力和普遍威慑力。即罚款的目的不仅在于制裁个案中的卡特尔企业（特殊威慑力），而且在于阻止其他企业参与或继续实施违反《欧共体条约》第81条、第82条的卡特尔行为，即罚款对其他企业产生普遍威慑力。

第5条：为达到罚款的威慑力，欧盟委员会在计算罚款基数时有权考量卡特尔行为持续期间的销售金额，即把与卡特尔行为有关联的产品和服务所对应的经济价值全部纳入罚款基数。

第6条：对卡特尔企业作出的罚金应基于卡特尔行为的持续期限和销售金额，且该罚金能真实客观地反映卡特尔行为造成的经济影响，以及每个卡特尔企业在整个侵权行为中的权重。

第13条：为确定罚款基数，欧盟委员会有权对欧洲经济区内某一特定地点或区域发生的卡特尔行为展开调查，查明与该卡特尔行为直接或间接关联的产品和服务所对应的经济价值。

……

第35条：经卡特尔企业请求，欧盟委员会可以结合该企业所处的社会和经济背景以评估该企业是否无法缴纳罚金。只有在这种特殊情形下，即依据《2006年罚款指南》缴纳罚款会严重影响该企业的经济、财务状况，甚至会损失其全部资产价值，欧盟委员会可以据此降低罚金。这是欧盟委员会降低罚金的唯一情形。除此之外，欧盟委员会不会因企业财务状况恶化无法缴纳罚金而决定降低罚金。

Background to the dispute and the decision at issue

4 As is apparent from paragraphs 1 to 12 and 36 of the judgment under appeal, the Commission, in the decision at issue, found that a number of undertakings, including the appellants, had participated in a single and continuous infringement of Article 81(1)EC, consisting in the concerted allocation, in the automotive glass sector, of contracts concerning the supply of carglass pieces and/or carsets, generally consisting of a windscreen, sidelights and backlights, to the major car manufacturers in the EEA. With regard to the appellants, the Commission found that there had been an infringement over the period from 10 March 1998 to 3 September 2002 and for that reason imposed on them, jointly and severally, a fine of EUR 370 million(Article 2(c) of the decision at issue).

5 On 28 February 2013, the Commission adopted Decision C(2013)1119 final, amending Decision C(2008)6815 final with respect to, inter alia, the calculation of the fine imposed on the appellants. By that decision, the Commission essentially sought to correct two errors which it believed it had made in that calculation. As a result of that decision, the new amount of the fine imposed on the appellants was set at EUR 357 million instead of the original amount of EUR 370 million.

The procedure before the General Court and the judgment under appeal

6 By application lodged at the Registry of the General Court on 18 February 2009, as modified by a letter received at the Registry of the General Court on 15 March 2013, the appellants lodged an application for annulment of the decision at issue, raising six pleas in law in support. Only the third, fifth and sixth pleas in law, relating to the calculation of the fine imposed on the appellants, are relevant for the purposes of the present appeal. The appellants also requested the General Court, independently of those grounds of annulment, where applicable, to exercise its unlimited jurisdiction by reducing the fine imposed on them.

7 By the judgment under appeal, the General Court dismissed the action in its entirety.

Forms of order sought by the parties to the appeal

8 By their appeal, the appellants claim that the Court should:

–set aside the judgment under appeal, to the extent that it dismisses the action brought against Article 2(c) of the decision at issue;

–reduce the fine imposed on them in Article 2(c) of the decision at issue; and

–order the Commission to pay the costs.

争议背景以及欧盟委员会的决定

4 初审判决在第1~12段及第36段阐述了案件背景：欧盟委员会发现，包括上诉人在内的若干企业通过协同行为参与了欧洲经济区内汽车玻璃行业单一、持续的卡特尔行为。上述企业与欧洲经济区内主要汽车制造商达成关于汽车挡风玻璃、侧灯及尾灯的车辆玻璃供应卡特尔协议，因此违反了《欧共体条约》第81条第1款的规定。欧盟委员会据此认定，上诉人于1998年3月10日至2002年9月3日期间实施了非法卡特尔行为，并对其对作出37 000万欧元的罚款决定（欧盟委员会决定第二部分C项）。欧盟委员会认定上诉人应对其行为承担连带责任。

5 2013年2月28日，欧盟委员会通过第1119号最终决定，该决定修正了此前第6815号决定中两处关于上诉人罚款数额计算方法的错误。上诉人应缴纳的最终罚款金额应为35 700万欧元，而非此前的37 000万欧元。

初审法院的审理程序及判决

6 2009年2月18日，上诉人首次向初审法院提出上诉请求。2013年3月15日，上诉人再次向初审法院提交了一份修正后的诉状。上诉人要求初审法院认定欧盟委员会决定无效，为此，上诉人提出了6项理由。其中，仅有第3、5、6项涉及罚款计算方法，与当前的上诉请求有关。此外，上诉人请求初审法院依法行使其罚款数额决定权，降低针对上诉人的罚款数额。

7 初审法院在其判决中驳回了上诉人的全部诉讼请求。

当事人提交到欧盟法院的诉讼请求

8 上诉人请求欧盟法院判决：

——撤销初审判决，或撤销欧盟委员会决定中第2部分C项的决定；

——欧盟委员会应降低其依据决定第2部分C项作出的罚款金额；

——责令欧盟委员会支付诉讼费用。

9 The Commission contends that the Court should dismiss the appeal and order the appellants to pay the costs.

The appeal

10 The appellants put forward three grounds in support of their appeal.

The first ground of appeal, alleging an error of law in the interpretation of point 13 of the 2006 Guidelines

Arguments of the parties

11 By their first ground of appeal, directed against paragraphs 217 to 227 of the judgment under appeal, the appellants criticise the General Court for finding that the Commission was fully entitled, when determining the basic amount of the fine imposed on them, to take into account sales made pursuant to contracts that pre-dated the infringement period and that were not renegotiated during the infringement period ('the sales at issue').

12 The appellants submit that the General Court thus relied on an incorrect interpretation of the concept of 'the value of the undertaking's sales of goods or services to which the infringement directly or indirectly relates' within the meaning of point 13 of the 2006 Guidelines. According to the appellants, this concept does not entitle the Commission to take into account the sales at issue, in so far as it is obvious, in the appellants' opinion, that these could not in any way have formed part of the infringement, even though the objective of the latter was the overall stabilisation of the infringement market. Therefore, the appellants claim that taking those sales into account does not serve as an 'appropriate proxy', within the meaning of point 6 of the 2006 Guidelines, because it overestimates the economic importance of the infringement, the relative weight of the undertaking that achieved such sales in the context of the infringement, and the harm caused by the infringement.

13 The appellants emphasise that none of the reasons given by the General Court in paragraph 225 of the judgment under appeal, relating to the mode of operation of the infringement and the objective which it pursues, can prove that the sales at issue formed part of the infringement.

14 The Commission contends that the appellants' arguments should be rejected as unfounded.

9 欧盟委员会认为，欧盟法院应驳回上诉人的上诉请求并判决由上诉人承担全部诉讼费用。

上诉

10 上诉人提出3项理由以支持其上诉请求。

第一项理由认为初审法院对《2006年罚款指南》第13条的解释有误。

争议双方的观点

11 上诉人在卡特尔行为发生前曾与部分玻璃制造商订立了合同，约定了销售金额，上诉人在卡特尔行为期间并未改变或重新约定之前已经确定的销售金额（“争议销售金额”）。针对初审判决书中第217~227段，上诉人认为初审法院错误地认为欧盟委员会在决定罚款金额时有权将这一“争议销售金额”纳入考量范围。

12 上诉人认为，初审法院对《2006年罚款指南》第13条项下关于“涉案企业的销售或服务金额认定应与侵权行为有直接或间接关联”的相关规定解释有误。即使欧盟委员会审查的目的是维持整个汽车玻璃市场的稳定，上诉人认为侵权行为发生前订立的合同涉及的金额不属于罚款金额考量范围。依据《2006年罚款指南》第6条的规定，此类合同金额不属于“罚款金额的合理考量范围”。若被纳入罚款基数考量范围，则会过高认定侵权行为对相关行业的经济影响、各涉案企业在侵权行为中的权重，以及侵权导致的损害结果。

13 上诉人认为，初审法院在其判决书第225段列举的侵权行为和侵权目的，均无法证明欧盟委员会在计算罚金时可以将争议销售金额作为罚金基数的一部分。

14 欧盟委员会对上述理由不予认可并请求法院依法驳回。

Findings of the Court

15 By their first ground of appeal, the appellants submit, in essence, that the General Court erred in law in finding that, under 'the undertaking's sales of goods or services to which the infringement directly or indirectly relates', within the meaning of point 13 of the 2006 Guidelines, the Commission could include the sales at issue in the sales to be taken into account when determining the amount of the fine imposed on them.

16 With regard to the imposition of a fine pursuant to Article 23(2) of Regulation No 1/2003, the Court has held that the Commission must assess, in each specific case and having regard to both the context and the objectives pursued by the scheme of penalties created by that regulation, the intended impact on the undertaking concerned, in particular by taking into account a turnover which reflects the undertaking's real economic situation during the period in which the infringement was committed (judgment of 9 July 2015, InnoLux v Commission, C-231/14 P, EU:C:2015:451, paragraph 46 and the case-law cited).

17 In that context, it is permissible, for the purpose of setting the amount of the fine, to have regard both to the overall turnover of the undertaking, which gives an indication, albeit approximate and imperfect, of its size and of its economic power, and to the proportion of that turnover accounted for by the goods in respect of which the infringement was committed, which gives an indication of the scale of the infringement (judgment of 9 July 2015 in *InnoLux* v *Commission*, C-231/14 P, EU:C:2015:451, paragraph 47 and the case-law cited).

18 As provided in point 13 of the 2006 Guidelines: 'in determining the basic amount of the fine to be imposed, the Commission will take the value of the undertaking's sales of goods or services to which the infringement directly or indirectly ... relates in the relevant geographic area within the EEA'. In the introductory section of the 2006 Guidelines, point 6 specifies that 'the combination of the value of sales to which the infringement relates and of the duration of the infringement is regarded as providing an appropriate proxy to reflect the economic importance of the infringement as well as the relative weight of each undertaking in the infringement'.

本院查明的事实及观点

15 上诉人认为，初审法院在认定罚款金额时错误地解释了《2006年罚款指南》第13条项下关于"涉案企业的销售或服务金额认定应与侵权行为有直接或间接关联"的相关概念。

16 初审法院认为，欧盟委员会在依据《第1/2003号条例》第23条第2款作出罚款决定前，应充分考虑到以下因素：该条例设定罚款的具体条文、罚款所要达到的目标、罚款对企业产生的影响，以及作出的罚金能否反映该企业在侵权行为期间真实的经济情况和营业额。（参见判例：2015年7月9日，InnoLux v Commission，C−231/14 P，EU：C：2015：451，第46段）

17 据此，欧盟委员会还应考量罚金是否可以大体反映该企业体量和经济实力的总营业额。同时，还应考虑侵权行为发生期间、涉及卡特尔行为的部分销售额，进而判断卡特尔行为的规模和程度。（参见判例：2015年7月9日，InnoLux v Commission，C−231/14 P，EU：C：2015：451，第47段）

18 《2006年罚款指南》第6条和第13条均强调欧盟委员会决定的罚金应适当反映卡特尔行为造成的经济影响和每个涉案企业在卡特尔行为中的权重。

19 It follows that point 13 of the 2006 Guidelines pursues the objective of adopting, as the starting point for the calculation of the fine imposed on an undertaking, an amount which reflects the economic significance of the infringement and the size of the undertaking's contribution to it. Consequently, while the concept of the 'value of sales' referred to in point 13 of the Guidelines admittedly cannot extend to encompassing sales made by the undertaking in question which do not come within the scope of the alleged cartel, it would, however, be contrary to the goal pursued by that provision if that concept were to be understood as applying only to turnover achieved by the sales in respect of which it is established that they were actually affected by that cartel (judgments of 11 July 2013, *Team Relocations and Others* v *Commission*, C-444/11 P, not published, EU: C: 2013: 464, paragraph 76, and of 12 November 2014, *Guardian Industries and Guardian Europe* v *Commission*, C-580/12 P, EU: C: 2014: 2363, paragraph 57).

20 However, while, as the appellants argue, the sales at issue were made pursuant to contracts which pre-date the infringement period, the fact remains that the General Court was correct in finding, in paragraph 226 of the judgment under appeal, that the Commission was entitled to include those sales in the value of the sales calculated in accordance with point 13 of the 2006 Guidelines, for the purpose of determining the basic amount of the fine, on the same basis as the sales made pursuant to supply contracts concluded during the infringement period but which were not shown to have specifically been the subject of collusion.

21 As is apparent from paragraphs 222 to 225 of the judgment under appeal, the General Court approved the method of calculation used by the Commission, by examining the grounds relating to the mode of operation of the infringement and its objectives, which formed the basis for that institution's finding that taking the sales at issue into account was justified in so far as those sales were capable of reflecting the economic importance of the infringement.

22 The General Court thus held, inter alia, in paragraphs 224 and 225 of the judgment under appeal, that taking the sales at issue into account was justified in view of the scope of the cartel, its mode of operation and its overall objective of stabilising market shares, with the result that it was not necessary to collude on each supply contract in order to achieve that objective. In that regard, the General Court rightly found that, in those circumstances, the need for collusion on a given supply contract depended on the allocation of supplies, the perceived need to take measures to maintain the respective market shares, and the ability of each individual contract to bring about an appreciable change in the share of the overall supplies envisaged by each cartel participant.

19 《2006年罚款指南》第13条规定，罚金应反映侵权行为造成的经济影响以及涉案企业在影响中的权重。其第13条项下关于“营业额”的概念显然不能扩大解释为涉案企业在卡特尔侵权行为以外产生的销售额；但也不能限缩解释为仅与侵权行为有实质关联的营业额（参见判例：2013年7月11日，Team Relocations and Others v Commission，C-444/11 P，未公布，EU：C：2013：464，第76段，以及 2014年11月12日，Guardian Industries and Guardian Europe v Commission，C-580/12 P，EU：C：2014：2363，第57段）。

20 初审法院在其判决书第226段认定，欧盟委员会有权将争议营业额纳入计算罚款基数的考量范围。即使如上诉人所言，争议营业额源于侵权行为前订立的合同，初审法院的认定依然是正确的。本院认为，对于在侵权行为发生期间订立的，但未被特别认定为与此次卡特尔行为有关联的合同，欧盟委员会有权将此类合同涉及的金额纳入罚款基数；同理，欧盟委员会也有权将在侵权行为发生前订立的合同涉及的争议营业额纳入罚款基数范围。

21 初审法院在其判决书第222~225段说明，将争议营业额纳入罚款基数可以更好地反映出该案侵权行为的运作模式和其造成的经济影响，因此支持欧盟委员会采纳的罚金计算方法。

22 初审法院判决书第224段和第225段阐明，争议营业额纳入基数可以反映出该案卡特尔的范围、运作方式。同时，争议金额也能反映卡特尔企业分割相关市场份额的共谋目的。事实上，卡特尔企业并不需要共谋或履行每一份供应合同，便可达到分割市场份额的目的。因此，初审法院的判决是正确的，涉案企业对一份供应合同是否参与共谋会考量以下因素：货物供应的分配、为维持某企业的市场份额所要采取哪些行动、每份独立合同能否发挥其作用，进而达到卡特尔企业分割维持市场份额的目的。

23 Contrary to the appellants' claims, those considerations are not irrelevant. The cartel's overall plan was to allocate supplies of automotive glass between the cartel participants, with respect to both existing supply contracts and new contracts. As is apparent from the finding of fact made by the General Court in paragraph 24 of the judgment under appeal, the allocation affected the whole activity of the cartel participants on the relevant market, which is confirmed, inter alia, by the mode of operation of the cartel, which included correcting measures which took existing supply contracts into account. It follows that the sales made pursuant to contracts predating the infringement period and not renegotiated during that period were to be regarded as falling within the scope of the cartel, for the purposes of the case-law cited in paragraph 19 above.

Consequently, it must be held that, if the Commission were not entitled to include those sales in the value of the sales calculated in accordance with point 13 of the 2006 Guidelines, the amount of the resulting fine would not reflect the economic significance of the infringement. The General Court therefore did not err in law in finding that the sales at issue were covered by that infringement.

24 The first ground of appeal must therefore be rejected as unfounded.

The second ground of appeal, alleging an error of law in the interpretation of the second subparagraph of Article 23(2) of Directive No 1/2003.

Arguments of the parties

25 By their second ground of appeal, directed against paragraphs 410 to 423 of the judgment under appeal, the appellants criticise the General Court for finding that the final amount of the fine imposed on them by the Commission did not exceed the ceiling of 10% of the total turnover in the business year preceding the adoption of the decision at issue, referred to in the second subparagraph of Article 23(2) of Regulation No 1/2003 ('the statutory ceiling of the fine').

26 According to the appellants, the General Court erred in law in finding that the Commission was justified, for the purpose of converting that total turnover—which, for the appellants, is denominated in pounds sterling—in using the average exchange rate of the European Central Bank (ECB) applicable in the period between 1 April 2007 and 31 March 2008, and not the exchange rate applicable at the date on which the decision at issue was adopted, namely on 12 November 2008. In the appellants' opinion, the maximum amount that the Commission was entitled to impose on them was capped at EUR 317 547 860, that is to say, EUR 39 452 140 less than the fine ultimately imposed on them.

23 因此，与上诉人的理由相反，上述因素对确定罚款基数至关重要。本案卡特尔的最终目的是通过已订立和尚未订立的合同，在卡特尔的企业间约定针对汽车玻璃行业的货物分配和供应。初审法院在其判决书第24段指出：影响卡特尔企业在相关市场活动的重要因素是货物供应和分配。卡特尔企业通过订立货物供应和分配合同来实现市场分割的目的，这一事实已被初审法院核实。同时，基于初审判决第19段援引的判例，依据侵权行为前订立的且在侵权行为发生过程中尚未重新修订的合同产生的销售额也属于卡特尔范畴。

因此，若欧盟委员会无权依据《2006年罚款指南》第13条，将争议营业额纳入罚款基数，那么本案的罚款金额就无法全面反映侵权行为的经济影响。所以，初审法院适用法律正确，欧盟委员会有权将争议营业额纳入罚款基数。

24 综上，上诉人第1项上诉理由不成立。

上诉人的第2项上诉理由是，初审法院对《第1/2003号条例》第23条第2款解释有误。

争议双方的观点

25 上诉人针对初审法院判决第410~423段指出，初审法院认定欧盟委员会对上诉人的罚款符合《第1/2003号条例》第23条第2款的规定，即欧盟委员会处罚的罚金未超出决定作出前上一营业年度总营业额的10%（“罚金法定上限”）。上诉人指出，初审法院支持欧盟委员会的判决有误。

26 上诉人总营业额的计价货币为英镑。计算罚金需要进行汇率换算，而欧盟委员会在汇率换算时使用了欧洲央行（ECB）在2007年4月1日到2008年3月31日期间的平均汇率，而非决定作出时（2008年11月12日）的即期汇率。据此，上诉人认为，欧盟委员会对其作出的罚款上限应为317 547 860欧元，应该比此前的最终决定减少39 452 140欧元。

27 First, the appellants submit that the General Court's interpretation is not consistent with the purpose of the statutory ceiling of the fine set out in Article 23(2) of Regulation No 1/2003, which is designed to offer protection against currency fluctuations preceding the adoption of the Commission decision, in other words, the date on which the fine becomes payable.

28 In that regard, the appellants claim that the General Court wrongly relied on the case-law relating to the applicable exchange rate for the calculation of the basic amount of the fine, which, they maintain, cannot be transposed to the context of determining the statutory ceiling of the fine because, by setting that ceiling, the EU legislature pursues an objective that is distinct and autonomous by comparison with the criteria of the gravity and duration of the infringement. According to the appellants, the purpose of that ceiling is precisely to offer absolute protection against the harmful consequences of the monetary fluctuations that may occur up to the date of adoption of the Commission decision, as they claim is apparent from the case-law of the Court and, in particular, from paragraph 59 of the judgment of 16 November 2000, Enso Española v. Commission (C-282/98 P, EU:C:2000:628), from paragraph 89 of the judgment of 16 November 2000, Sarrió v. Commission (C-291/98 P, EU:C:2000:631), from paragraph 606 of the judgment of 15 October 2002, Limburgse Vinyl Maatschappij and Others v. Commission (C-238/99 P, C-244/99 P, C-245/99 P, C-247/99 P, C-250/99 P to C-252/99 P and C-254/99 P, EU:C:2002:582), and from paragraph 63 of the judgment of 4 September 2014, YKK and Others v. Commission (C-408/12 P, EU:C:2014:2153).

29 Secondly, the appellants dispute the finding of the General Court in paragraph 418 of the judgment under appeal that undertakings have to bear the risk of currency fluctuations between the preceding business year and the date on which the Commission decision is adopted, which, they claim, entails significant costs for those undertakings. The appellants argue that that finding is not consistent with the objective of Article 23(2) of Regulation No 1/2003 and has no basis in the case-law of the Court.

30 Thirdly, according to the appellants, the approach of the General Court fails to ensure equal treatment between undertakings which keep their accounts in currencies other than the euro and those which keep their accounts in euros, since the former are exposed to the risk that the level of the statutory ceiling of the fine may vary substantially depending on currency fluctuations, while the latter are not exposed to that risk.

31 Fourthly, the appellants claim that the General Court's approach fails to ensure legal certainty, since it creates uncertainty with regard to the maximum financial risk borne by undertakings with an accounting currency other than the euro.

32 The Commission contends that this ground of appeal must be rejected as unfounded.

27 第一，上诉人认为，《第1/2003号条例》第23条的立法目的是规避可能面临的汇率波动风险。在本案中就涉及欧盟委员会决定作出前（应付罚款金额之日前）企业可能面临的汇率风险。而初审法院对该条的解释与立法目的不符。

28 上诉人指出，初审法院对有关汇率适用的判例解读有误，并且错误地适用平均汇率来计算罚金。上诉人称，欧洲立法者设定罚款上限的立法目的在于，确保罚金与卡特尔行为的时间周期和严重程度相匹配。同时，上诉人也指出，卡特尔企业在欧盟委员会决定作出前可能面临极大的货币、汇率风险及不利影响。因此，设定罚金上限的根本目的在于为涉案企业规避此类风险并提供法律上的保护。为支持其抗辩，上诉人援引了以下判例。[参见判例：Enso Española v Commission（C−282/98 P，EU：C：2000：628），第59段；Sarrió v Commission（C−291/98 P，EU：C：2000：631），第89段；Limburgse Vinyl Maatschappij and Others v Commission（C−238/99 P，C−244/99 P，C−245/99 P，C−247/99 P，C−250/99 P to C−252/99 P and C−254/99 P，EU：C：2002：582），第606段；YKK and Others v Commission（C−408/12 P，EU：C：2014：2153，第63段）]。

29 第二，上诉人针对初审法院判决第418段提出，初审法院认定欧盟委员会决定作出前的汇率风险应该由企业承担，该项认定不合理。因为这将过分加重了企业的成本负担。上诉人认为，初审法院这一判断与《第1/2003号条例》立法目的不符，且初审法院援引的判例无法支持其作出判决的理由。

30 第三，上诉人认为，相较于使用非欧元货币计价的企业，使用欧元计价的企业面临的汇率风险相对较低。因此，初审判决未能遵从平等待遇原则，即未能保证平等对待使用不同货币（欧元或其他货币）计价的企业。

31 第四，上诉人认为，初审判决未能遵从法律确定性原则，即使用非欧元货币计价的企业须承担巨大的汇率风险。

32 欧盟委员会对上述理由不予认可，并请求欧盟法院予以驳回。

Findings of the Court

33 By their second ground of appeal, the appellants essentially criticise the General Court for having found that the Commission was entitled to determine the statutory ceiling of the fine by reference to the average exchange rate applicable in the business year preceding the adoption of the decision at issue, rather than by reference to the exchange rate applicable at the time when the decision was adopted. The appellants submit that, in doing so, the General Court misinterpreted the purpose of the statutory ceiling and the case–law of the Court, and failed to have regard for the principles of equal treatment and legal certainty.

34 The second subparagraph of Article 23(2) of Regulation No 1/2003 provides that, for each undertaking and association of undertakings participating in the infringement, the fine may not exceed 10% of its total turnover in the preceding business year.

35 The appellants, the total turnover of which in the preceding business year is denominated in pounds sterling, do not dispute the Commission's right to set in euros the fines which it imposes under Article 23 of Regulation No 1/2003. That provision does not, however, contain any indication as to the exchange rate to be used when determining the statutory ceiling of the fine, in the case where the total turnover referred to in the second subparagraph of Article 23(2) of Regulation No 1/2003 is denominated in a currency other than the euro.

36 In that regard, for the purpose of assessing the merits of the method of conversion used by the Commission, it must be noted that the General Court, without being challenged by the appellants on that point, referred to the objective pursued by the statutory ceiling of the fine, as the Court specified in paragraphs 281 and 282 of the judgment of 28 June 2005, *Dansk Rørindustri and Others* v. *Commission* (C–189/02 P, C–202/02 P, C–205/02 P to C–208/02 P and C–213/02 P, EU: C: 2005: 408) and as the General Court recalled in paragraph 414 of the judgment under appeal. That objective is to avoid the imposition of fines in respect of which it is foreseeable that the undertakings, owing to their size, as determined—albeit approximately and imperfectly—by their total turnover, will be unable to pay them.

37 As is apparent from the case–law of the Court, the amount of the fine that may be imposed on an undertaking is subject to a quantifiable and absolute ceiling, with the result that the maximum amount of the fine that can be imposed on a given undertaking can be determined in advance (see, to that effect, judgment of 9 July 2015, *InnoLux* v. *Commission*, C–231/14 P, EU: C: 2015: 451, paragraph 48 and the case–law cited).

本院查明的事实及观点

33 上诉人的第二项理由实际上是批评初审法院错误地认为欧盟委员会采用决定作出前上一营业年度的平均汇率来计算罚款（而非决定作出时的即期汇率）这一做法是对的。上诉人认为初审法院的认定违反了法定上限的立法目的、平等待遇原则和法律确定性原则。

34 《第1/2003条例》第23条第2款第2段规定：对于每一个参与违法的企业或企业协会，对其处以的罚款额不应超过其前一营业年度总营业额的10%。

35 本院认为，欧盟委员会有权依据《第1/2003号条例》第23条的规定，以欧元作为罚款计价货币，上诉人对此并无异议。第23条第2款规定了罚款计算方法，但没有规定采用哪一个时间段的欧元汇率。

36 因此，为阐明欧盟委员会使用的汇率换算方法的合理性，本院认为，要特别注意的是，在上诉人对初审法院换算方法无异议的前提下，初审法院的做法与《第1/2003号条例》第23条第2款的立法目的是一致的。该条立法目的在于保证基于企业规模和营业总额作出的罚款金额具有可预见性，且可以为企业所负担。对此，初审法院援引了2005年6月28日作出的“Dansk Rørindustri and Others v Commission”判决书中的第281段和第282段（参见判例：C 189/02 P, C 202/02 P, C 205/02 P to C 208/02 P and C 213/02 P, EU: C: 2005: 408），并在其初审判决第414段中有所论证。

37 显然，依据初审法院援引的判例，针对企业的罚款金额上限应当是某一精确的可量化的数额，并且在决定作出前可以预见罚款的具体最高金额。（参见判例：InnoLux v Commission, C-231/14 P, EU: C: 2015: 451，第48段及该段引用的判例）

38 Therefore, in the light of that objective, the General Court cannot be criticised for finding, in paragraph 415 of the judgment under appeal, that the upper limit derived from the second subparagraph of Article 23 (2) of Regulation No 1/2003 must be determined, as a rule, by reference to the economic reality as it appeared in the business year preceding the adoption of the decision penalising an infringement of Article 81 EC.

39 As the Advocate General emphasised in point 51 of her Opinion, that finding is consistent with the choice made by the EU legislature to take, as a rule, the turnover figures for the last full business year preceding the adoption of the decision setting the amount of the fine as the reference value, ascertainable in advance, that is most likely to reflect the financial capacity of an undertaking at the time when the undertaking is identified as responsible for the infringement and a financial penalty is imposed on it by the Commission.

40 However, contrary to the appellants' assertions, the choice made by the EU legislature also justifies the use of the exchange rate applicable during that period to convert the reference value in the case where that value is expressed in a currency other than the euro.

41 The Court notes, first, that, with regard to the assessment of an undertaking's financial capacity, it is consistent with the choice of the EU legislature to refer, for that purpose, not to the exchange rate applicable at the time of the decision imposing the fine but to the average exchange rate in the business year preceding the adoption of that decision, since the latter is more likely to reflect the economic reality as it appeared in the course of that business year.

42 In that regard, contrary to the assertions of the appellants, it cannot be inferred from the case-law of the Court that, with regard to the conversion of the maximum amount of the fine, it has held it necessary to refer to the exchange rate applicable at the time when the decision imposing the fine was adopted. On the contrary, the Court notes that that line of case-law confirms the finding of the General Court, in paragraph 415 of the judgment under appeal, that, in essence, where the economic reality is to be assessed as it appeared at a given time, it is reasonable to refer to the exchange rates applicable during that period. Otherwise, the assessment of the economic reality would necessarily be distorted by extrinsic and uncertain factors, such as the changes in exchange rates over a period subsequent to that business year (see, by analogy, judgement of 16 November 2000, *Sarrió* v *Commission*, C-291/98 P, EU: C: 2000: 631, paragraphs 86 and 88).

38 因此，从立法目的来看，初审法院在判决书第415段的表述是对的，即根据第23条第2款第2项罚款上限的规定。按一般规则，法庭是参考《欧共体条约》第81条对违法行为的罚款依据，即企业上一营业年度的经济状况来确定（罚款金额）。

39 如佐审官在其意见书中第51段指出，初审法院的做法与设定罚款金额的立法目的一致，且由此计算出的罚款金额可以更为准确地反映企业在侵权行为发生时的经济状况。

40 此外，与上诉人的上诉理由相反，欧盟立法者允许使用侵权行为期间内欧元平均汇率（即使企业的计价货币为非欧元）来计算罚款金额。

41 本院认为，首先，基于《第1/2003号条例》第23条第2款立法目的和对企业实际营业额的考量，适用平均汇率能更准确地反映企业在侵权行为发生过程中的经济状况。其次，依据上诉人援引的欧盟法院判例，也无法得出适用决定作出时的即期汇率计算罚金更合理的结论。

42 相反，本院认为，上述判例确定的审判尺度与初审法院的做法一致。初审判决书第415段提到，适用的汇率应当准确反映企业在卡特尔行为期间的经济状况（参见判例：Sarrió v Commission，C-291/98 P，EU：C：2000：631，第86段、第88段）。

43 Secondly, the method of conversion endorsed by the General Court in paragraph 416 of the judgment under appeal meets the requirement of predictability for the statutory ceiling of the fine, referred to in paragraph 37 above, in so far as that method is based on an exchange rate ascertainable prior to the adoption of the decision of the Commission imposing the fine, and according to which the upper limit of the fine can be determined in advance.

44 Thirdly, the Court must reject the appellants' argument that the General Court misinterpreted the purpose of the statutory ceiling in that, they claim, it is designed to ensure absolute protection against monetary fluctuations up to the date on which the decision imposing the fine is adopted.

45 As the Advocate General observed in point 55 of her Opinion, such protection is not an independent purpose of the statutory ceiling of the fine, but rather a feature of the protection offered by that ceiling against excessive and disproportionate fines (see, by analogy, judgment of 28 June 2005, *Dansk Rørindustri and Others* v *Commission*, C-189/02 P, C-202/02 P, C-205/02 P to C-208/02 P and C-213/02 P, EU:C:2005:408, paragraph 281). Thus, as regards the purpose of the statutory ceiling of the fine, the appellants cannot rely on the case-law cited in paragraph 28 above to support their claim. While that case-law relating to the conversion of the value of sales in the context of determining the basic amount of the fine acknowledges that the statutory ceiling limits the possible harmful consequences of monetary fluctuations, it does not follow from that line of authority that that ceiling constitutes an absolute protection against such fluctuations, nor that the relevant exchange rate for determining that ceiling is that applicable at the time when the decision imposing the fine is adopted.

46 As regards the alleged impact of monetary fluctuations on the level of the statutory ceiling of the fine, converted into euros, the Court notes that the appellants have failed to provide any particulars capable of demonstrating that the General Court erred in finding, in paragraph 415 of the judgment under appeal, that the method for calculating the statutory ceiling of the fine chosen by the Commission limits the possible harmful consequences of those monetary fluctuations. As is apparent from paragraph 42 of the present judgment, that method, which is based on the average historical rates applicable over the course of the business year preceding the adoption of the decision imposing the fine, rather than on the exchange rate applicable at the time of the decision, tends, by its very nature, to neutralise the effect which those fluctuations have on the level of the statutory ceiling of the fine up to the date on which that decision is adopted. The Court cannot accept the appellants' arguments in that respect, since a method of conversion based on a daily exchange rate is bound to be uncertain and unpredictable, unlike the method chosen by the General Court.

43 第二，初审法院在其判决书第416段适用的换算方法符合法定上限可预期的要求（见本判决第37段）。该方法所确定的平均汇率在决定作出前已经确定且依据该汇率可以确定罚款金额的上限。

44 第三，上诉人认为初审法院错误地解释罚款上限的立法目的，并且认为其立法目的是为确保企业规避决定作出前可能面临的一切汇率波动风险。对此，本院不予支持。

45 正如佐审官在其意见书第55段提出，所谓的风险规避并非设定罚款上限的立法目的，设定罚款上限是用来规避过分或不合理罚款的一种表现形式（参见判例：Dansk Rørindustri and Others v Commission，C–189/02 P，C–202/02 P，C–205/02 P to C–208/02 P and C–213/02 P，EU：C：2005：408，第281段）。因此，上诉人无法依据本判决第28段所援引的判例来证明其上诉理由成立。上述关于汇率换算的判例说明设定罚款上限可以限制汇率波动导致的不利后果，但并不能得出罚款上限可以规避一切汇率风险，更不能证明应适用即期汇率换算罚金。

46 对于上诉人有关汇率波动导致不利后果的上诉理由，本院认为，上诉人未能向法院提供任何细节或证据以证明初审法院在其判决第415段使用的换算方法于法无据，或该方法未能达到规避决定作出前汇率波动的风险。初审判决第42段指出，平均汇率最基本的属性是可以降低或规避决定作出前汇率波动的风险。反之，使用即期汇率的方法则缺乏确定性和可预期性。

47 The Court consequently finds that the General Court did not err in law in holding, in paragraph 416 of the judgment under appeal, that the method of conversion used by the Commission to determine the statutory ceiling of the fine was consistent with the purpose of that ceiling.

48 Furthermore, the appellants cannot argue that undertakings which keep their accounts in a currency other than the euro face unequal treatment as against undertakings which keep their accounts in euros, as a result of the former being exposed to currency risk. Since the appellants do not dispute that the fine imposed on them may be set in euros, they are inevitably exposed to currency fluctuations. In that context, the General Court was fully entitled to find, in paragraph 418 of the judgment under appeal, that currency fluctuations are an element of chance which may produce advantages and disadvantages which undertakings realising part of their sales on export markets have to deal with regularly in the course of their business activities and the very existence of which is not such as to render inappropriate the amount of a fine lawfully fixed on the basis of the gravity and the duration of the infringement.

49 Moreover, the appellants' contention alleging infringement by the General Court of the principle of legal certainty is based, as established in paragraph 46 above, on the false premise that the method of calculation approved by the General Court exposed them to the risk of changes in the level of the statutory ceiling of the fine depending on currency fluctuations between the end of the previous business year and the date of the decision at issue.

50 Those arguments must therefore be rejected as unfounded.

51 In the light of all of the foregoing, the General Court did not err in law in finding, in paragraph 421 of the judgment under appeal, that the Commission was entitled to calculate the statutory ceiling of the fine by reference to the appellants' total turnover in the preceding business year, which was converted into euros by application of the average exchange rate applicable in that business year.

52 The appellants' second ground of appeal must therefore be rejected as unfounded.

The third ground of appeal, alleging infringement of the principles of equal treatment and proportionality and also failure by the General Court to exercise its unlimited jurisdiction.

Arguments of the parties

53 The appellants' third ground of appeal, directed against paragraphs 396 to 402, 434, 438 and 440 to 444 of the judgment under appeal, is divided into two parts.

47 因此，本院认为，初审法院在其判决第416段适用的换算方法于法有据且符合设定罚款上限的初衷。

48 此外，上诉人认为，使用非欧元货币计价的企业将面临更大的汇率风险，因此初审法院的做法违反了平等待遇原则。但上诉人此前并未对以欧元计算罚款的可能性提出异议，因此上诉人应该承担汇率波动的风险。所以，初审法院完全有权在其判决书第418段认定，参与出口贸易的企业面临汇率风险已是常态，且汇率波动可能带来利好或不利的后果。存在汇率风险并不能说明使用平均汇率换算的罚金与卡特尔行为的严重性和期限不符的结论。

49 此外，上诉人认为，初审法院适用上一营业年度末至决定作出前这一时间段的平均汇率的做法使其面临更大的汇率波动风险，因此违反了法律确定性原则（见本判决第46段）。本院认为，这一理由也不成立（理由同上）。

50 本院对上述理由予以驳回。

51 综上，本院认为，初审法院在其判决书第421段适用法律正确，即认定欧盟委员会有权将上诉人上一年度的营业总额作为罚款基数，并适用侵权行为期间的平均汇率计算应缴罚款的法定上限。

52 本院对上诉人第二项理由予以驳回。

第三项上诉理由是初审法院判决违反了平等待遇和比例原则，及初审法院未依法行使罚款数额决定权。

争议双方的观点

53 上诉人第3项理由针对初审判决第396~402段、第434段、第438段，及第440~444段，其包括两部分内容。

54 By the first part of this ground of appeal, the appellants claim that the General Court erred in law by misapplying the principles of equal treatment and proportionality when it rejected their plea in law alleging that the fine imposed on them by the Commission was proportionally higher than that imposed on other cartel participants by reason of the less diversified nature of the appellants' activity.

55 According to the appellants, the General Court thus ignored their argument that, when the harmful consequences of a fine on an undertaking are disproportionate in comparison with the fine imposed on the other addressees of the decision, as illustrated by the proportion of the amount of the fine in relation to the total annual turnover of those undertakings, the Commission must ensure that there is compliance with the principles of proportionality and equal treatment. In the present case, the appellants submit, that state of affairs was predictable at the time when the decision at issue was adopted, as is indicated in the report of the consulting firm submitted to the General Court. In that regard, the appellants claim that the General Court misinterpreted the purpose of that report, which was submitted not as evidence of facts that occurred after the decision at issue had been adopted but as evidence of the fact that the imposition of a large fine on the appellants would have a disproportionate impact and would lead to a serious deterioration of their financial situation in comparison with the other participants in the infringement.

56 The appellants also maintain that the General Court misinterpreted their argument alleging that the Commission should have taken into account not the possible financial losses of undertakings that are less well adapted to market conditions but the impact that a large fine might have on the financial situation of the undertakings and, in particular, of those with the least diversified activity.

57 Lastly, in the appellants' opinion, the General Court overlooked the fact that arguments similar to those which they raised have been taken into account by the Commission in previous decisions, and by the General Court, inter alia, in the judgment of 12 December 2012, *Nováke chemické závody* v *Commission* (T-352/09, EU:T:2012:673).

58 By the second part of their third ground of appeal, the appellants allege that the General Court erred in law in failing to exercise its unlimited jurisdiction with the intensity required in order to remedy the unequal treatment to which they were subject as against the other participants in the infringement that resulted in the decision at issue. The appellants submit that the General Court, when exercising its unlimited jurisdiction, should have taken into account the financial difficulties which the payment of that fine might entail for them, without those difficulties having necessarily to amount to exceptional circumstances, as the General Court held in paragraph 443 of the judgment under appeal. According to the appellants, in order for the amount of the fine to be rectified, it suffices that those difficulties might have a significant impact on the appellants, resulting in unequal treatment in comparison with the other cartel participants.

54 第一部分，上诉人认为，初审法院未能正确适用平等待遇原则和比例原则。欧盟委员会错误认定上诉人的卡特尔行为相对集中，其罚款金额远高于其他卡特尔成员企业，而初审法院驳回了上诉人要求认定欧盟委员会对其罚款金额不合理的诉讼请求。

55 上诉人认为，初审法院无视他们的主张，即卡特尔企业依照其营业总额的一定比例缴纳的罚金应当与其因此承担的不利后果相适应。相比本案中其他卡特尔企业，上诉人认为，其承担的不利后果更为严重。因此，欧盟委员会在作出罚款决定时必须遵守比例原则和平等对待原则。上诉人认为，本案中，其已经向欧盟委员会提交了一份由咨询公司出具的关于罚款将对其导致不利后果的报告（“咨询报告”）。上诉人认为，罚款和不利后果在欧盟委员会决定作出前是可预见的。该报告本意是用于证明，罚款将使其财务情况（相比其他接受处罚的企业）严重恶化。而欧盟委员会却错误地认定该报告是对决定作出后的各项事实的陈述。

56 上诉人认为，欧盟委员会作出罚款时应考量巨额罚款可能对不同企业（特别是业务集中程度较高的企业）造成的财务状况恶化及不利后果。

57 最后，上诉人提出，初审法院忽视了其提出的部分事实和抗辩理由。而此类事实和理由在此前的欧盟委员会决定中，特别是初审法院的一份判决中有所体现［参见判例：Novácke chemické závody v Commission（T−352/09，EU：T：2012：673）］。但是，初审法院在本案中并未参照此前的判例。

58 在第二部分，上诉人认为，初审法院未能依法行使其罚款数额决定权，进而对上诉人相对于其他卡特尔行为参与企业面临的不平等待遇作出救济裁决。上诉人认为，初审法院应该行使罚款数额决定权，综合考虑高额罚款可能对上诉人造成的财务困难（而该等困难并非一定要达到例外情形）。因此，上诉人认为初审法院判决第443段的说理过于牵强，于法无据。上诉人认为，相比其他卡特尔参与企业，当上述财务困难的影响对上诉人可能造成显著的不利后果时，初审法院应该对罚款金额作出调整。

59 The Commission contends that this ground of appeal must be rejected as unfounded.

Findings of the Court

60 By the first part of this ground of appeal, the appellants essentially claim that, in the context of reviewing the legality of the decision at issue under Article 263 TFEU, the General Court misapplied the principles of equal treatment and proportionality. The appellants are of the opinion that those principles required the General Court to hold that, when determining the amount of the fines, the Commission ought to have taken into consideration that the impact of the fine imposed on the appellants would evidently be more detrimental than the impact on the other cartel participants because their activity was less diversified, as reflected by the difference in the proportion represented by the fine in relation to the total turnover of the undertakings concerned.

61 With regard to the information contained in the consulting firm' s report referred to in paragraph 400 of the judgment under appeal, it is apparent from paragraph 401 of that judgement that it was, in essence, for the reasons set out in paragraphs 274 and 275 of the judgment under appeal, namely that the report concerned the development of the appellants' financial situation after the decision at issue had been adopted and that it could therefore not have had any effect on the legality of that decision in the context of the review carried out under Article 263 TFEU, that the General Court held that there was no need to take this information into account when assessing the legality of the fine.

62 While it is indeed true that the appellants implicitly invoked a distortion of that evidence, in particular by claiming that the General Court misinterpreted the purpose of that report, a mere allusion to such a distortion does not satisfy the requirements laid down by the case-law of the Court under which an appellant must indicate precisely the evidence alleged to have been distorted and must show the errors of appraisal which, in that appellant' s view, led the General Court to make that distortion (see, to that effect, judgment of 7 January 2004, *Aalborg Portland and Others* v *Commission*, C-204/00 P, C-205/00 P, C-211/00 P, C-213/00 P, C-217/00 P and C-219/00 P, EU: C: 2004: 6, paragraph 50).

63 Next, with regard to the argument concerning the failure to take account of the proportion represented by the amount of the fine imposed on the appellants in relation to their overall turnover in comparison with the other addressees of the decision at issue, and the alleged resulting unequal treatment, the Court finds that, contrary to the appellants' assertions, the General Court did address that issue, in paragraphs 397 to 399 of the judgment under appeal.

59 欧盟委员会对上述理由不予认可并请求欧盟法院依法驳回。

本院查明的事实及观点

60 上诉人在其第3项理由的第一部分特别提出，依据《欧盟运行条约》第263条对初审判决的合法性审查的规定，初审法院未能遵照平等对待原则和比例原则。上诉人认为，依据上述原则，初审法院在审理中应考虑到欧盟委员会对上诉人卡特尔行为相对集中而作出的罚款，其罚金多少对不同的卡特尔企业会造成不同的财务影响，还应该考虑到这些罚金会对卡特尔企业造成极为不利的后果；但是初审法院根本没有考虑这些因素。

61 关于初审判决中第400段出现的咨询公司报告，初审法院在其判决第401段已经表明，正如初审判决书第274~275段阐明的理由，咨询报告的内容仅对决定作出后上诉人财务发展状况的说明，而这并非是初审法院依据《欧盟运行条约》第263条对欧盟委员会罚款决定的合法性作出审查时应考虑的。

62 上诉人的第3项理由中的确暗指初审法院误解了咨询报告的意图。但根据欧盟法院的判例，若上诉人仅辩称初审法院对其提交的报告解读有误，但未能承担举证责任，提供证据证明初审法院误解的具体事实是什么，那么欧盟法院可以对其辩称不予采纳。（参见判例：Aalborg Portland and Others v Commission，C–204/00 P，C–205/00 P，C–211/00 P，C–213/00 P，C–217/00 P and C–219/00 P，EU：C：2004：6，第50段）。

63 此外，上诉人辩称，初审法院在认定罚款时对上诉人和其他卡特尔企业适用了不同比例的罚款可能造成的不同影响，因此违反了平等待遇原则。对此抗辩，本院认为，初审法院在审理中已经考虑了这一问题，并在初审判决第397~399段对此作出了说明。

64 In particular, the General Court was fully entitled to hold, in paragraph 398 of the judgment under appeal, that it is not contrary to the principles of proportionality and equal treatment that, through the application of the method of calculation of the basic amount of fines set out in point 13 of the 2006 Guidelines, an undertaking, the activities of which are more focused than others on the sale of goods or services connected directly or indirectly to the infringement, may receive a fine which represents a proportion of its overall turnover that is greater than that represented by the fines imposed respectively on each of the other undertakings. The General Court found that it is inherent in that method of calculation, which is not based on the overall turnover of the undertakings concerned, that disparities may appear between those undertakings as to the relationship between their overall turnover and the amount of the fines imposed on them.

65 As the General Court found in paragraph 397 of the judgment under appeal, it is apparent from the case–law of the Court that the Commission is not required, when determining the amount of fines, to ensure, where such fines are imposed on a number of undertakings involved in the same infringement, that the final amounts of the fines reflect any distinction between the undertakings concerned in terms of their overall turnover (judgment of 28 June 2005, *Dansk Rørindustri and Others* v *Commission*, C–189/02 P, C–202/02 P, C–205/02 P to C–208/02 P and C–213/02 P, EU: C: 2005: 408, paragraph 312).

66 With regard to the alleged infringement of the principle of equal treatment invoked by the appellants, on the assumption that this ground of appeal seeks to demonstrate that the Commission ought to have departed from that method by deciding, as regards the appellants, to reduce the amount of the fine because of the less diversified nature of their activity, the Court notes, as did the Advocate General in point 100 of her Opinion, that the difference in the proportion represented by the fine in relation to the total turnover of the undertakings concerned does not, as such, constitute a sufficient justification for departing from the method of calculation that the Commission imposed on itself. That would be tantamount to conferring an advantage on the least diversified undertakings on the basis of criteria that are irrelevant in the light of the gravity and the duration of the infringement. When the amount of the fine is determined, there cannot, by the application of different methods of calculation, be any discrimination between the undertakings which have participated in an agreement or a concerted practice contrary to Article 101 (1) TFEU (see, to that effect, judgment of 19 July 2012, *Alliance One International and Standard Commercial Tobacco* v *Commission and Commission* v *Alliance One International and Others*, C–628/10 P and C–14/11 P, EU: C: 2012: 479, paragraph 58 and the case–law cited).

64 本院认为，初审法院有权认定（初审判决第398段），依据《2006年罚款指南》第13条的规定，若某一卡特尔企业的侵权行为，直接或间接的经营行为相比其他企业更加集中，那么该企业面临的罚款数占总营业额的比例可能会高于其他企业所占的比例。初审法院的这一认定与《2006年罚款指南》第13条的规定一致。即罚款的计算方法并不一定以某一企业的总营业额为基准。针对不同企业的罚款金额与其总营业额之比可能有所不同。

65 如初审法院在其判决第397段指出，依据欧盟法院判例，欧盟委员会在确定罚款金额时有权作出相关决定，即不需要确保针对卡特尔企业的罚款金额必须反映各企业之间在罚金占总营业额之比例上有所区别。

66 上诉人所援引的违反平等待遇原则，是为了证明其上诉理由的依据。即证明欧盟委员会不应该采用其罚款方法，应减少上诉人因为其集中行为而承担的过多的罚款数额。本院观点与佐审官的意见一致（见意见书第100段）。罚款金额的不同与有关企业总营业额的比例差异，这本身并不能说明欧盟委员会错误地采用了其计算罚款的方法。如果上诉人的观点可以成立，这无疑会偏袒集中企业的行为，导致处罚与侵权行为的严重程度和持续时间没有关联性。当罚款数额已经确定时，即不得通过采用不同的计算方法，对参与违反《欧盟运行条约》第101条的某一协议或某一协同集中行为的企业进行区别对待。

67 With regard to the appellants' argument based on the alleged impact that a large fine would have on their financial situation, it must be noted that the Court has repeatedly held that the Commission is not required, when determining the amount of the fine, to take account of the economic situation of the undertaking concerned, and, in particular, of its financial capacity, since recognition of such an obligation would be tantamount to conferring unfair competitive advantages on the undertakings least well adapted to market conditions (judgment of 10 May 2007, *SGL Carbon* v *Commission*, C-328/05 P, EU: C: 2007: 277, paragraph 100 and the case-law cited).

68 Lastly, the appellants cannot reasonably argue that account was taken of such considerations in other decisions of the Commission, given that, according to the Court's settled case-law, the Commission's practice in previous decisions does not serve as a legal framework for the fines imposed in competition matters (judgement of 23 April 2015, *LG Display and LG Display Taiwan* v *Commission*, C-227/14 P, EU: C: 2015: 258, paragraph 67 and the case-law cited).

69 In those circumstances, the first part of the third ground of appeal cannot be accepted.

70 By the second part of the third ground of appeal, the appellants claim that the General Court failed adequately to exercise its unlimited jurisdiction under Article 261 TFEU, read in combination with Article 31 of Regulation No 1/2003, by not reducing the amount of the fine in order to ensure equal treatment between the cartel participants.

71 It must be borne in mind that, in accordance with the provisions referred to in the previous paragraph, the General Court is empowered, in addition to the mere review of the legality of the fines imposed by the Commission, to substitute its own assessment for that of the Commission, and, consequently, to cancel, reduce or increase the fine or penalty payment imposed (see, to that effect, judgment of 21 January 2016, *Galp Energía España and Others* v *Commission*, C-603/13 P, EU: C: 2016: 38, paragraph 75 and the case-law cited).

72 By contrast, it is not for the Court of Justice, when ruling on questions of law in the context of an appeal, to substitute, on grounds of fairness, its own assessment for that of the General Court exercising its unlimited jurisdiction to rule on the amount of fines imposed on undertakings for infringements of EU law (judgment of 18 July 2013, *Schindler Holding and Others* v *Commission*, C-501/11 P, EU: C: 2013: 522, paragraph 164 and the case-law cited).

73 It is only in so far as the Court of Justice considers that the level of the penalty is not merely inappropriate, but also excessive to the point of being disproportionate, that it would have to find that the General Court erred in law, due to the inappropriateness of the amount of a fine (judgment of 18 July 2013, *Schindler Holding and Others* v *Commission*, C-501/11 P, EU: C: 2013: 522, paragraph 165 and the case-law cited).

67 此外，对于上诉人提出的缴纳高额罚金将使其财务状况恶化的理由，本院一再强调，欧盟委员会在确定罚款金额时无须考虑涉案企业的经济情况，尤其无须考虑其财务能力和经营情况。若欧盟委员会有考虑上述因素的义务，即相当于使市场适应能力较差（与市场匹配度低）的企业享受不正当的竞争优势（参见判例：2015年4月23日判决书，LG Display and LG Display Taiwan v Commission，C-227/14 P，EU：C：2015：258，paragraph 67 and the case-law cited）。

68 最后，上诉人未能合理论证欧盟委员会在确定罚金时应考虑其提出的其他若干因素。因为依据本院援引的判例，欧盟委员会在以往决定中使用的罚金计算方法并不构成在其他有关竞争法案例中确定罚金的先例。

69 综上，本院驳回上诉人第3项第一部分的上诉理由。

70 上诉人在其第3项上诉理由的第二部分提出，初审法院未能行使其在《欧盟运行条约》第261条项下的罚款数额决定权；未能依据《欧盟第1/2003号条例》第31条减免罚金。因而，初审法院判决不符合平等待遇原则。

71 本院强调，针对欧盟委员会的罚款决定，初审法院不仅有权对其进行合法性审查，也有权自行决定罚金的计算方法，从而撤销、增减罚金或损害赔偿金（参见判例：Galp Energía España and Others v Commission，C-603/13 P，EU：C：2016：38，第 75段及该段引用的判例）。

72 相反，欧盟法院在针对上诉案件的争议问题上无权适用相关法律，即无权依据公平原则自行决定本应由初审法院的权限作出的罚金计算方法，进而对参与卡特尔企业作出罚款（参见判例：Schindler Holding and Others v Commission，C-501/11 P，EU：C：2013：522，第164段及该段引用的判例）。

73 只有当欧盟法院认为罚款数额非常不合理且不符合比例原则时，才会认定初审法院适用法律错误，从而作出合理的罚款决定。

74 In that respect, as is apparent from paragraphs 433, 438 and 441 of the judgment under appeal, with regard to the allegedly disproportionate nature of the fine imposed on the appellants, the General Court, under its unlimited jurisdiction, examined the appellants' arguments alleging, in the first place, that, due to the less diversified nature of their activity, the amount of the fine would have a greater impact on their financial situation in comparison with the fine imposed on the other undertakings concerned, and, in the second place, that the fine would lead to a deterioration of their financial situation. In that context, the General Court took into account the information contained in the consulting firm's report referred to in paragraph 55 above.

75 With regard to the first argument, as is apparent from paragraph 64 above, the General Court was fully entitled to find, in paragraph 438 of the judgment under appeal, that the circumstances invoked by the appellants, were they established, would not have been relevant for the purpose of assessing whether the fine was proportionate.

76 As for the second argument, it is apparent from paragraphs 441 and 442 of the judgment under appeal that the General Court acted correctly in taking the view that the existence of possible financial difficulties is capable of justifying, as such, a reduction of the fine only in exceptional circumstances, where justified by an overriding interest. As the General Court observed, in essence, in paragraph 441 of the judgment under appeal, the fines imposed on undertakings by the Commission pursuant to Article 23(2) of Regulation No 1/2003 would be deprived of their deterrent effect if such difficulties were automatically to be taken into account.

77 Thus, contrary to what the appellants contend, the finding of the General Court was not that its unlimited jurisdiction may be exercised only in exceptional circumstances but that the reduction of a fine based on the existence of alleged financial difficulties may be carried out only if those difficulties are exceptional in nature. In paragraphs 434 and 443 of the judgment under appeal, the General Court found that, on the basis of the available information, that was not the position in the case before it.

78 Therefore, the second part of the third ground of appeal must be rejected to the extent to which, on the one hand, it is based on a misinterpretation of the judgment under appeal and, on the other hand, its objective is to secure a re-examination of the appraisal of the facts by the General Court, something which the Court of Justice cannot do in the context of an appeal.

79 In the light of all of the foregoing, the third ground of appeal must be rejected as being in part inadmissible and in part unfounded.

80 Since none of the three grounds of appeal raised by the appellants in support of their appeal can be upheld, the appeal must be dismissed in its entirety.

74 在这一点上，从初审法院判决第433段、第438段、第441段可以看出，关于上诉人声称对其罚款本质上违反了比例原则。初审法院应该根据其罚款数额决定权，认真审查上诉人的理由：其一，由于上诉人的卡特尔行为比其他企业更为集中，因此罚金对其财务状况的影响会比其他企业更为显著；其二，这种不利影响可能会导致其财务状况恶化。此外，初审法院应该重视其提交的咨询报告（本判决书第55段及以上段落）。

75 本院认为，关于上诉人第一点提出的比例原则的抗辩（见本判决书第63段、第64段），初审法院有权审查上诉人针对比例原则提出的罚金将导致其财务状况恶化的事实，也有权认定即使该事实查证属实，也并不违反对卡特尔企业适用平等待遇的原则（在初审法院判决第438段）。

76 关于上诉人提出的第二点罚款导致财务状况恶化的理由（见本判决第67段），本院认为，初审法院说理正确。即若罚款对企业造成财务影响，只有在特殊情况下，为保护更高的利益，初审法院才可以减少罚金（在原审判决第441~442段说明）。

77 因此，初审法院判决第434段、第443段的观点正确。根据已查明的事实，上诉人的上诉理由于法无据。

78 本院判决驳回上诉人第3项上诉理由第二部分。 方面，上诉人对初审法院判决的对应部分解读有误；另一方面，上诉人的请求目的是要求本院再次审查初审法院已经认定的事实，该请求超出了本院针对上诉案件可以行使的职权范围。

79 综上，基于上诉人提交的证据、事实不可采信以及有关说理依据不足，本院判决驳回上诉人第3项上诉理由。

80 因上诉人提出的3项理由均不成立，本院全部予以驳回。

Costs

81 Under Article 184(2) of the Rules of Procedure of the Court of Justice, where the appeal is unfounded, the Court is to make a decision as to the costs. Under Article 138(1) of those rules, which applies to the procedure on appeal by virtue of Article 184(1) thereof, the unsuccessful party must be ordered to pay the costs if they have been applied for in the successful party's pleadings. Since the appellants have been unsuccessful and the Commission has applied for costs to be awarded against them, the appellants must be ordered to pay the costs relating to the present appeal proceedings.

On those grounds, the Court (Fourth Chamber) hereby:

1.Dismisses the appeal;

2.Orders Pilkington Group Ltd, Pilkington Automotive Ltd, Pilkington Automotive Deutschland GmbH, Pilkington Holding GmbH and Pilkington Italia SpA to pay the costs.

诉讼费用

81 依据《欧盟法院程序规则》第184条第2款的规定，上诉人诉讼请求不成立，本院应对本案诉讼费用作出判决。依据《欧盟法院程序规则》第138条第1款有关上诉案件诉讼程序的规定，同时适用该规则第184条第1款，若上诉案件中，胜诉方提出由败诉方承担上诉费用的请求，那么败诉方则应当承担全部诉讼费用。本案中，欧盟委员会已提出诉讼费由败诉方负担费用的请求。因此，本案诉讼费用应由上诉人承担。

根据上述法律规定，本院（第五法庭）判决如下：

1.驳回全部上诉请求；

2.由上诉人承担本案全部诉讼费用。

4

Colruyt公司
诉
欧盟委员会

(Etablissements Fr. Colruyt NV v
European Commission)

(*Case C-221/15*)

案例导读*

一、案例基本信息

法　院	欧盟法院		
提请法院	比利时布鲁塞尔上诉法院	判决时间	2016年9月21日
案　号	Case C–221/15		
关键词	烟草制品；定价；印花税		
当事人	上 诉 人：Colruyt公司（Etablissements Fr. Colruyt NV） 被上诉人：欧盟委员会（European Commission）		

二、案例涉及的欧盟法规

（一）《欧盟运行条约》第101条①规定：

"1.下列行为因与内部市场相冲突而应予以禁止：一切可能影响成员国间的贸易且其目标或结果会阻碍、限制或扭曲内部市场竞争的企业之间的协定、企业联合组织的决定和协同行为，特别是：

（1）以直接或间接方式规定收购或销售价格或其他交易条件；

（2）限制或控制生产、市场、技术发展或投资；

（3）分配市场或供货渠道；

（4）对与其他商业伙伴的同等交易适用不同的条件，从而使之在竞争中处于不利地位；

（5）以其他缔约方接受附加义务为条件缔结合同，这些条件从其本

* 作者：朱玥。

① 程卫东、李靖堃：《欧洲联盟基础条约》，社会科学文献出版社2010年版，第86页。

质上说或者根据商业惯例与此等合同的主题无关。

2.本条所禁止的任何协议或决定应自动无效。

3.但在下列情形下可宣告本条第1款不适用：

——企业之间的任何协议或任何类型的协议；

——企业联合组织的任何决定或任何类型的决定；

——任何协同行为或任何类型的协同行为。

上述措施应有助于改善商品的生产或销售，或有助于推动技术或经济进步，同时保证消费者公平分享由此带来的收益，并且做到：

（1）不对有关企业施加并非为达到这些目标所必不可少的限制；

（2）不为有关企业提供在相关产品的实质部分消除竞争的可能性。”

（二）《关于食品和其他商品的消费者健康保护法》第7条第1款规定：

“禁止为烟草、以烟草为主的产品和类似产品（以下简称烟草制品）做广告或拉赞助。任何直接或间接旨在促进销售的通信或行为，不论地点，通信方式和所采用的技术，均被视为是做广告或赞助。”

（三）《第2011/64/EU号指令》

1.第1条规定：

“本指令规定了各成员国协调烟草制品消费税税收结构和税率的一般规则。”

2.第2条规定：

“欧盟关于烟草产品的财政立法应确保内部市场的正常运行，同时，还要保证更高水平的健康保护……”

3.第3条规定：

“《欧盟条约》的目标之一是维持经济联盟，类似于一个具有良性竞争的国内市场。实现这一目标的前提是，各成员国关于烟草制品的课税政策对这一部门中产品消费的影响，不会扰乱竞争条件，也不会阻碍产品在欧盟内部的自由流动。”

4.第7条第1款规定：

“在欧盟生产和从非欧盟国家进口的卷烟，均应以包含关税的最高零售价为计税基数，适用从价计征的消费税。同时也应按单位课征从量计征的消费税。”

5.第9条规定：

“在各成员国开放的国内市场中，消费税结构的协调必然不会让市场竞争因课税而被扰乱，尤其是同一种类内不同品种的烟草制品之间的竞争。”

6.第10条规定：

“对竞争的迫切需求意味着针对所有品种烟草制品的自由定价制度。”

7.第15条第1款规定：

“在适当的情况下，制造商或者制造商在欧盟的代表或授权代理人，以及从非欧盟国家进口烟草的进口商，有权自由决定面向欧盟成员国销售的产品的最高零售价。”

三、案件事实和审理过程

Colruyt是一家在比利时经营的连锁超市。比利时公诉机关经调查发现，Colruyt连锁超市低价促销烟草制品，给予烟草制品数量折扣以及露营折扣，[①]使烟草制品的零售价低于制造商或进口商在对烟草制品贴花[②]时所基于的定价。而比利时法律禁止在比利时直接或间接的促销烟草制品。2013年5月10日，比利时布鲁塞尔刑事法院作出判决，Colruyt针对烟草制品促销活动违反了比利时《关于食品和其他商品的消费者健康保护法》第7条第1款，并对Colruyt处以27万欧元的罚款。Colruyt认为比利时法律——“禁止烟草制品的零售价低于制造商或进口商在对烟草制品贴花时所基于的定价”，违背了商品自由流动的原则，违反了《第

① 露营折扣(camping discount)，青年运动会给每个成员分发青年卡，成员在超市消费时可以出示青年卡，获得相应的折扣。这样的折扣被称为露营折扣。——译者注

② 贴花，即缴纳印花税。——译者注

2011/64/EU号指令》第15条第1款、《欧盟运行条约》第34条和第101条，向比利时布鲁塞尔上诉法院提起上诉。考虑到这些问题，比利时布鲁塞尔上诉法院中止了诉讼程序，于 2015年5月5日请求欧盟法院作出先行裁决，欧盟法庭于2015年5月13日收到申请，2016年9月21日作出判决。

四、争议焦点和主要法律观点

先行裁决申请涉及以下三个问题。

（一）比利时法律是否与《第2011/64/EU号指令》第15条第1款相违背？

Colruyt认为比利时《关于食品和其他商品的消费者健康保护法》第7条第1款与《第2011/64/EU号指令》相违背，欧盟法院则认为，《第2011/64/EU号指令》不排除成员国制定法律——禁止烟草制品的零售价低于制造商或进口商对烟草制品贴花时所基于的定价。《第2011/64/EU号指令》第15条第1款规定制造商或者以及从非欧盟国家进口烟草的进口商，有权自由决定其面向欧盟成员国销售的烟草制品的最高零售价。而比利时法律并没有限制烟草制品的制造商和进口商的上述权利。制造商和进口商设定的价格可以低于比利时政府设定的最高价，以有效利用较低的成本价格带来的竞争优势。此外，指令确保了各成员国烟草制品消费税的计税基数是其最高零售价格，既保证税收的完整性，也不会对竞争造成不良影响。可见零售商不在《第2011/64/EU号指令》涉及的主体范围之内。

（二）比利时法律是否与《欧盟运行条约》第34条相违背？

Colruyt认为，比利时《关于食品和其他商品的消费者健康保护法》第7条第1款与《欧盟运行条约》第34条相违背，欧盟法院则认为，《欧盟运行条约》第34条不排除成员国制定法律来禁止烟草制品的零售价低于制造商或进口商对烟草制品贴花时所基于的定价。《欧盟运行条约》第34条禁止的是对进口实行数量限制以及一切具有同等效果的措施。而《关于食品和其他商品的消费者健康保护法》第7条第1款仅是关于商品的销售安排，并没有阻碍其他成员国商品进入比利时国内市场，所以没有违反《欧盟运行条约》第34条。

（三）比利时法律是否与《欧盟运行条约》第101条相违背？

Colruyt认为，比利时《关于食品和其他商品的消费者健康保护法》第7条第1款与《欧盟运行条约》第101条相违背，欧盟法院则认为，《欧盟运行条约》第101条不排除成员国制定法律禁止烟草制品的零售价低于制造商或进口商对烟草制品贴花时所基于的定价。《欧盟运行条约》第101条虽仅规制企业行为，而不涉及成员国的法律或条例，但该条可以与《欧盟条约》第4条第3款一起来解读，即赋予欧盟和成员国之间合作的责任，要求欧盟和成员国不要采取或者继续实施可能使适用于企业的竞争规则无效的强制措施，甚至是制定法律或条例。而《关于食品和其他商品的消费者健康保护法》第7条第1款并没有鼓励供应商和零售商之间达成固定最高转售价格的纵向垄断协议，因此不违反《欧盟运行条约》第101条。

五、本案的意义及其启示

价格和税收是调节商品产销的最有力杠杆。由于烟草制品不同于普通消费品，它具有较大的负外部性，[①]世界上绝大多数国家都对烟草制品实行严格的价格和税收管控。

比利时颁布《关于食品和其他商品的消费者健康保护法》禁止烟草制品的零售价低于制造商或进口商在对烟草制品贴花时所基于的定价，禁止任何形式的针对烟草制品的推广促销行为。而我国对烟草行业实行的“统一领导、垂直管理、专卖专营”，烟草制品的定价权在国家手中，任何市场主体不能擅自上涨或下调烟草制品的价格，属于国家垄断。我国《反垄断法》第7条规定：“国有经济占控制地位的关系国民经济命脉和国家安全的行业以及依法实行专营专卖的行业，国家对其经营者的合法经营活动予以保护，并对经营者的经营行为及其商品和服务的价格依法实施监管和调控，维护消费者利益，促进技术进步。前款规定行业的经营者应当依法经营，诚实守信，严格自律，接受社会公众的监督，不得利用其控制地位

① “负外部性”是指生产商的某些产品对社会的成本大于生产商自己的成本。以烟草为例，每生产一吨烟草，社会成本都包括生产商的私人成本加上受到污染的大气、人群健康等成本。所以国家会对此类产生负外部性的产品进行税收和价格管控，从而激励买卖双方都考虑该产品的负外部性影响。——译者注

或者专营专卖地位损害消费者利益。”为实行烟草专卖管理，有计划地组织烟草专卖品的生产和经营，提高烟草制品质量，维护消费者利益，保证国家财政收入，我国颁布了《烟草专卖法》。该法明确规定国家对烟草专卖品的生产、销售、进出口依法实行专卖管理，并实行烟草专卖许可证制度。同时禁止对烟草制品的促销行为，即禁止在广播电台、电视台、报刊播放、刊登烟草制品广告。相比之下，我国将促销行为限定在广告的形式上，且对广告平台作了有限列举。我国不妨可以再细化相关规定，借鉴比利时的做法，将任何直接或间接地，旨在提高烟草制品销量的行为都归于促销行为，从而更加严格、有效地实施《烟草专卖法》。

此外，欧盟《第2011/64/EU号指令》是针对烟草消费税的规定。根据这一指令，目前欧盟需要课征消费税的烟草制品包括卷烟、雪茄、小雪茄、细切烟丝和其他用于吸烟的制品。对于卷烟，该指令明确规定，在欧盟生产和从非欧盟国家进口的卷烟都要同时适用从价计征的消费税和按单位课征的从量消费税。卷烟总体的消费税负担，即从量计征的消费税加上从价计征的消费税，应该占投入消费的卷烟零售价加权平均数的至少57%。不管零售价的加权平均数为多少，1000支卷烟的消费税不能低于64欧元。那些对1000支卷烟至少课征101欧元消费税的国家，可以不必遵守57%的条件。从量计征的消费税占卷烟间接税（从量消费税+从价消费税+增值税）税负的比重不能低于5%，同时不能高于76.5%。对于除卷烟之外的其他烟草制品，欧盟国家可以选择采用从价计征方式，或从量计征方式，或者两种方式混合使用。但总体的消费税负担不得低于如下标准：雪茄或小雪茄，包含所有税收的零售价的5%，或每千支/千克12欧元；为卷制香烟而切割的吸用烟草，零售价加权平均数的40%或每千克40欧元；其他吸用烟草，包含所有税收的零售价的20%，或每千克22欧元。消费税课征环节为生产环节或进口环节，但后移至产品首次投入消费之时课征。这些具体规定和可操作性值得我们借鉴。

我国烟草消费税征收情况如表4–1所示：

表4-1 烟草消费税税目税率

税目	税率	征收环节
烟		
1.卷烟		
工业		
(1)甲类卷烟	56%加0.003元/支	生产环节
[调拨价70元(不含增值税)/条以上(含70元)]		
(2)乙类卷烟	36%加0.003元/支	生产环节
[调拨价70元(不含增值税)/条以下]		
商业批发	11%加0.005元/支	批发环节
2.雪茄	36%	生产环节
3.烟丝	30%	生产环节

可以看出我国对于卷烟在生产环节征收消费税,适用从价计征和从量计征相结合的方式;在批发环节征收消费税,适用从价计征的方式。与欧盟的做法一样,我国并未将征收环节后移至零售环节,因为如果这样做会使烟草消费税纳税人数较少、管控便利的优势就会丧失大半,税源流失可能性将剧增,征管成本也会相应提高。

我国烟草消费税税率也在逐年上调。虽然我国卷烟零售价格低于世界平均水平,但卷烟税收占零售价格的比率已高于世界平均水平,特别是高于许多中低收入国家。虽然从理论上说提高烟草税收有利于加强烟草控制,但过高的烟草税收也会增强地方政府发展烟草行业的积极性。因此,我们应从我国国情和烟草行业实际出发,烟草税收政策设计应统筹兼顾控烟履约和行业发展的关系,有效发挥烟草税收约束作用,加快促进烟草产品结构调整,努力避免政策初衷与最终目标背道而驰。烟草税制的目标定位应该是"寓禁于征",即控制烟草消费,而不是保障政府财政收入。

表4-2　C-221/15（2016）涉及的法律

序号	原文	中文名称	所在段落
1	Treaty on the Functioning of the European Union（TFEU）	《欧盟运行条约》	1、11、12、15、32、33、36、40、41、42、43、44、45、48、49、50
2	Council Directive 2011/64/EU	《第2011/64/EU号指令》	1、3、4、5、6、11、12、13、16、19、20、21、22、23、26、27、29、30、31、50
3	Law on the protection of consumer health in relation to foodstuffs and other goods	《关于食品和其他商品的消费者健康保护法》	7、9、13、16、28、37、38、46、
4	Treaty on the European Union（TEU）	《欧盟条约》	1、11、12、42、43、44、45、49、50
5	Charter of Fundamental Rights of the European Union	《欧盟基本权利宪章》	1、12、19、30、

表4-3　C-221/15（2016）涉及的判例

序号	判例名称	案号	所在段落
1	Sommer Antriebs-und Funktechnik	EU：C：2015：491	14
2	dos Santos Palhota and Others	EU：C：2010：589	15
3	Commission v. France	EU：C：2010：111	24、25
4	GB-Inno-BM	EU：C：1977：185	27
5	Dassonville	EU：C：1974：82	33
6	Scotch Whisky Association and Others	EU：C：2013：366	33
7	Rewe-Zentral	EU：C：1979：42	34
8	Commission v. Italy	EU：C：2009：66	35、36

续表

序号	判例名称	案号	所在段落
9	Fachverband der Buch- und Medienwirtschaft	EU: C: 2009: 276	37
10	API and Others	EU: C: 2014: 2147	43、44
11	Cullet and Chambre syndicale des réparateurs automobiles et détaillants de produits pétroliers	EU: C: 1985: 29	45
12	Ohra Schadeverzekeringen	EU: C: 1993: 887	45

JUDGMENT OF THE COURT（Sixth Chamber）

21 September 2016（*）

（Reference for a preliminary ruling—Directive 2011/64/EU—Article 15（1）—Free determination, by the manufacturers and importers, of the maximum retail selling prices of manufactured tobacco products—National regulation prohibiting the sale of such products by retailers at prices lower than those indicated on the revenue stamp—Free movement of goods—Article 34 TFEU—Selling arrangements—Article 101 TFEU, read in conjunction with Article 4（3）TEU）

In Case C-221/15,

REQUEST for a preliminary ruling under Article 267 TFEU from the hof van beroep te Brussel（Court of Appeal, Brussels, Belgium）, made by decision of 5 May 2015, received at the Court on 13 May 2015, in the criminal proceedings against Etablissements Fr. Colruyt NV.

判例正文*

欧盟法院判决（第六法庭）
2016年9月21日

（提请先行裁决—《第2011/64/EU号指令》—第15条第1款—制造商和进口商关于烟草制品最高零售价格的自由决定—国家规定禁止零售商以低于对烟草制品贴花时基于的定价销售烟草制品—商品的自由流动—《欧盟运行条约》第34条—销售安排—对《欧盟运行条约》第101条及《欧盟条约》第4条第3款的解读）

案号：C-221/15

2015年5月5日，比利时布鲁塞尔上诉法院决定依据《欧盟运行条约》第267条的规定，就本案向欧盟法院请求先行裁决，本庭于2015年5月13日在针对荷兰Colruyt公司（以下简称Colruyt）的刑事诉讼中收到该先行裁决申请。

* 初译者：朱玥；校对者：林燕萍、戴娜。

THE COURT (Sixth Chamber),

composed of A. Arabadjiev (Rapporteur), President of the Chamber, J.C. Bonichot and C.G. Fernlund, Judges,

Advocate General: N. Wahl,

Registrar: M. Ferreira, Principal Administrator,

having regard to the written procedure and further to the hearing on 17 February 2016,

after considering the observations submitted on behalf of:

–Etablissements Fr. Colruyt NV, by R. Verstraeten and H. De Bauw, advocaten,

–the Belgian Government, initially by N. Zimmer, J. Van Holm and M. Jacobs, and subsequently J. Van Holm and M. Jacobs, acting as Agents, and A. Fromont, advocaat,

–the French Government, by G. de Bergues, D. Colas, J. Bousin and S. Ghiandoni, acting as Agents,

–the Portuguese Government, by L. Inez Fernandes, A. Brigas Afonso and M. Rebelo, acting as Agents,

–the European Commission, by E. Manhaeve, H. van Vliet and F. Tomat, acting as Agents,

after hearing the Opinion of the Advocate General at the sitting on 21 April 2016, gives the following

欧盟法院（第六法庭）

由审判长阿拉巴吉耶夫（判决书起草人）、法官J.-C.博尼科特、法官C.G.弗恩隆德组成。

佐审官：N.尼瓦尔；

书记官：M.费雷拉（首席行政官）；

本院进行了所有的书面程序之后，于2016年2月17日开庭审理了本案，并听取了以下各方意见：

——荷兰Colruyt公司，代理律师R.韦斯特拉滕和H.德鲍；

——比利时政府，原代理人N.齐莫、J.凡·霍姆和M.雅各布斯，现代理人范霍尔姆和雅各布斯、代理律师A.弗摩；

——法国政府，代理人G.德·伯格斯、D.格拉斯、J.波斯顿和S.吉安多尼；

——葡萄牙政府，代理人L.因斯·费南迪斯、A.布里加斯·阿方索和M.瑞贝罗；

——欧盟委员会，代理人E.曼海夫、H.范弗利特和F.托马特。

以及在2016年4月21日听取了佐审官的意见之后，经审理，本院作出如下判决：

Judgment

1 This request for a preliminary ruling concerns the interpretation of Article 15(1) of Council Directive 2011/64/EU of 21 June 2011 on the structure and rates of excise duty applied to manufactured tobacco (OJ 2011 L 176, p. 24), read in conjunction with Articles 20 and 21 of the Charter of Fundamental Rights of the European Union ('the Charter'), of Article 34 TFEU, and of Article 101 TFEU read in conjunction with Article 4(3) TEU.

2 The request has been made in the criminal proceedings brought against Établissements Fr. Colruyt NV ('Colruyt') concerning the sale by Colruyt of tobacco products at a unit price below the price indicated by the manufacturer or importer on the revenue stamp affixed to those products.

Legal context

EU law

3 Recitals 2, 3, 9 and 10 of Directive 2011/64 state:

'(2) The Union's fiscal legislation on tobacco products needs to ensure the proper functioning of the internal market and, at the same time, a high level of health protection ...

(3) One of the objectives of the Treaty on European Union is to maintain an economic union, whose characteristics are similar to those of a domestic market, within which there is healthy competition. As regards manufactured tobacco, achievement of this aim presupposes that the application in the Member States of taxes affecting the consumption of products in this sector does not distort conditions of competition and does not impede their free movement within the Union.

...

(9) As far as excise duties are concerned, harmonisation of structures must, in particular, result in competition in the different categories of manufactured tobacco belonging to the same group not being distorted by the effects of the charging of the tax and, consequently, in the opening of the national markets of the Member States.

(10) The imperative needs of competition imply a system of freely formed prices for all groups of manufactured tobacco.'

判　决

1 先行裁决申请涉及解释2011年6月21日发布的《关于烟草制品的消费税结构和税率的第2011/64/EU号指令》(OJ 2011 L 176, p. 24)第15条第1款，并结合《欧盟基本权利宪章》第20条和第21条进行解读，以及解释《欧盟运行条约》第34条、第101条，并结合《欧盟条约》第4条第3款进行解读。

2 述先行裁决申请源于针对Colruyt销售的烟草制品的单价低于制造商和进口商对烟草制品贴花时所基于的定价的刑事诉讼。

法律背景

欧盟法

3 《第2011/64/EU号指令》第2条、第3条、第9条、第10条规定如下：

"(2)欧盟关于烟草产品的财政立法应确保内部市场的正常运行，同时，还要保证更高水平的健康保护……

(3)《欧盟条约》的目标之一是维持经济联盟，类似于一个具有良性竞争的国内市场。实现这一目标的前提是，各成员国关于烟草制品的课税政策对这一部门中产品消费的影响，不会扰乱竞争环境，也不会阻碍产品在欧盟内部的自由流动。

……

(9)在各成员国开放的国内市场中，消费税结构的协调必然不会让市场竞争因课税而被扰乱，尤其是同一种类内不同品种的烟草制品之间的竞争。

(10)对竞争的迫切需求意味着针对所有品种烟草制品的自由定价制度。"

4 Article 1 of that directive, in Chapter 1, entitled 'Subject-matter', provides:

'This Directive lays down general principles for the harmonisation of the structure and rates of the excise duty to which the Member States subject manufactured tobacco.'

5 The first subparagraph of Article 7(1) of Directive 2011/64 provides:

'Cigarettes manufactured in the Union and those imported from third countries shall be subject to an ad valorem excise duty calculated on the maximum retail selling price, including customs duties, and also to a specific excise duty calculated per unit of the product.'

6 Article 15(1) of that directive is worded as follows:

'Manufacturers or, where appropriate, their representatives or authorised agents in the Union, and importers of tobacco from third countries shall be free to determine the maximum retail selling price for each of their products for each Member State for which the products in question are to be released for consumption.

The first subparagraph may not, however, hinder implementation of national systems of legislation regarding the control of price levels or the observance of imposed prices, provided that they are compatible with Union legislation.'

Belgian Law

7 Article 7(2*bis*)(1) of the Wet betreffende de bescherming van de gezondheid van de gebruikers op het stuk van de voedingsmiddelen en andere producten (Law on the protection of consumer health in relation to foodstuffs and other goods, *Belgisch Staatsblad* (*Official Journal*) of 8 April 1977, p. 4501), of 24 January 1977, at the date of the facts in the main proceedings ('the Law on Health Protection'), provides:

'It is prohibited to display advertisements for, or to organise sponsorship by, tobacco, tobacco-based products and similar products, hereinafter referred to as tobacco products.

Any communication or act which is directly or indirectly aimed at promoting sales, irrespective of the place, method of communication or techniques used, shall be regarded as constituting advertising or sponsorship.'

The dispute in the main proceedings and the questions referred for a preliminary ruling

8 Colruyt operates a chain of supermarkets in Belgium under the same name.

4 该指令第一章第1条“本条主旨”规定：“本指令规定了各成员国协调烟草制品消费税税收结构和税率的一般规则。”

5 《第2011/64/EU号指令》第7条第1款第1小段规定：“在欧盟生产和从非欧盟国家进口的卷烟，均应以包含关税的最高零售价为计税基数，适用从价计征的消费税。同时也应按单位课征从量计征的消费税。”

6 该指令第15条第1款规定：“在适当的情况下，制造商或者制造商在欧盟的代表或授权代理人，以及从非欧盟国家进口烟草的进口商，有权自由决定面向欧盟成员国销售的产品的最高零售价。

但是，在符合欧盟立法的前提下，第一小段不得妨碍执行关于控制价格水平的国家立法体系或遵守定价。”

比利时法律

7 1977年1月24日《关于食品和其他商品的消费者健康保护法》(以下简称《消费者健康保护法》)，刊登在1977年4月8日比利时官方公报第4501页，其第7条第1款，规定：

“禁止为烟草、以烟草为主的产品和类似产品(以下简称烟草制品)做广告或拉赞助。

任何直接或间接旨在促进销售的通信或行为，不论地点、通信方式和所采用的技术如何，均被视为做广告或赞助。”

主诉讼程序中的争议和提请先行裁决的问题

8 Colruyt集团在比利时经营与其同名的连锁超市。

9 Following an investigation by the federale overheidsdienst van volksgezondheid (Federal Public Service for Public Health, Belgium), the openbaar ministerie (the Public Prosecution Service, Belgium) found that Colruyt made use, in its supermarkets, of tobacco advertising measures prohibited under Article 7(2*bis*)(1) of the Law on Health Protection. Colruyt is thereby alleged to have sold a variety of tobacco products:

–at a unit price lower than the price indicated by the manufacturer or importer on the revenue stamp affixed to those products;

–with a quantity discount, which was marked by a yellow and red background on the display rail;

–with a temporary general discount of 3% to all customers;

–with a general discount of 3% to a specific category of persons, namely the members of youth movements by means of the 'camping discount' ('*kampkorting*').

10 By a judgment of the correctionele rechtbank te Brussel (Criminal Court, Brussels, Belgium) of 10 May 2013, Colruyt was ordered to pay, inter alia, a fine of EUR 270 000 for breach of the provision in question.

11 Colruyt brought an appeal against that judgment before the hof van beroep te Brussel (Court of Appeal, Brussels, Belgium), submitting, in particular, that the prohibition on applying retail prices which are lower than the price indicated by the manufacturer or importer on the revenue stamp affixed to the tobacco products is incompatible with Article 15(1) of Directive 2011/64, Article 34 TFEU and Article 101 TFEU read in conjunction with Article 4(3) TEU.

12 In those circumstances the hof van beroep te Brussel (Court of Appeal, Brussels) decided to stay the proceedings and to refer the following questions to the Court of Justice for a preliminary ruling:

'(1) Does Article 15(1) of Directive 2011/64, whether or not read in conjunction with Articles 20 and 21 of the [Charter], preclude a national measure which requires retailers to respect minimum prices by prohibiting the application of a price for tobacco products which is lower than the price that the manufacturer/importer has affixed to the revenue stamp?

(2) Does Article 34 TFEU preclude a national measure which requires retailers to respect minimum prices by prohibiting the application of a price for tobacco products which is lower than the price that the manufacturer/importer has affixed to the revenue stamp?

9 根据比利时联邦公共卫生服务部门的调查，比利时公诉机关发现：Colruyt实施了《消费者健康保护法》第7条第1款所禁止的烟草广告的行为。Colruyt被指控销售大量烟草制品：

（1）单价低于制造商或进口商对烟草制品贴花时所基于的定价；

（2）给予货架上用红色和黄色背景标记的烟草制品数量折扣；

（3）给予所有消费者3%的临时折扣；

（4）给予特定人群3%的一般折扣，即给予青年运动的成员“露营折扣”。

10 根据2013年5月10日比利时布鲁塞尔刑事法院的判决，Colruyt因违反上述条款需要支付罚款27万欧元。

11 Colruyt在比利时布鲁塞尔上诉法院提起上诉，认为禁止设定的零售价低于制造商或进口商在对烟草制品贴花时所基于的定价，违反《第2011/64/EU号指令》第15条第1款，同时参阅《欧盟运行条约》第34条和《欧盟条约》第4条第3款的规定。

12 考虑到这些问题，布鲁塞尔上诉法院决定中止诉讼程序，将下列问题提交至本院，请求本院作出先行裁决：

（1）《第2011/64/EU号指令》第15条第1款以及《欧盟基本权利宪章》第20条、第21条是否禁止成员国制定这样的国内法，即该国内法要求“零售商出售的烟草制品的价格不得低于制造商或进口商对烟草制品贴花时所基于的定价”？

（2）《欧盟运行条约》第34条是否禁止成员国制定这样的国内法，即该国内法要求“零售商出售的烟草制品的价格不得低于制造商或进口商对烟草制品贴花时所基于的定价”？

(3) Does Article 4(3)[TEU], read in conjunction with Article 101 TFEU, preclude a national measure which requires retailers to respect minimum prices by prohibiting the application of a price for tobacco products which is lower than the price that the manufacturer/importer has affixed to the revenue stamp?'

Admissibility of the request for a preliminary ruling

13 The Belgian Government submits that the request for a preliminary ruling is inadmissible on the ground that, first, Article 7(2*bis*)(1) of the Law on Health Protection bears no relation to the purpose of the main proceedings, since the retail selling prices of tobacco products in Belgium are governed by other Belgian law provisions. It submits, secondly, that the interpretation of Directive 2011/64 is irrelevant in resolving the present dispute, because Article 7(2*bis*)(1) is not intended to transpose that directive into Belgian law. It submits, thirdly, that the order for reference does not fulfil the conditions laid down in Article 94 of the Rules of Procedure of the Court, since it neither contains sufficient information on the legal and factual context of the dispute nor a statement of the precise reasons which prompted the referring court to inquire about the interpretation of the provisions of EU law. The French Government has also raised doubts as to the admissibility of the request for a preliminary ruling.

14 In that regard, it should be borne in mind that, according to settled case-law of the Court, questions on the interpretation of EU law referred by a national court in the factual and legislative context which that court is responsible for defining and the accuracy of which is not a matter for the Court to determine enjoy a presumption of relevance. The Court may refuse to rule on a question referred for a preliminary ruling from a national court only where it is quite obvious that the interpretation of EU law that is sought bears no relation to the actual facts of the main action or its purpose, where the problem is hypothetical, or where the Court does not have before it the factual or legal material necessary to give a useful answer to the questions submitted to it (judgment of 16 July 2015, Sommer Antriebs- und Funktechnik, C-369/14, EU:C:2015:491, paragraph 32 and the case-law cited).

（3）《欧盟条约》第4条第3款的规定以及《欧盟运行条约》第101条是否禁止成员国制定这样的国内法，即该国内法要求“零售商出售的烟草制品的价格不得低于制造商或进口商对烟草制品贴花时所基于的定价”？

该先行裁决申请是否可被受理

13 比利时政府认为，该先行裁决申请不应被受理。理由如下：

第一，《消费者健康保护法》第7条第1款与主要诉讼程序的目的无关，因为烟草制品的零售价由比利时其他法律规制。

第二，对于《第2011/64/EU号指令》的解释与解决涉案争议是不相干的，因为第7条第1款并没有将指令转化为比利时国内法的意图。

第三，先行裁决申请不符合法院程序规则第94条规定的条件，因为它既不包含关于争议的法律和事实问题，也不包含要求欧盟法院解释欧盟法的确切理由。

此外，法国政府也对先行裁决申请是否受理提出质疑。

14 关于这一问题，根据欧盟法院以往的判例，成员国法院就事实和法律问题向欧盟法院提出申请，要求对相关欧盟法进行解释。欧盟法院有义务确定成员国提交的问题的性质是否属于欧盟法的解释问题，是否属于欧盟法院的管辖范围。如果仅是一个假定性的问题，欧盟法院不应受理。如果成员国法院提交的有关欧盟法的解释问题明显与主要诉讼的事实或目的没有关联，欧盟法院也可以拒绝对成员国法院提交先行裁决的问题进行裁决。例如，问题是假设性的，或者欧盟法院没有收到提交先行裁决所需要的相关事实和法律材料。（参见判例：2015年7月16日，Sommer Antriebs-und Funktechnik案，C-369/14，EU：C：2015：491，第32段以及所引述的判例）

15 As regards the first plea of inadmissibility in respect of the request for a preliminary ruling, it is sufficient to note that, in the context of the procedure laid down in Article 267 TFEU, it is not for the Court to rule on the interpretation of national laws or regulations or to decide whether the referring court's interpretation of them is correct (judgment of 7 October 2010, *dos Santos Palhota and Others*, C-515/08, EU:C:2010:589, paragraph 18).

16 As regards the second plea of inadmissibility raised by the Belgian Government, it is not obvious that the situation at issue in the main proceedings is excluded from the scope of Directive 2011/64 or, at the very least, that Article 7(2bis)(1) of the Law on Health Protection would in no way be capable of rendering certain provisions of that directive ineffective and that the interpretation of that directive requested bears no relation to the actual facts of the main action or its purpose. In addition, that objection of inadmissibility relates to the substance of the first question referred for a preliminary ruling.

17 As regards the third plea of inadmissibility, it must be found that the referring court has, in the present case, set out the legal and factual context of the dispute in the main proceedings sufficiently precisely in order to enable the Court to give a useful answer to the questions submitted to it and the interested parties referred to in Article 23 of the Statute of the Court of Justice to submit observations. In addition, it is apparent from the order for reference that the referring court is uncertain as to whether the national legislation in the main proceedings is compatible with the provisions of EU law whose interpretation is sought and that, if that legislation were not compatible with those provisions, the allegations against Colruyt would be considered unfounded.

18 Having regard to the foregoing, it must be held that the request for a preliminary ruling is admissible.

Consideration of the questions referred

The first question

19 By its first question the referring court asks, in essence, whether Article 15(1) of Directive 2011/64, read in conjunction with Articles 20 and 21 of the Charter, must be interpreted as precluding national legislation, such as that at issue in the main proceedings, which prohibits retailers from selling tobacco products at a unit price lower than the price indicated by the manufacturer or importer on the revenue stamp affixed to those products.

15 关于比利时政府认为不可受理该先行裁决申请的第一条理由，需要注意的是：根据《欧盟运行条约》第267条规定的程序，欧盟法院不应对成员国国内的法律解释作出裁决，也不应由欧盟法院裁决成员国法院对该条文的解释是否正确。（参见判例：2010年10月7日，dos Santos Palhota and Others，C 515/08，EU：C：2010：589，第18段）

16 关于比利时政府认为不可受理该先行裁决申请的第二条理由，主诉讼程序中涉及的领域明显在《第2011/64/EU号指令》的范围之内，或者至少，《消费者健康保护法》第7条第1款不可能使该指令的某些条款失去效力，对指令的解释与主要诉讼的事实和目的无关。此外，这些反对意见还涉及提交先行裁决的第一个问题的实质内容。

17 关于比利时政府认为不可受理该先行裁决申请的第三条理由，必须注意的是，在本案中比利时布鲁塞尔上诉法院在审理案件中已经足够准确地阐述了涉案的法律和事实背景，以便欧盟法院能够对提交先行裁决的问题给出有用的回答；这些材料也便于根据《法院规约》第23条所述的有利害关系的当事人提交意见。此外，在先行裁决申请中也可以看到，比利时布鲁塞尔上诉法院对于主要诉讼程序中有关成员国国内法立法是否符合欧盟法的要求，对这一问题，申请书中并没有明确提出来。如果成员国立法不符合欧盟法的规定，那么针对Colruyt的诉讼也就没有事实依据了。

18 基于以上理由，本院认为该先行裁决申请可以受理。

欧盟法院对提请法院所提问题的分析

第一个问题

19 比利时布鲁塞尔上诉法院提出的第一个问题，《第2011/64/EU号指令》第15条第1款以及《欧盟基本权利宪章》第20条、第21条是否禁止成员国制定这样的国内法，即该国内法要求“零售商出售的烟草制品的价格不得低于制造商或进口商对烟草制品贴花时所基于的定价”？

20 As is apparent from Article 1, Directive 2011/64 is designed to lay down general principles for the harmonisation of the structure and rates of the excise duty to which the Member States subject manufactured tobacco. Directive 2011/64 falls, therefore, within the European Union's fiscal legislation on tobacco products, which, in the words of recital 2 of that directive, is designed to ensure the proper functioning of the internal market.

21 It is apparent, in addition, from recital 3 of Directive 2011/64 that, in order to achieve that aim, that directive seeks to ensure that the application in the Member States of taxes affecting the consumption of products in the manufactured tobacco sector does not distort conditions of competition and does not impede their free movement within the European Union. In particular, recital 9 of that directive states that harmonisation of excise duty structures must result in competition in the different categories of manufactured tobacco belonging to the same group not being distorted by the effects of the charging of the tax and, consequently, in the opening of the national markets of the Member States.

22 It follows from the foregoing that Directive 2011/64 is designed to ensure the proper functioning of the internal market as regards the application in the Member States of the excise duty on products in the manufactured tobacco sector.

23 The first subparagraph of Article 15(1) of that directive must be interpreted in the light of that aim. It provides that manufacturers or, where appropriate, their representatives or authorised agents in the European Union, and importers of tobacco from third countries are to be free to determine the maximum retail selling price for each of their products for each Member State for which the products in question are to be released for consumption, the aim being to ensure effective competition between them.

24 The Court has held that that provision seeks, first, to ensure that the determination of the tax base of the proportional excise duty on tobacco products, that is the maximum retail selling price of those products, is subject to the same rules in all the Member States and, secondly, to maintain the freedom of the economic operators, by which they may make effective use of the competitive advantage resulting from any lower cost prices (see, by analogy, judgment of 4 March 2010, *Commission* v *France*, C-197/08, EU:C:2010:111, paragraph 36).

25 In addition, the provision is part of the machinery for the taxation of tobacco, which implies that the price determined by the manufacturer or the importer and approved by the public authorities is binding as a maximum price and must be observed as such at every stage of the distribution chain until it is sold to the consumer in order to ensure that the integrity of tax revenue is not undermined by the exceeding of imposed prices (see, to that effect, judgment of 4 March 2010, *Commission* v *France*, C-197/08, EU:C:2010:111, paragraph 43).

20 《第2011/64/EU号指令》第1条已经明确，该指令规定了各成员国协调烟草制品税收结构和税率的一般规则。因此，《第2011/64/EU号指令》属于欧盟国家关于烟草制品的财政立法，正如该指令第2条所述，其目的是确保欧盟内部市场的正常运转。

21 此外，《第2011/64/EU号指令》第3条已经明确，为了实现这一目标，该指令旨在确保成员国课税对于烟草制品部门的产品消费产生的影响不会扭曲竞争条件，以及不妨碍其在欧盟内的自由流动。特别是该指令的第9条指出，就消费税而言，在各成员国开放的国内市场中，其课税结构的协调是为了不让市场竞争因课税被扰乱，尤其是同一种类内不同品种的烟草制品之间的竞争关系。

22 综上所述，《第2011/64/EU号指令》的立法目的在于协调各成员国在烟草制品部门的产品课征消费税方面确保欧盟内部市场的正常运转。

23 考虑到《第2011/64/EU号指令》的立法目的，应当这样来理解该指令第15条第1款的第一段：在一般情况下，为了确保经营者之间的有效竞争，制造商或者制造商在欧盟的代表或授权代理人，以及从非欧盟国家进口烟草的进口商，有权自由决定面向欧盟成员国销售的产品的最高零售价。

24 本院认为该条款目的是：首先，明确各成员国烟草制品消费税的计税基数是这些产品的最高零售价格；其次，为了保证经营者的自由，他们可以有效利用由较低的成本价格所带来的竞争优势。（参见判例：2010年3月4日，Commission v France，C-197/08，EU：C：2010：111，第36段）

25 此外，该条款属于烟草税制的一部分。指令规定了将制造商或进口商确定的并经政府当局批准的价格强制作为最高价格，并且分销链的每个阶段都必须遵守这些规定，直到将其出售给消费者，以确保税收的完整性和不受超出规定的价格影响。（参见判例：2010年3月4日，Commission v France，C-197/08，EU：C：2010：111，第43段）

26 The first subparagraph of Article 15(1) of Directive 2011/64 is, therefore, designed to ensure that the application of the rules relating to the excise duty on tobacco products does not harm the imperative needs of competition which imply, as is clear from recital 10 of that directive, a system of prices, formed freely by the producers or importers, for all groups of manufactured tobacco.

27 Consequently, the Court has held, in essence, that Article 15(1) of Directive 2011/64 cannot be interpreted as precluding legislation whereby a selling price, namely the price stated on the tax label, is imposed for the sale to the consumer of imported or home-produced tobacco products, provided that that price has been freely determined by the manufacturer or importer (see, by analogy, judgment of 16 November 1977, *GB-Inno-BM*, 13/77, EU: C: 1977: 185, paragraphs 63 and 64).

28 As regards the case at issue in the main proceedings, a provision of national legislation such as Article 7(2*bis*)(1) of the Law on Health Protection, which, according to the information provided by the referring court, prohibits retailers, inter alia, from selling tobacco products at a unit price lower than the price indicated by the manufacturer or importer on the revenue stamp affixed to those products, results indeed—having regard to the specific features of the machinery for the taxation of tobacco—in the price affixed to that stamp being imposed on those operators as regards the sale of those products to the consumer. However, it is not apparent from the documents submitted to the Court that that provision is intended to govern the setting of the price indicated by the producer or importer on the revenue stamp nor indeed that that provision concerns in any other manner the application of the excise duty on tobacco products.

29 Consequently, such a national provision is not encompassed by the situation referred to in Article 15(1) of Directive 2011/64. That article does not, therefore, preclude such a provision.

30 That interpretation is not called in question by Colruyt's argument, according to which not allowing retailers the freedom, under Article 15(1), to set the sales price of tobacco products to the consumer, constitutes unjustified discrimination, contrary to Articles 20 and 21 of the Charter, as between retailers who are also importers and those which are not. Those provisions of the Charter cannot, in any event, result in the scope of Directive 2011/64 being extended to the setting of the minimum price charged by retailers, which is not, as a rule, concerned by the application of the excise duty on tobacco products.

26 可见,《第2011/64/EU号指令》第15条第1款的第1段是为了确保关于烟草制品消费税规则的适用不会对公平竞争造成损害。从该指令第10条也可以清楚地看出,烟草制品的价格体系是由生产者或进口商自由建立的。

27 所以,本院认为,《第2011/64/EU号指令》第15条第1款并没有禁止各成员国在国内针对销售价格的立法,即以税收标签所示的价格分别将进口的或国内生产的烟草制品销售给消费者,有关价格可以由制造商或进口商自由决定。(参见判例:1977年11月16日,GB-Inno-BM案,13/77,EU:C:1977:185,第63和64段)

28 本案中,本院认为,根据比利时布鲁塞尔上诉法院提供的资料,考虑到烟草税制的特点,例如,《消费者健康保护法》第7条第1款"禁止零售商出售的烟草制品的单价低于制造商或进口商对烟草制品贴花时所基于的定价",这样的法律规定可能造成固定"贴花定价"成为零售商向消费者出售商品的价格。但是,从递交给本院的文件材料中并不能看出,《消费者健康保护法》第7条第1款的目的是规制制造商或进口商设定贴花时所基于的定价或者其他课征烟草制品消费税的方式,也就是说制造商或进口商设定贴花定价是自由的、不受限制的。

29 因此,《第2011/64/EU号指令》第15条第1款没有禁止上述成员国可以进行国内立法,即成员国可以制定类似《消费者健康保护法》第7条第1款这样的规定。

30 Colruyt在其提出的疑问中并没有对上述指令的解释提出质疑。但是,根据该指令第15条第1款的规定,如果不允许零售商自由设定向消费者出售的烟草制品的销售价格,则那些既是零售商也是进口商的商家有权自由定价,但是仅是零售商的商家无权自由定价,这样就构成了不合理的歧视,违反了《欧盟基本权利宪章》的第20条和第21条。根据这些宪章条款,在任何情况下《第2011/64/EU号指令》的适用范围都不能扩大到零售商设定的最低价格。这些价格一般不用于对烟草制品课征的消费税。

31 It follows from all the foregoing considerations that the answer to the first question is that Article 15(1) of Directive 2011/64 must be interpreted as not precluding national legislation, such as that at issue in the main proceedings, which prohibits retailers from selling tobacco products at a unit price lower than the price indicated by the manufacturer or importer on the revenue stamp affixed to those products, in so far as that price has been freely determined by the manufacturer or importer.

The second question

32 By its second question the referring court asks, in essence, whether Article 34 TFEU must be interpreted as precluding national legislation, such as that at issue in the main proceedings, which prohibits retailers from selling tobacco products at a retail price which is lower than the price indicated by the manufacturer or importer on the revenue stamp affixed to those products.

33 Article 34 TFEU prohibits quantitative restrictions on imports and all measures having equivalent effect. In accordance with settled case-law, all measures of a Member State which are capable of hindering, directly or indirectly, actually or potentially, trade within the European Union are to be considered as measures having an effect equivalent to quantitative restrictions within the meaning of Article 34 TFEU (judgments of 11 July 1974, *Dassonville*, 8/74, EU: C: 1974: 82, paragraph 5, and 23 December 2015, *Scotch Whisky Association and Others*, C-333/14, EU: C: 2015: 845, paragraph 31).

34 Hence, in the absence of harmonisation of national legislation, obstacles to the free movement of goods which are the consequence of applying, to goods coming from other Member States where they are lawfully manufactured and marketed, rules that lay down requirements to be met by such goods constitute measures of equivalent effect to quantitative restrictions even if those rules apply to all products alike (see, to that effect, judgment of 20 February 1979, *Rewe-Zentral*, '*Cassis de Dijon*', 120/78, EU: C: 1979: 42, paragraphs 6, 14 and 15).

35 The application to products from other Member States of national provisions restricting or prohibiting certain selling arrangements is not such as to hinder directly or indirectly, actually or potentially, trade between Member States for the purposes of that case-law, on condition that those provisions apply to all relevant traders operating within the national territory and that they affect in the same manner, in law and in fact, the marketing of domestic products and of those from other Member States. Provided that those conditions are fulfilled, the application of such rules to the sale of products from another Member State meeting the requirements laid down by that State is not by nature such as to prevent their access to the market or to impede access any more than it impedes the access of domestic products (judgment of 10 February 2009, *Commission* v *Italy*, C-110/05, EU: C: 2009: 66, paragraph 36).

31 基于上述理由可以看出，对第一个问题的回答是：《第2011/64/EU号指令》第15条第1款允许成员国根据本国情况制定相关国内法（如本案所示国内法），规定“零售商出售的烟草制品的单价不得低于制造商或进口商对烟草制品贴花时所基于的定价”，只要该贴花时所基于的定价是制造商或进口商自由决定的即可。

第二个问题

32 比利时布鲁塞尔上诉法院提出的第二个问题：《欧盟运行条约》第34条是否禁止成员国制定这样的国内法，即该国内法要求“零售商出售的烟草制品的价格不得低于制造商或进口商对烟草制品贴花时所基于的定价”？

33 《欧盟运行条约》第34条禁止对进口实行数量限制以及一切具有同等效果的措施。根据以往的判例，各成员国采取的任何直接或间接、实际或潜在地在欧盟范围内阻碍贸易的措施都应被视为《欧盟运行条约》第34条“具有同等效果”的措施。（参见判例：1974年7月11日，Dassonville案，8/74，EU：C：1974：82，第5段，以及2015年12月23日，Scotch Whisky Association and Others，C－333 / 14，EU：C：2015：845，第31段）

34 因此，在各成员国立法不统一的情况下，成员国采取以下措施——如对国内商品与在其他成员国合法制造的和销售的商品之间的自由流通设置障碍，或对其他成员国合法制造并销售的商品设置门槛——都属于“具有同等的数量限制效果”的措施，即使这些措施普遍适用于所有类似产品也不例外。（参见判例：1979年2月20日，Rewe－Zentral，“Cassis de Dijon”，120/78，EU：C：1979：42，第6段、第14和15段）

35 成员国若要避免“直接或间接、实际或潜在地妨碍成员国之间的贸易”，除非要满足这样的条件，即对来自其他成员国商品采取的限制或禁止某些销售的措施，和成员国在国内对所有相关的贸易适用同样的限制措施，并且在法律和事实上这些措施都以同样的方式影响成员国的国内商品销售和来自其他成员国的商品销售。在这种情况下，对于其他成员国的商品所采取的措施并不是为了阻止其他成员国商品进入其国内市场或妨碍其进入市场，因为这些措施也同样阻碍了其国内商品进入市场。（参见判例：2009年2月10日，Commission v Italy，C－110/05，EU：C：2009：66，第36段）

36 Consequently, measures adopted by a Member State the object or effect of which is to treat products coming from other Member States less favourably are to be regarded as measures having equivalent effect to quantitative restrictions on imports within the meaning of Article 34 TFEU, as are the measures referred to in paragraph 34 of the present judgment. Any other measure which hinders access of products originating in other Member States to the market of a Member State is also covered by that concept (see, to that effect, judgment of 10 February 2009, *Commission* v *Italy*, C-110/05, EU: C: 2009: 66, paragraph 37).

37 In that regard, in so far as the national provisions on tobacco product pricing, such as those in Article 7(2*bis*)(1) of the Law on Health Protection, do not concern the characteristics of those goods, but solely the arrangements under which they may be sold, they must be regarded as concerning selling arrangements (see, by analogy, judgment of 30 April 2009, *Fachverband der Buch- und Medienwirtschaft*, C-531/07, EU: C: 2009: 276, paragraph 20).

38 As to whether such provisions fulfil the conditions set out in paragraph 35 above, it must be found, first, that a national provision such as Article 7(2*bis*)(1) of the Law on Health Protection, which prohibits retailers from selling tobacco products at a unit price lower than the price indicated by the manufacturer or importer on the revenue stamp affixed to those products, applies to all relevant traders operating within the national territory.

39 Secondly, since that provision does not concern the determination by importers of the products from other Member States of the price indicated on the revenue stamp and those importers remain free to set that price, it is not of such a kind as to prevent access to the Belgian market of tobacco products from another Member State or to impede access any more than it impedes the access of domestic tobacco products.

40 Consequently, such legislation does not constitute a measure having an effect equivalent to quantitative restrictions on imports, prohibited by Article 34 TFEU.

41 In the light of the foregoing considerations, the answer to the second question is that Article 34 TFEU must be interpreted as not precluding national legislation, such as that at issue in the main proceedings, which prohibits retailers from selling tobacco products at a unit price lower than the price indicated by the manufacturer or importer on the revenue stamp affixed to those products, in so far as that price has been freely determined by the importer.

36 因此，如果成员国所采取的措施，其目的或效果是给予其他成员国的商品较低的优惠待遇，则应被视为与《欧盟运行条约》第34条“具有同等的进口数量限制效果”的措施。正如本判决第34段提到的这些措施。任何阻碍其他成员国商品进入某一成员国市场的其他措施也包含在这一概念之内。（参见判例：2009年2月10日，Commission v. Italy，C-110/05，EU：C：2009：66，第37段）

37 但是，就成员国关于烟草制品定价的规定而言，这些规定应该被视为相关销售安排。如《消费者健康保护法》第7条第1款并没有涉及这些商品的特性，而仅是关于商品销售的安排。（参见判例：2009年4月30日，Fachverband der Buch-und Medienwirtschaft，C-533/07，EU：C：2009：276，第20段）

38 至于上述规定是否符合上文第35段所述的条件，首先，要看这项规定是否对本国境内所有相关的贸易都适用。如《消费者健康保护法》第7条第1款，禁止零售商出售的烟草制品的单价低于制造商或进口商对烟草制品贴花时所基于的定价。这是一项国内法的规定。

39 其次，由于该条款没有限制进口商对来自其他成员国的商品贴花时所基于的定价，进口商可以自由设定贴花定价，所以该条款并没有阻止其他成员国烟草制品进入比利时市场，或者妨碍商品的进入。这条对国内烟草制品的进入也同样适用。

40 因此，这项国内立法并不是《欧盟运行条约》第34条所禁止的进口数量限制具有同等效果的措施。

41 基于以上理由，对第二个问题的回答是：《欧盟运行条约》第34条允许成员国根据本国情况制定相关国内法（如本案所示国内法），规定“零售商出售的烟草制品的单价不得低于制造商或进口商对烟草制品贴花时所基于的定价”，只要该贴花时所基于的定价是进口商自由决定的即可。

The third question

42 By its third question the referring court asks, in essence, whether Article 101 TFEU, read in conjunction with Article 4(3) TEU, must be interpreted as precluding national legislation, such as that at issue in the main proceedings, which prohibits retailers from selling tobacco products at a unit price lower than the price indicated by the manufacturer or importer on the revenue stamp affixed to those products.

43 As is apparent from the Court's settled case-law, although Article 101 TFEU is concerned solely with the conduct of undertakings and not with laws or regulations emanating from Member States, that article, read in conjunction with Article 4(3) TEU, which lays down a duty of cooperation between the European Union and the Member States, none the less requires the latter not to introduce or maintain in force measures, even of a legislative or regulatory nature, which may render ineffective the competition rules applicable to undertakings (judgment of 4 September 2014, *API and Others*, C-184/13 to C-187/13, C-194/13, C-195/13 and C-208/13, EU:C:2014:2147, paragraph 28 and the case-law cited).

44 Article 101 TFEU, read in conjunction with Article 4(3) TEU, is infringed where a Member State requires or encourages the adoption of agreements, decisions or concerted practices contrary to Article 101 TFEU or reinforces their effects, or where it divests its own rules of the character of legislation by delegating to private economic operators responsibility for taking decisions affecting the economic sphere (judgment of 4 September 2014, *API and Others*, C-184/13 to C-187/13, C-194/13, C-195/13 and C-208/13, EU:C:2014:2147, paragraph 29).

45 However, rules such as those which are not intended to compel suppliers and retailers to conclude agreements or to take any other action of the kind referred to in Article 101(1) TFEU but which, on the contrary, entrust to the public authorities responsibility for fixing prices to the consumer do not infringe that provision, read in conjunction with Article 4(3) TEU (see, to that effect, judgment of 29 January 1985, *Cullet and Chambre syndicale des réparateurs automobiles et détaillants de produits pétroliers*, 231/83, EU:C:1985:29, paragraphs 17 and 18). Similarly, rules which lay down a prohibition which is self-sufficient neither require nor favour the conclusion of anti-competitive agreements (see, to that effect, judgment of 17 November 1991, *Ohra Schadeverzekeringen*, C-245/91, EU:C:1993:887, paragraph 11).

第三个问题

42 比利时布鲁塞尔上诉法院提出的第三个问题,《欧盟条约》第4条第3款的规定以及《欧盟运行条约》第101条是否禁止成员国制定这样的国内法,即该国内法要求“零售商出售的烟草制品的价格不得低于制造商或进口商对烟草制品贴花时所基于的定价”?

43 从欧盟法院以往的判例可知,尽管《欧盟运行条约》第101条仅涉及企业行为,不涉及成员国的国内法律或条例,该条必须与《欧盟条约》第4条第3款一起理解,即欧盟和成员国之间的合作关系,要求欧盟和成员国不要采取或者继续实施可能使适用于企业的竞争规则无效的强制措施,甚至制定相关法律或条例。(参见判例:2014年9月4日,API and Others,C-184/13至C-187/13,C-194/13,C-195/13和C-208/13,EU:C:2014:2147,第28段以及所引述的判例)

44 如果成员国要求或鼓励通过与《欧盟运行条约》第101条相抵触的协议、决议或一致行动,或相关措施,或通过委托私营经济主体作出影响经济领域的决策来规避本国的法律规则,则违反了《欧盟运行条约》第101条及《欧盟条约》第4条第3款的规定。(参见判例:2014年9月4日,API and Others,C-184/13至C-187/13,C-194/13,C-195/13和 C-208/13,EU:C:2014:2147,第29段)

45 但是,有些国内法规则并不强迫供应商和零售商签订协议或采取任何《欧盟运行条约》第101条第1款禁止的其他行为,反而将定价的责任委托给政府当局,这些规则并不违反《欧盟运行条约》第101条及《欧盟条约》第4条第3款。(参见判例:1985年1月29日,Cullet and Chambre syndicale des réparateurs automobiles et détaillants de produits pétroliers,231/83,EU:C:1985:29,第17和18段)同样,自动生效的、既不需要也不利于缔结反竞争协议的限制性规则也是如此。(参见判例:1991年11月17日,Ohra Schadeverzekeringen,C-245/91,EU:C:1993:887,第11段)

46 As has been found in paragraph 28 above, a provision of national legislation such as Article 7(2*bis*)(1) of the Law on Health Protection results in a sale price being imposed on retailers, for the sale of tobacco products to the consumer, namely, that indicated by the manufacturer or importer on the revenue stamp affixed to those products. Such legislation neither requires nor encourages the adoption of agreements between suppliers and retailers, but is self–sufficient since the direct effect of the legislation is to set the price charged by retailers. In addition, it is not apparent from the file that the adoption of Article 7(2*bis*)(1) of the Law on Health Protection was preceded by an agreement on sale prices imposed in the tobacco products sector.

47 In addition, Article 7(2*bis*)(1) does not delegate to private operators responsibility for setting the price charged by retailers or for taking other decisions affecting the economic sphere.

48 In those circumstances, legislation such as that at issue in the main proceedings is not capable of rendering Article 101(1) TFEU ineffective.

49 It follows from the foregoing considerations that the answer to the third question is that Article 101 TFEU, read in conjunction with Article 4(3) TEU, must be interpreted as not precluding national legislation, such as that at issue in the main proceedings, which prohibits retailers from selling tobacco products at a unit price lower than the price indicated by the manufacturer or importer on the revenue stamp affixed to those products.

Costs

50 Since these proceedings are, for the parties to the main proceedings, a step in the action pending before the national court, the decision on costs is a matter for that court. Costs incurred in submitting observations to the Court, other than the costs of those parties, are not recoverable.

On those grounds, the Court (Sixth Chamber) hereby rules:

1.Article 15(1) of Directive 2011/64/EU of 21 June 2011 on the structure and rates of excise duty applied to manufactured tobacco must be interpreted as not precluding national legislation, such as that at issue in the main proceedings, which prohibits retailers from selling tobacco products at a unit price lower than the price indicated by the manufacturer or importer on the revenue stamp affixed to those products, in so far as that price has been freely determined by the manufacturer or importer.

46 正如上文第28段所述，成员国立法，如《消费者健康保护法》第7条第1款规定零售商向消费者出售的烟草制品的价格不得低于制造商或进口商对商品贴花时所基于的定价，这种立法既不要求也不鼓励供应商和零售商之间达成某种协议。因为立法的直接作用是设定零售价格，供应商和零售商之间的零售价格是自动生效的。此外，从现有材料中也不能看出，在实施《消费者健康保护法》第7条第1款之前，在烟草制品部门实行了销售价格协议。

47 此外，《消费者健康保护法》第7条第1款也没有授权私营经营者设定零售价格或作出影响经济领域的其他决定。

48 在这种情况下，本案中所涉及的成员国国内法并不因其违反《欧盟运行条约》第101条第1款而无效。

49 基于上述理由，对于第三个问题的回答是：《欧盟运行条约》第101条及《欧盟条约》第4条第3款允许成员国根据本国情况制定相关国内法（如本案所示国内法），规定“零售商出售的烟草制品的单价不得低于制造商或进口商对烟草制品贴花时所基于的定价”。

诉讼费用

50 对本案双方当事人而言，现在的程序只是提交国内法院的先行步骤，对费用作出裁定是国内法庭的事。对于当事人向本院提出申请时所支出的费用，均不予偿付。

综上所述，欧盟法院（第六法庭）作出如下裁决：

1.《第2011/64/EU号指令》第15条第1款“烟草制品消费税税收结构和税率”条款允许成员国根据本国情况制定相关国内法（如本案所示国内法），规定“零售商出售的烟草制品的单价不得低于制造商或进口商对烟草制品贴花时所基于的定价”，只要该贴花时所基于的定价是制造商或进口商自由决定的即可。

2.Article 34 TFEU must be interpreted as not precluding national legislation, such as that at issue in the main proceedings, which prohibits retailers from selling tobacco products at a unit price lower than the price indicated by the manufacturer or importer on the revenue stamp affixed to those products, in so far as that price has been freely determined by the importer.

3.Article 101 TFEU, read in conjunction with Article 4(3) TEU, must be interpreted as not precluding national legislation, such as that at issue in the main proceedings, which prohibits retailers from selling tobacco products at a unit price lower than the price indicated by the manufacturer or importer on the revenue stamp affixed to those products.

2.《欧盟运行条约》第34条允许成员国根据本国情况制定相关国内法（如本案所示国内法），规定“零售商出售的烟草制品的单价不得低于制造商或进口商对烟草制品贴花时所基于的定价”，只要该贴花时所基于的定价是进口商自由决定的即可。

3.《欧盟运行条约》第101条及《欧盟条约》第4条第3款允许成员国根据本国情况制定相关国内法（如本案所示国内法），规定“零售商出售的烟草制品的单价不得低于制造商或进口商对烟草制品贴花时所基于的定价”。

Landmark Cases
on EU Competition Law

5

阿克苏诺贝尔公司等诉欧盟委员会

（Akzo Nobel NV and Others v European Commission）

（*C-516/15P*）

案例导读*

一、案例基本信息

阿克苏诺贝尔公司案基本信息

法　院	欧盟法院		
提请法院	初审法院	判决时间	2017年4月27日
案　号	Case C-516/15P		
关 键 词	母公司责任；时限；《第1/2003号条例》		
当 事 人	上 诉 人：阿克苏诺贝尔公司（Akzo Nobel NV） 阿克苏诺贝尔化学（德国）公司 （Akzo Nobel Chemicals GmbH） 阿克苏诺贝尔化学（荷兰）公司 （Akzo Nobel Chemicals BV） 被上诉人：欧盟委员会（European Commission）		

二、案例涉及的欧盟法规

（一）《第1/2003号条例》第7条第1款规定：

"当欧盟委员会依投诉采取行动或者主动采取行动而查明存在条约第81条和第82条项下的违法行为时，它可以作出决定要求相关高管企业和企业协会停止该违法行为……如果委员会有正当的理由，它也可以就过去已经发生的违法行为作出决定。"

* 作者：应嘉毅。

（二）《第1/2003号条例》第23条第2款规定：

“欧盟委员会可以通过决定对企业或企业协会处以罚款，如果企业或企业协会有意地或疏忽地从事了下列行为：

a）它们违反了条约第81条或第82条……”

（三）《第1/2003号条例》第25条第1款、第2款和第3款规定：

“1.第23条赋予的权力应当服从下列时限的规定：

（a）如果违反了有关索取信息或进行检查的条款，时限是3年；

（b）如果是所有其他的违法行为，时限是5年。

2.时间从违法行为实施之日开始计算。但是，在违法行为持续发生或重复发生的情况下，时间应当从违法行为结束之日起计算。

3.当欧盟委员会或成员国竞争主管部门对违法行为进行调查或采取行动时，应中断对处罚或定期支付罚款时限的计算……”

三、案件事实和审理过程

自20世纪90年代以来，在锡稳定剂行业以及ESBO/酯类行业中，众多企业通过签订垄断协议的方式，固定价格、通过销售配额分割市场、分配客户以及交换关于客户、生产和销售的商业敏感信息。这类行为违反了《欧共体条约》第81条以及《欧洲经济区协议》第53条的规定。

基于此，欧盟委员会作出决定，对20家公司的相关违法行为做出处罚。在这20家公司中，有的公司直接实施了上述违法行为而承担责任，有的公司作为母公司为子公司的违法行为承担责任。在本案中，阿克苏诺尔贝公司是阿克苏诺贝尔化学（德国）公司、阿克苏诺贝尔化学（荷兰）公司的母公司因此对其子公司实施的违法行为承担责任。

2010年1月27日，阿克苏诺贝尔公司、阿克苏诺贝尔化学（德国）公司公司、阿克苏诺贝尔化学（荷兰）公司以及艾科化学公司作为原告，对欧盟委员会提起诉讼。初审程序中的原告认为，根据《第1/2003号条例》第25条的规定，欧盟委员会对本案所涉的违法行为的惩罚权力的时限为5年，欧盟委员会对于阿克苏诺贝尔化学（德国）公司和阿克苏诺贝尔化学（荷兰）公司1993年6月28日之前的违法行为的处罚权已过时限，故请求初审法院撤销欧盟委员会的决定，或者减少对其罚款金额。

然而，初审法院仅撤销了欧盟委员会决定中对于阿克苏诺贝尔化学（德国）公司和阿克苏诺贝尔化学（荷兰）公司在1993年6月28日之前的违法行为的处罚，但驳回了其他诉讼请求。初审法院仍然认定，母公司阿克苏诺贝尔公司应当对于其子公司的违法行为承担责任。因此，阿克苏诺贝尔公司、阿克苏诺贝尔化学（德国）公司、阿克苏诺贝尔化学（荷兰）公司提起了上诉。欧盟法院受理了上诉人的上诉，在对本案进行了书面审理程序之后，于2016年12月21日听取了佐审官的意见，于2017年4月17日作出了最终判决。

四、争议焦点和主要法律观点

欧盟委员会将1987年2月24日起至1993年6月28日的时间称为“第一阶段违法期”。荷兰阿克苏公司与瑞典诺贝尔公司于1994年合并为阿克苏诺贝尔公司，是本案中阿克苏诺贝尔化学（德国）公司和阿克苏诺贝尔化学（荷兰）公司的最终控股母公司。在第一阶段违法期内，欧盟委员会发现，阿克苏诺贝尔公司间接全资控股了阿克苏诺贝尔化学（德国）公司和阿克苏诺贝尔化学（荷兰）公司。在该期间内，子公司阿克苏诺贝尔化学（德国）公司参与实施了锡稳定剂行业的违法行为，而阿克苏诺贝尔化学（荷兰）公司参与实施了ESBO/酯类行业的违法行为。子公司阿克苏诺贝尔化学（德国）公司和阿克苏诺贝尔化学（荷兰）公司于1993年6月28日均停止了上述违法行为。欧盟委员会据此对母公司阿克苏诺贝尔公司以及该两家子公司均作出了罚款决定。

根据《第1/2003号条例》第25条的规定，欧盟委员会对本案所涉的违法行为的惩罚权的时限为5年，即从1998年6月28日起，欧盟委员会便无权对上述两家子公司进行惩罚。而欧盟委员会于2003年年初才对相关违法行为进行调查。因此，初审法院因时限问题，撤销了欧盟委员会对上述两家子公司的惩罚。但是，初审法院却未撤销在该第一阶段违法期内母公司应承担的相应的惩罚责任。

本案的争议焦点是：母公司是否应为子公司的违法行为承担责任？当欧盟委员会对子公司的处罚权超过时限时，母公司是否仍需承担责任？

上诉人根据欧盟法院的判例和平等原则提出，当母公司为子公司的违法行为承担责任时，其承担的责任不可能多于子公司的责任。即当欧盟委员会针对子公司的罚款部分或全部撤销时，母公司也应该同样减少部分或全部责任。因此，在本案中，当欧盟委员会撤销了对两家子公司于第一阶段违法期的罚款后，应当同时撤销对母公司在第一阶段违法期内完全因子公司的违法行为而承担的部分或全部责任。

初审法院和上诉法院认为，母子公司之间因经济、组织以及法律上的关联，形成了一个整体，即为欧盟竞争法所规制的对象——单一经济单位。母公司对子公司具有决定性的重大影响，从而决定了子公司的市场行为。因此，母公司理应对子公司的违法行为承担责任。即使母公司未对子公司施加影响，子公司独立实施违法行为时，母公司作为单一经济单位的组成部分，也应当承担衍生性质的责任。在第一阶段违法期内，母公司间接拥有两家子公司的全部股权，且对于子公司施加了决定性的影响，母子公司之间是一个经济单位，因此子公司所实施的违法行为应被认定为是母公司的行为。而且，在子公司停止实施了相应的违法行为后，母公司并未停止实施，而是通过其他方式实施了相应的违法行为。因此，母公司理应为子公司的违法行为负责，即使当欧盟委员会因时限问题撤销了对子公司的处罚时，母公司仍然需要承担责任。

五、本案的意义及其启示

本案不仅梳理了欧盟竞争法对母子公司责任认定的规定和欧盟法院的一些判例，还着重分析了有关处罚时限问题，即当欧盟委员会对子公司的处罚超过时限规定时，母公司是否仍然需要承担责任。根据欧盟法院的观点，第一，当母公司对子公司施加了决定性的影响，母子公司之间形成了单一经济单位时，子公司所实施的违法行为应被认定为母公司自身实施的行为。因此,母公司须为子公司的违法行为承担责任;第二,在子公司停止实施了相应的违法行为后,母公司并未停止实施,而是通过其他方式一直在参与实施违法行为。因此即使当欧盟委员会因时限问题撤销了对子公司的处罚时,母公司仍然需要承担责任。可见,欧盟法院为了防止母公司利用其子公司实施违法行为,在认定母公司的责任时采取了比较严格的标准。这一点更加体现了欧盟竞争法的宗旨在于保护消费者利益、维护市场内正常的竞争秩序。

我国《反垄断法》对于母子公司实施垄断行为的责任认定问题未作出具体的规定。由于子公司具有独立的法人资格,能够独立地承担法律责任,因此在无法律明确规定的情况下,很难追究母公司的法律责任。因此,母公司可利用该法律漏洞,让子公司实施违法行为,自身却置身事外,这将动摇整个市场经济的根基,扭曲市场公平竞争机制。因此,从严认定母公司的法律责任,能够对消费者提供更为有力的保护,同时也对其他企业给予警示。本案反映了欧盟竞争法对母公司责任认定的最新态度。

表5-1　C-516/15P(2017)涉及的法律

序号	原文	中文名称	所在段落
1	(Treaty establishing the European Community)EC	《欧共体条约》	1、6、46
2	(the Agreement on the European Economic Area)EEA	《欧洲经济区协议》	1、6
3	Council Regulation(EC)No 1/2003	《第1/2003号条例》	2、3、4、24、34、36、40、41、51、68、70
4	Treaty on the Functioning of the European Union(TFEU)	《欧盟运行条约》	34、46
5	the Rules of Procedure of the Court of Justice	《欧盟法院程序规则》	79、80

表5-2　C-516/15P（2017）涉及的判例

序号	判例名称	案号	所在段落
1	ArcelorMittal Luxembourg v Commission and Commission v ArcelorMittal Luxembourg and Others	C-201/09 P and C-216/09 P, EU: C: 2011: 190	20、33、49、63
2	Akzo Nobel and Akcros Chemicals v Commission	T 485/11, EU: T: 2015: 517	22
3	Total v Commission	C-597/13 P, EU: C: 2015: 613	29、52、62
4	Commission v Tomkins	C-286/11 P, EU: C: 2013: 29	30、59、60、61
5	Kendrion v Commission	C-50/12 P, EU: C: 2013: 771	31、56、58
6	FLSmidth v Commission	C-238/12 P, EU: C: 2014: 284	31
7	AC-Treuhand v Commission	C-194/14 P, EU: C: 2015: 717	38
8	Schindler Holding and Others v Commission	C-501/11 P, EU: C: 2013: 522	46
9	ETI and Others	C-280/06, EU: C: 2007: 775	47
10	General Química and Others v Commission	C-90/09 P, EU: C: 2011: 21	48
11	Akzo Nobel and Others v Commission	C-97/08 P, EU: C: 2009: 536	50、57
12	Team Relocations and Others v Commission	C-444/11 P,	51
13	Imperial Chemical Industries v Commission	48/69, EU: C: 1972: 70	52、56
14	AEG-Telefunken v Commission	107/82, EU: C: 1983: 293	52

续表

序号	判例名称	案号	所在段落
15	Team Relocations and Others v Commission	C−444/11 P, not published, EU: C: 2013: 464	52、53
16	GroupeGascogne v Commission	EU: C: 2013: 770	54
17	Evonik Degussa and AlzChem v Commission	C−155/14 P, EU: C: 2016: 446	55
18	Metsä−Serla and Others v Commission	C−294/98 P, EU: C: 2000: 632	56
19	Bolloré v Commission	C−414/12 P, not published, EU: C: 2014: 301	56
20	FLS Plast v Commission	C−243/12 P, EU: C: 2014: 2006	58

JUDGMENT OF THE COURT (Fifth Chamber)

27 April 2017 (*)

(Appeal—Agreements, decisions and concerted practices—European markets in tin stabilisers and in ESBO/esters heat stabilisers—Price fixing, market allocation and exchange of commercially sensitive information—Whether the unlawful conduct of the subsidiaries may be attributed to the parent company—Regulation (EC) No 1/2003—Article 25(1)—Limitation period for the imposition of penalties on subsidiaries—Effects on the legal position of the parent company)

In Case C-516/15 P,

APPEAL under Article 56 of the Statute of the Court of Justice of the European Union, brought on 24 September 2015,

Akzo Nobel NV, established in Amsterdam (Netherlands),

Akzo Nobel Chemicals GmbH, established in Düren (Germany),

Akzo Nobel Chemicals BV, established in Amersfoort (Netherlands),

represented by C. Swaak and R. Wesseling, advocaten,

appellants,

the other parties to the proceedings being:

Akcros Chemicals Ltd, established in Warwickshire (United Kingdom),

applicant at first instance,

European Commission, represented by V. Bottka and P. Rossi, acting as Agents,

defendant at first instance,

判例正文*

欧盟法院判决（第五法庭）
2017年4月27日

（上诉—协议、决定和协同行为—欧洲经济区内锡稳定剂行业和ESBO/酯类热稳定剂行业—固定价格、分配市场以及交换商业敏感信息—子公司的违法行为能否归因于母公司—《第1/2003号条例》—第25条第1款—对子公司的惩罚已过时限—对母公司承担法律责任的影响）

案号：C-516/15 P

2015年9月24日，上诉人根据《欧盟法院规约》第56条向本院提起上诉。

上诉人（初审原告）：

阿克苏诺贝尔公司，成立于荷兰阿姆斯特丹；

阿克苏诺贝尔化学（德国）公司，成立于德国迪伦；

阿克苏诺贝尔化学（荷兰）公司，成立于荷兰的阿默斯福特；

代理律师是C.斯瓦克和R.韦瑟林。

初审原告中的其他参与人：

艾科化学公司，成立于英格兰沃里克郡。

被上诉人（初审被告）：

欧盟委员会，代理人为V.博特卡和P.罗西。

---

* 初译者：应嘉毅；校对者：林燕萍、戴娜。

THE COURT（Fifth Chamber），

composed of J.L. da Cruz Vilaça（Rapporteur），President of the Chamber，M. Berger，A. Borg Barthet，E. Levits and F. Biltgen，Judges，

Advocate General：N. Wahl，

Registrar：A. Calot Escobar，

having regard to the written procedure，after hearing the Opinion of the Advocate General at the sitting on 21 December 2016，

gives the following：

欧盟法院（第五法庭）

由本庭庭长J. L.达·克鲁兹·维拉萨（判决书起草人）、法官M.伯格、A.博格·巴塞特、E.列维兹和F.比尔特根组成。

佐审官：N.尼瓦尔；

书记官：A.卡洛特·艾博卡；

本院在进行了书面审理程序之后，于2016年12月21日听取了佐审官的意见。

经审理，本院作出如下判决：

Judgment

1 By their appeal, Akzo Nobel NV, Akzo Nobel Chemicals GmbH and Akzo Nobel Chemicals BV ask the Court to set aside the judgment of the General Court of the European Union of 15 July 2015, Akzo Nobel and Others v Commission (T 47/10, 'the judgment under appeal', EU: T: 2015: 506), by which the General Court upheld only in part their action for, principally, annulment of Commission Decision C(2009)8682 final of 11 November 2009 relating to a proceeding under Article 81 EC and Article 53 of the EEA Agreement (Case COMP/38589—Heat Stabilisers) ('the decision at issue'), and, in the alternative, a reduction of the amount of the fines imposed on them.

Legal context

2 Article 7 of Council Regulation (EC) No 1/2003 of 16 December 2002 on the implementation of the rules on competition laid down in Articles 81 and 82 [EC] (OJ 2003 L 1, p. 1), entitled 'Finding and termination of infringement', provides in paragraph 1:

'Where the Commission, acting on a complaint or on its own initiative, finds that there is an infringement of Article 81 or of Article 82 [EC], it may by decision require the undertakings and associations of undertakings concerned to bring such infringement to an end. ... If the Commission has a legitimate interest in doing so, it may also find that an infringement has been committed in the past.'

3 Article 23 of that regulation, entitled 'Fines', provides in paragraph 2:

'The Commission may by decision impose fines on undertakings and associations of undertakings where, either intentionally or negligently:

(a) they infringe Article 81 or Article 82 [EC]...

4 Article 25 of that regulation, entitled 'Limitation periods for the imposition of penalties', provides in paragraphs 1 to 3:

'1.The powers conferred on the Commission by [Article 23] shall be subject to the following limitation periods:

判　决

1 在初审程序中，上诉人阿克苏诺贝尔公司、阿克苏诺贝尔化学（德国）公司和阿克苏诺贝尔化学（荷兰）公司，请求撤销欧盟委员会于2009年11月11日依据《欧共体条约》第81条和《欧洲经济区协议》第53条作出的第C（2009）8682号决定（COMP/38589，以下简称欧盟委员会决定），而初审法院仅支持了上诉人部分诉讼请求。因此，上诉人在上诉程序中提出如下请求：第一，撤销初审法院作出的“诺贝尔集团诉欧盟委员会案”的判决（T-47/10，EU：T：2015：506，以下简称初审法院判决）；第二，若上述请求不能得到支持，请求减少罚款数额。

法律背景

2 《关于实施〈欧共体条约〉第81条、第82条的第1/2003号条例》（OJ 2003 L 1，p. 1，以下简称《第1/2003号条例》）《第1/2003号条例》第7条“违法行为的查明及终止”第1款规定：

“当欧盟委员会依投诉采取行动或者主动采取行动而查明存在条约第81条和第82条项下的违法行为时，它可以作出决定要求企业或企业联合组织停止该违法行为……如果欧盟委员会有正当的理由，也可以对以往已经发生的违法行为作出决定。”

3 《第1/2003号条例》第23条“罚款”项下第2款规定：

“欧盟委员会可以通过决定对企业或企业协会处以罚款，如果企业或企业协会有意地或疏忽地从事了下列行为：

（a）它们违反了条约第81条或第82条……”

4 以及，《第1/2003号条例》第25条“处罚的时限”中第1款、第2款和第3款规定：

“1.第23条赋予的权力应当服从下列时限的规定：

(a) three years in the case of infringements of provisions concerning requests for information or the conduct of inspections;

(b) five years in the case of all other infringements.

2.Time shall begin to run on the day on which the infringement is committed. However, in the case of continuing or repeated infringements, time shall begin to run on the day on which the infringement ceases.

3.Any action taken by the Commission or by the competition authority of a Member State for the purpose of the investigation or proceedings in respect of an infringement shall interrupt the limitation period for the imposition of fines or periodic penalty payments...'

Background to the dispute

5 The background to the dispute is set out in paragraphs 1 to 50 of the judgment under appeal. In order to ensure that the present case is understood, it is important to note the following.

6 By the decision at issue, the Commission found that a number of undertakings had infringed Article 81 EC and Article 53 of the Agreement on the European Economic Area of 2 May 1992 (OJ 1994 L 1, p. 3) by participating in two sets of anticompetitive agreements and concerted practices covering the territory of the European Economic Area and relating, first, to the tin stabilisers sector and, secondly, to the epoxidised soybean oil and esters sector ('the ESBO/esters sector').

7 According to Article 1 of the decision at issue, both of the infringements found by the Commission, which related to those two categories of heat stabilisers, consisted of price fixing, allocation of markets through sales quotas, allocation of customers and exchange of commercially sensitive information, in particular on customers, production and sales.

8 The decision at issue states that the undertakings concerned participated in those infringements during various periods between 24 February 1987 and 21 March 2000, in relation to the tin stabilisers sector, and between 11 September 1991 and 22 March 2000, in relation to the ESBO/esters sector.

9 The decision at issue was addressed, with respect to each infringement, to 20 companies, which had either participated directly in the infringements involved or were liable as parent companies.

(a)如果违反了有关索取信息或进行检查的条款，时限是3年；

(b)如果是所有其他的违法行为，时限是5年。

2.时间从违法行为实施之日开始计算。但是，在违法行为持续发生或重复发生的情况下，时间应从违法行为结束之日起计算。

3.当欧盟委员会或成员国竞争主管部门对违法行为进行调查或采取行动时，应中断对处罚或定期支付罚款时限的计算……”

争议的背景

5 本案争议的背景载于初审法院判决的第1段至第50段。为了确保能够准确理解本案，需要重点关注以下内容。

6 欧盟委员会在其决定中写道，其在调查中发现一些企业通过签订两个不同类型的涉嫌反竞争的协议，在欧洲经济区内实施协同行为，涉及的行业包括锡稳定剂行业和环氧化大豆油酯类行业（ESBO/酯类行业）两大行业。这些企业的行为违反了《欧共体条约》第81条和《欧洲经济区协议》第53条的规定。

7 欧盟委员会决定的第1条指出，上述两类与热稳定剂行业有关的违法行为包括固定价格、通过销售配额分配市场、分配客户，以及交换关于客户、生产和销售的商业敏感信息。

8 关于实施违法行为的时间，欧盟委员会认为，在1987年2月24日至2000年3月21日的不同时间段内，相关企业在锡稳定剂行业实施了违法行为；在1991年9月11日至2000年3月22日的不同时间段内，相关企业在ESBO/酯类行业实施了违法行为。

9 欧盟委员会对20家企业的违法行为均作出了相应的处理，这20家企业或直接参与了违法行为，或作为母公司对子公司应承担相应的责任。

10 As regards attribution of the infringements, Article 1 of the decision at issue holds Akzo Nobel, Akzo Nobel Chemicals GmbH and Akcros Chemicals Ltd liable for their participation in the infringement relating to tin stabilisers from 24 February 1987 until 21 March 2000 in the case of Akzo Nobel, from 24 February 1987 until 28 June 1993 in the case of Akzo Nobel Chemicals GmbH, and from 28 June 1993 until 21 March 2000 in the case of Akcros Chemicals.

11 Similarly, Article 1 of the decision at issue holds Akzo Nobel, Akzo Nobel Chemicals BV and Akcros Chemicals liable for their participation in the infringement relating to the ESBO/esters sector from 11 September 1991 until 22 March 2000 in the case of Akzo Nobel, from 11 September 1991 until 28 June 1993 in the case of Akzo Nobel Chemicals BV, and from 28 June 1993 until 22 March 2000 in the case of Akcros Chemicals.

12 In addition, the Commission divided the participation of Akzo Nobel, Akzo Nobel Chemicals GmbH, Akzo Nobel Chemicals BV and Akcros Chemicals in the infringements into three separate infringement periods.

13 With regard to the infringement period before 28 June 1993 ('the first infringement period'), the Commission found that some companies, which were indirectly wholly owned by Akzo NV, which became Akzo Nobel, had participated directly in the infringements, namely Akzo Nobel Chemicals GmbH, for the infringement relating to tin stabilisers, and Akzo Nobel Chemicals BV, for the infringement relating to the ESBO/esters sector.

14 With regard to the second infringement period, from 28 June 1993 to 2 October 1998, the Commission found that the direct participant in the infringements had been the Akcros Chemicals partnership, which had centralised the heat stabilisers production and sales activities of the Akzo Group, which did not have a legal personality in its own right.

15 With regard to the third infringement period, from 2 October 1998 to 21 March 2000, in the case of tin stabilisers, and from 2 October 1998 to 22 March 2000, in the case of the ESBO/esters sector, the Commission found that Akcros Chemicals, which had absorbed the business of the Akcros Chemicals partnership, had participated directly in the infringements.

10 关于违法行为的归责问题，欧盟委员会决定的第1条指出，关于锡稳定剂行业的违法行为，阿克苏诺贝尔公司应对1987年2月24日至2000年3月21日的违法行为负责；阿克苏诺贝尔化学（德国）公司应对1987年2月24日至1993年6月28日的违法行为负责；艾科化学公司应对1993年6月28日至2000年3月21日的违法行为负责。

11 同样地，欧盟委员会决定的第1条指出，关于ESBO/酯类行业的违法行为，阿克苏诺贝尔公司应对1991年9月11日至2001年3月22日的违法行为负责；阿克苏诺贝尔化学（德国）公司应对1991年9月11日至1993年6月28日的违法行为负责；艾科化学公司应对1993年6月28日至2000年3月22日的违法行为负责。

12 此外，欧盟委员会对阿克苏诺贝尔公司、诺贝尔化学（德国）公司、诺贝尔化学（荷兰）公司以及艾科化学公司等公司实施的违法行为的时间分为3个阶段来计算。

13 欧盟委员会将1993年6月28日之前的行为划分为"第一阶段违法期"。在这一时期内，欧盟委员会发现，阿克苏诺贝尔化学（德国）公司参与了锡稳定剂行业的违法行为，阿克苏诺贝尔化学（荷兰）公司参与了ESBO/酯类行业的违法行为。并且，这两家公司都是荷兰阿克苏公司间接全资拥有的子公司。之后，荷兰阿克苏公司变更为阿克苏诺内尔公司。①

14 第二阶段违法期是指1993年6月28日至1998年10月2日。欧盟委员会发现，在这一阶段，违法行为的直接参与者是艾科化学公司的合伙企业，该合伙企业集中了阿克苏集团的热稳定剂生产和销售活动。但这个企业不具有独立的法人资格。

15 对于锡稳定剂行业来说，第三阶段违法期是1998年10月2日至2000年3月21日；对于ESBO/酯类行业来说，第三阶段违法期是1998年10月2日至2000年3月22日。在第三阶段违法期内，欧盟委员会发现艾科化学公司兼并了其合伙企业的业务，从而直接参与了违法行为。

---

① 荷兰阿克苏公司和瑞典诺贝尔公司于1994年合并为阿克苏诺贝尔公司，也就是阿克苏诺贝尔化学（德国）公司和阿克苏诺贝尔化学（荷兰）公司的母公司。——译者注

16 Accordingly, in the decision at issue, Akzo Nobel, as the ultimate parent company of a group of companies, some of which had participated directly in the cartels, was held liable for the entire infringement period, that is to say, from 24 February 1987 until 22 March 2000.

17 As regards the attribution of the fines, Article 2 of the decision at issue states the following:

'For the [infringement] in the tin stabiliser sector ..., the following fines are imposed:

...

(4) [Akzo Nobel], Akzo Nobel Chemicals GmbH and [Akcros Chemicals] are jointly and severally liable for: EUR 1 580 000;

...

(6) [Akzo Nobel] and Akzo Nobel Chemicals GmbH are jointly and severally liable for: EUR 9 820 000;

(7) [Akzo Nobel] is liable for: EUR 1 432 700;

...

For the [infringement] in the ESBO/esters sector ..., the following fines are imposed:

...

(21) [Akzo Nobel], Akzo Nobel Chemicals BV and [Akcros Chemicals] are jointly and severally liable for: EUR 2 033 000;

...

(23) [Akzo Nobel] and Akzo Nobel Chemicals BV are jointly and severally [liable] for: EUR 3 467 000;

(24) [Akzo Nobel] is liable for: EUR 2 215 303;

...'

18 By decision of the Commission of 30 June 2011, the decision at issue was amended to the extent that it was addressed to Akzo Nobel and to Akcros Chemicals ('the amending decision').

16 因此，欧盟委员会决定认为，由于阿克苏诺贝尔公司的众多子公司直接参与了卡特尔，阿克苏诺贝尔公司作为这些公司的母公司，应当对整个3个阶段违法期内（1987年2月24日至2000年3月22日）的违法行为承担责任。

17 关于罚款的归因问题，欧盟委员会决定的第2条陈述如下：

针对锡稳定剂行业的违法行为，作出如下罚款决定：

……

（4）阿克苏诺贝尔公司、阿克苏诺贝尔化学（德国）公司 和艾科化学公司承担连带责任，罚款158万欧元；

……

（6）阿克苏诺贝尔公司和阿克苏诺贝尔化学（德国）公司承担连带责任，罚款982万欧元；

（7）阿克苏诺贝尔公司单独罚款1 432 700欧元；

……

针对ESBO/酯类行业的违法行为，作出如下罚款决定：

……

（21）阿克苏诺贝尔公司，阿克苏诺贝尔化学（荷兰）公司和艾科化学公司承担连带责任，罚款2 033 000欧元；

……

（23）阿克苏诺贝尔公司和阿克苏诺贝尔化学（荷兰）公司承担连带责任，罚款3 467 000欧元；

（24）阿克苏诺贝尔公司单独罚款2 215 303欧元；

……

18 欧盟委员会于2011年6月30日作出决定（以下简称修正决定），修改了针对阿克苏诺贝尔公司和艾科化学公司的处理结果。

19 In recital 1 of the amending decision, the Commission recalled that it had imposed fines in the decision at issue on Akzo Nobel and Akcros Chemicals 'jointly and severally' with Elementis plc, Elementis Holdings Limited and Elementis Services Limited.

20 In recital 2 of the amending decision, the Commission stated that, in the light of the judgment of 29 March2011, ArcelorMittal Luxembourg v Commission and Commission v ArcelorMittal Luxembourg and Others（C–201/09 P and C–216/09 P, EU：C：2011：190）, it had decided to repeal the decision at issue to the extent that it was addressed, inter alia, to Elementis and Elementis Holdings Limited.

21 Accordingly, the Commission amended the decision at issue to the extent that it was addressed to Akzo Nobel and Akcros Chemicals in so far as they had been held jointly and severally liable with Elementis for the fines imposed.

22 By application lodged at the General Court Registry on 12 September 2011, Akzo Nobel and Akcros Chemicals brought an action against the amending decision. That decision was annulled by the General Court by judgment of 15 July 2015, Akzo Nobel and Akcros Chemicals v Commission（T–485/11, EU：T：2015：517）.

The procedure before the General Court and the judgment under appeal

23 By application lodged at the General Court Registry on 27 January 2010, Akzo Nobel, Akzo Nobel Chemicals GmbH, Akzo Nobel Chemicals BV and Akcros Chemicals sought annulment of the decision at issue and, in the alternative, a reduction of the fines that had been imposed on them.

24 In support of their action, those companies put forward five pleas in law, the first of which alleged infringements of the rules on limitation. In the first part of the first plea, alleging infringement of Article 25（1）（b）of Regulation No 1/2003, they submitted

that the Commission could no longer take action against Akzo Nobel Chemicals GmbH and Akzo Nobel Chemicals BV from 28 June 1998, since their participation in the infringements had ended on 28 June 1993. In consequence, neither they, nor Akzo Nobel, as their parent company, could be held liable for the first infringement period.

19 在修正决定的第一部分中，欧盟委员会重申，其已经在欧盟委员会决定中对阿克苏诺贝尔公司和艾科化学公司处以罚款，并由Elementis有限公司、Elementis控股公司和Elementis 服务有限公司3家公司承担连带责任。

20 在修正决定的第二部分中，欧盟委员会表示，参考欧盟法院于2011年3月29日作出的“卢森堡荷兰安赛乐米塔尔公司与欧盟委员会互诉案”（C-201/09 P和C-216/09 P, EU: C: 2011: 190）判决，其撤销了对Elementis公司 和 Elementis控股公司的处罚决定。

21 此前欧盟委员认定阿克苏诺贝尔公司、艾科化学公司和Elementis公司承担连带责任，因为现在撤销了对Elementis公司的处罚，故欧盟委员会对阿克苏诺贝尔公司和艾科化学公司的处罚作了相应修改。

22 阿克苏诺贝尔公司和艾科化学公司于2011年9月12日向初审法院针对欧盟委员会的修正决定提起诉讼。2015年7月15日，初审法院对“阿克苏诺贝尔公司和艾科化学公司诉欧盟委员会案”（T-485/11, EU: T: 2015: 517）作出判决，撤销了欧盟委员会的修正决定。

初审法院的审理程序及判决

23 2010年1月27日，阿克苏诺贝尔公司、阿克苏诺贝尔化学（德国）公司、阿克苏诺贝尔化学（荷兰）公司和艾科化学公司等在初审法院提起诉讼，请求撤销欧盟委员会的决定，或者减少他们的罚款金额。

24 上述公司提出了5项理由支持其诉请，第1项理由是欧盟委员会的处罚决定违反了时效规则。在第1项理由的第一部分中，他们声称阿克苏诺贝尔化学（德国）公司和阿克苏诺贝尔化学（荷兰）公司参与的违法行为在1993年6月28日已经结束了，根据《第1/2003号条例》第25条第1款b项的规定，欧盟委员会从1998年6月28日起不能再对其进行处罚。因此，阿克苏诺贝尔化学（德国）公司和阿克苏诺贝尔化学（荷兰）公司以及他们的母公司阿克苏诺贝尔公司均不应对这一段违法期内作出的违法行为负责。

25 By the judgment under appeal, the General Court annulled Article 2(4),(6),(21) and (23) of the decision at issue in respect of the fines imposed on Akzo Nobel Chemicals GmbH and Akzo Nobel Chemicals BV for the first infringement period because the limitation period had expired, and dismissed the action as to the remainder.

Forms of order sought

26 The appellants claim that the Court should:

–principally, set aside the judgment under appeal in so far as it holds that liability for the fines originally imposed on Akzo Nobel Chemicals GmbH and Akzo Nobel Chemicals BV for their participation in the infringements can still be attributed to Akzo Nobel after the annulment of those fines by the General Court;

–annul the decision at issue in so far as it establishes the participation of Akzo Nobel Chemicals GmbH and Akzo Nobel Chemicals BV in the infringements, and in particular Article 1(1)(b) and Article 1(2)(b) thereof;

–annul the decision at issue in so far as it attributes liability to, and/or imposes a fine on, Akzo Nobel on account of the unlawful conduct of Akzo Nobel Chemicals GmbH and Akzo Nobel Chemicals BV, and in particular Article 1(1)(a) for the period from 24 February 1987 to 28 June 1993 and Article 1(2)(a) for the period from 11 September 1991 to 28 June 1993 and/or Article 2(6) and (23);

–in the alternative, set aside the judgment under appeal and refer the case back to the General Court;

–order the Commission to pay the costs.

27 The Commission contends that the appeal should be dismissed and the appellants ordered to pay the costs.

25 在初审程序中，初审法院考虑到时效已过的原因，撤销了欧盟委员会决定中对于阿克苏诺贝尔化学（德国）公司和阿克苏诺贝尔化学（荷兰）公司第一段违法期的处罚，这些处罚决定分别载于欧盟委员会决定的第2条第4项、第6项、第21项以及第23项。除此之外，初审法院驳回了上诉人的其他诉讼请求。

提交到欧盟法院的诉讼请求

26 之后，上诉人向欧盟法院提出如下诉讼请求：

——驳回初审法院的判决。因为初审法院判决认为原先对阿克苏诺贝尔化学（德国）公司和阿克苏诺贝尔化学（荷兰）公司的处罚是错误的，所以，初审法院撤销了上述处罚。但初审法院仍然没有撤销对母公司阿克苏诺贝尔公司的处罚决定。

——撤销欧盟委员会关于认定阿克苏诺贝尔化学（德国）公司和阿克苏诺贝尔化学（荷兰）公司参与实施违法行为的决定，特别是欧盟委员会决定中的第1条第1款b项和第1条第2款b项。

——撤销欧盟委员会关于认定阿克苏诺贝尔化学（德国）公司和阿克苏诺贝尔化学（荷兰）公司的违法行为归因于母公司阿克苏诺贝尔公司的决定，以及/或者要求阿克苏诺贝尔公司承担相应的罚款，特别是欧盟委员会决定中的第1条第1款a项（针对1987年2月24日至1993年6月28日的违法行为）、第1条第2款a项（针对1991年9月11日至1993年6月28日的违法行为）及/或第2条第6款和第23款。

——或者，撤销初审法院判决，并将案件发回初审法院重审。

——判决欧盟委员会支付诉讼费用。

27 欧盟委员会认为，上诉法院应驳回所有的上诉请求，并判决上诉人承担相关费用。

The appeal

28 By their single ground of appeal, the appellants claim, in essence, that the General Court infringed the rules concerning the liability of parent companies for the unlawful conduct of their subsidiaries.

Arguments of the parties

29 The appellants note that the Court of Justice recently confirmed, in its judgment of 17 September 2015, Total v Commission (C–597/13 P, EU: C: 2015: 613), that, where the liability of a parent company is derived entirely from that of its subsidiary, the liability of the former cannot exceed that of the latter. In such situations, where the parent company has lodged an appeal with the same object as the subsidiary's, the parent company must benefit from the partial or full annulment of the fine imposed on the subsidiary.

30 Thus, the annulment of the fines imposed on Akzo Nobel Chemicals GmbH and Akzo Nobel Chemicals BV should have led to the annulment of the fine imposed on Akzo Nobel, as parent company, for the first infringement period, since that fine was imposed on it only on account of its subsidiaries' direct participation in the infringements. Akzo Nobel's liability was therefore purely derivative of that of its subsidiaries, within the meaning of the judgment of 22 January 2013, Commission v Tomkins (C–286/11 P, EU: C: 2013: 29).

31 They submit, in that regard, that the principle that a parent company's liability cannot exceed that of its subsidiaries seems to have been overlooked in the judgments of 26 November 2013, Kendrion v Commission (C–50/12 P, EU: C: 2013: 771), and of 30 April 2014, FLSmidth v Commission (C–238/12 P, EU: C: 2014: 284). However, as a general rule, the Court's reasoning is based on the premiss that, in a situation where the liability of the parent company is wholly derived from the actions of its subsidiary, to apply, in respect of the parent company, a fine which exceeds that for which its subsidiary is ultimately liable is tantamount to imposing a portion of a fine for which there is no legal basis.

上诉

28 上诉人主要一个上诉依据是，初审法院从本质上错误地适用了关于由母公司为其子公司的违法行为承担责任这一规则。

争议双方的观点

29 上诉人提出，欧盟法院在“道达尔公司诉欧盟委员会案”的判决中（参见判例：Total v Commission, C-597/13 P, EU: C: 2015: 613, 2015年9月17日）确认，若母公司要对子公司的行为完全负责，则母公司的责任不可能大于子公司的责任。当子公司因其被判承担责任而提出上诉，且母公司也因同样的理由提出上诉时，若撤销子公司部分或全部罚款的话，母公司也应相应减轻部分或全部罚款。

30 因此，当初审法院撤销了对阿克苏诺贝尔化学（德国）公司和阿克苏诺贝尔化学（荷兰）公司的罚款，便应同时撤销对母公司阿克苏诺贝尔公司的罚款。因为在第一阶段违法期内，母公司完全是因为其子公司直接参与实施了违法行为而被罚款。可见，母公司所承担的责任完全是由子公司的责任所衍生出来的，这与欧盟法院的“欧盟委员会诉汤金斯公司案”（参见判例：Commission v Tomkins, C-286/11 P, EU: C: 2013: 29, 2013年1月22日）说理部分是一致的。

31 对这一问题，上诉人提出欧盟法院作出的“肯德里安公司诉欧盟委员会”案判决（参见判例：C-50/12 P, EU: C: 2013: 771, 2013年11月26日）和“FLSmidth公司诉欧盟委员会案”判决（参见判例：C-238/12 P, EU: C: 2014: 284, 2014年4月30日）忽略了这样一个一般原则，即母公司所承担的责任不能超过其子公司所承担的责任。作为一项原则，法院的推理逻辑应该是：当母公司的责任完全来自其子公司的违法行为的情况下，如对母公司的处罚超过其子公司所承担责任的罚款，这就意味着这些超过部分的罚款是没有法律依据的。

32 The appellants submit that the application of the principle according to which the liability of a parent company cannot exceed that of its subsidiary is of particular importance in the present case since the cancellation of the fines imposed on Akzo Nobel Chemicals GmbH and Akzo Nobel Chemicals BV should have led to the annulment of the whole of the decision at issue vis-à-vis those two companies.

33 On that point, the appellants note that, following delivery of the judgment of 29 March 2011, ArcelorMittal Luxembourg v Commission and Commission v ArcelorMittal Luxembourg and Others (C-201/09 P and C-216/09 P, EU: C: 2011: 190), the Commission was confronted with the fact that its power to impose a fine on Elementis and on Ciba/BASF was time-barred. As was evident from the amending decision, the Commission therefore not only cancelled the fines but withdrew the finding as to any participation of those undertakings in the infringements.

34 In accordance with the principle of equal treatment, and so as to give full effect to the judgment under appeal, for the purposes of the first paragraph of Article 266 TFEU, the Commission should have adopted the same approach in relation to Akzo Nobel Chemicals GmbH and Akzo Nobel Chemicals BV. However, the decision at issue still contained a declaratory finding of an infringement addressed to those two undertakings. In addition, although Article 7 of Regulation No 1/2003 requires the Commission to have a legitimate interest for that type of finding, the Commission has no such interest in the present case, in the appellants' submission.

35 The Commission contends that the single ground of appeal put forward by the appellants should be rejected.

Findings of the Court

Admissibility

36 As regards the appellants' complaints concerning, first, the Commission's alleged breach of the principle of equal treatment and, secondly, the lack of a legitimate interest, within the meaning of the last sentence of Article 7(1) of Regulation No 1/2003, such as to justify the finding that Akzo Nobel Chemicals GmbH and Akzo Nobel Chemicals BV participated in the infringements at issue, it is apparent on examination of the file submitted to the Court that those complaints were not put forward at first instance.

32 上诉人认为，在本案中适用母公司责任不能超过其子公司责任这一原则特别重要，因为当撤销了对阿克苏诺贝尔化学（德国）公司和阿克苏诺贝尔化学（荷兰）公司的罚款责任时，事实上也就撤销了欧盟委员会针对两家公司罚款的决定。

33 上诉人进一步指出，欧盟法院对“卢森堡荷兰安赛乐米塔尔公司与欧盟委员会互诉案”（参见判例：C-201/09 P and C-216/09 P，EU：C：2011：190，2011年3月29日）作出判决后，就碰到了这样一个问题，即它对Elementis公司和Ciba/BASF公司处以罚款的权力已经丧失时效了。从修正决定中可以明显地看出，欧盟委员会不仅因此撤销了罚款，而且也撤回了关于这些企业参与违法行为的调查结果。

34 根据平等原则和《欧盟运行条约》第226条第1款，初审法院应阐明，欧盟委员会本应对阿克苏诺贝尔化学（德国）公司和阿克苏诺贝尔化学（荷兰）公司采取相同的措施。但是，欧盟委员会在其决定中仍然写了对这两家企业违法行为的调查结果。根据《第1/2003号条例》第7条的规定，欧盟委员会进行此类调查应该具有自身的合法利益，但从上诉人提交的文件材料来看，欧盟委员会在此类调查中并无相关的合法利益。

35 欧盟委员会认为，上诉人提出的这一上诉理由应该予以驳回。

本院查明的事实及观点

可采纳性

36 上诉人的上诉理由主要包含以下两点：其一，欧盟委员会违反了平等原则；其二，根据《第1/2003号条例》第7条第1款最后一段，欧盟委员会对相关调查结果缺乏合法利益。例如，为了证明阿克苏诺贝尔化学（德国）公司和阿克苏诺贝尔化学（荷兰）公司参与本案涉及的违法行为，欧盟委员会把一些调查结果的材料提交给初审法院，而上诉人在初审程序中并未提出该等请求。

37 The appellants merely claimed before the General Court that, in view of the expiry of the limitation period with respect to Akzo Nobel Chemicals GmbH and Akzo Nobel Chemicals BV, those companies could not be held liable.

38 According to settled case-law, to allow a party to put forward for the first time before the Court of Justice pleas and arguments which it did not raise before the General Court would be to authorise it to bring before the Court of Justice, whose jurisdiction in appeals is limited, a case of wider ambit than that which came before the General Court. In an appeal, the Court's jurisdiction is thus confined to examining the assessment by the General Court of the pleas and arguments aired before it (see, in particular, judgment of 22 October 2015, AC-Treuhand v Commission, C-194/14 P, EU:C:2015:717, paragraph 54).

39 These complaints put forward by the appellants must, therefore, be rejected as inadmissible.

Substance

40 By the judgment under appeal, the General Court accepted the appellants' arguments in so far as they maintained that Article 25(1)(b) of Regulation No 1/2003 prevented the Commission from imposing fines on Akzo Nobel Chemicals GmbH and Akzo Nobel Chemicals BV. The General Court therefore annulled Article 2(4), (6), (21) and (23) of the decision at issue in respect of the fines imposed on those companies for the first infringement period because the limitation period had expired.

41 The General Court stated, in essence, in paragraphs 121, 123 and 124 of the judgment under appeal, that the Commission's first actions for the purpose of the investigation or proceedings in respect of the infringements, within the meaning of Article 25(3) of Regulation No 1/2003, had been taken at the beginning of 2003, and thus after the expiry, for Akzo Nobel Chemicals GmbH and Akzo Nobel Chemicals BV, of the five-year period provided for in Article 25(1)(b) of that regulation, those companies having ceased to participate in the cartels on 28 June 1993.

42 By contrast, the General Court held, in essence, in paragraphs 125 and 126 of the judgment under appeal, that although the expiry of the limitation period could be invoked by Akzo Nobel Chemicals GmbH and Akzo Nobel Chemicals BV and had the effect of ensuring that they avoided penalties, it had no bearing on the liability of their parent company with regard to the first infringement period.

37 上诉人在初审法院审理中仅提出，鉴于针对阿克苏诺贝尔化学（德国）公司和阿克苏诺贝尔化学（荷兰）公司的时限已过，这两家公司不应再承担责任。

38 根据以往的判例，若允许一方当事人在欧盟法院提出其未在初审法院提出的请求或抗辩，那么该请求或抗辩应该得到批准后才能由欧盟法院审查。事实上，欧盟法院的上诉管辖权是受到限制的。若批准这种事由，会使欧盟法院对案件的审理范围大于初审法院。因此，在上诉案件中欧盟法院的管辖权局限于审查初审法院对于请求和抗辩的评判。（参见判例：AC-Treuhand v Commission，C-194/14 P，EU：C：2015：717，第54段）

39 因此，上诉人提出的这一上诉理由[①]不予采纳。本院予以驳回。

实体问题

40 上诉人提出欧盟委员会对阿克苏诺贝尔化学（德国）公司和阿克苏诺贝尔化学（荷兰）公司的罚款已经超过了时限，违反了《第1/2003号条例》的第25条第1款b项的规定。初审法院判决支持了上诉人的观点，并因时效问题已经撤销了欧盟委员会决定中的第2条第4项、第6项、第21项、第23项有关对上述两个公司在第一阶段违法期的罚款。

41 初审法院在其判决第121段、第123段和第124段中指出，欧盟委员会根据《第1/2003号条例》的第25条第3款的规定，针对相关违法行为的第一次调查是在2003年年初。因此，在欧盟委员会的处罚权已过时限后，根据《第1/2003号条例》的第25条第1款b项规定的5年诉讼时效，阿克苏诺贝尔化学（德国）公司和阿克苏诺贝尔化学（荷兰）公司确实在1993年6月28日已经停止参与卡特尔。

42 但初审法院在其判决第125段和第126段中指出，尽管对这2家公司的处罚权已过时限，可以免除他们的责任。但这一事实本身并不影响其母公司应该承担第一阶段违法期内的责任。

① 即欧盟委员会违反了平等原则。——译者注

43 In particular, the General Court held, in paragraph 126 of the judgment under appeal, that 'the mere fact that a subsidiary of a group of companies, in the sense of an economic unit, benefits from the expiry of the limitation period does not result in the parent company's liability being called into question and prevent proceedings being brought against that parent company'.

44 The appellants essentially dispute the validity of those findings of the General Court.

45 Consequently, it is necessary to consider whether the fact that the Commission's power to impose penalties on Akzo Nobel Chemicals GmbH and Akzo Nobel Chemicals BV was time-barred precluded Akzo Nobel from being held liable in respect of the first infringement period, contrary to the conclusion which the General Court reached in paragraph 126 of the judgment under appeal.

46 In this regard, it must be noted, in the first place, that the authors of the Treaties chose to use the concept of an undertaking to designate the perpetrator of an infringement of competition law, who is liable to be punished pursuant to Article 81 or 82 EC, now Article 101 or 102 TFEU (judgment of 18 July 2013, Schindler Holding and Others v Commission, C-501/11 P, EU: C: 2013: 522, paragraph 102).

47 It is apparent from the case-law of the Court of Justice that EU competition law refers to the activities of undertakings and that the concept of an undertaking covers any entity engaged in an economic activity, irrespective of its legal status and the way in which it is financed (judgment of 11 December 2007, ETI and Others, C-280/06, EU: C: 2007: 775, paragraph 38).

48 The Court has also stated that, in the same context, the term 'undertaking' must be understood as designating an economic unit even if in law that economic unit consists of several persons, natural or legal (judgment of 20 January 2011, General Química and Others v Commission, C-90/09 P, EU: C: 2011: 21, paragraph 35).

49 When such an economic entity infringes the competition rules, it is for that entity, according to the principle of personal responsibility, to answer for that infringement (judgment of 29 March 2011, ArcelorMittal Luxembourg v Commission and Commission v ArcelorMittal Luxembourg and Others, C-201/09 P and C-216/09 P, EU: C: 2011: 190, paragraph 95).

43 初审法院在其判决第126段中特别指出，集团公司旗下一个独立经济单位的子公司因时限已过而不受处罚，并不影响母公司应承担的责任，也不会影响欧盟委员会对母公司提起的调查程序。

44 上诉人对初审法院认定此类事实的合法性提出质疑。

45 因此，有必要考虑：欧盟委员会对阿克苏诺贝尔化学（德国）公司和阿克苏诺贝尔化学（荷兰）公司实施处罚的权力已经丧失时效后，这一事实能否让母公司阿克苏诺贝尔公司免于承担第一阶段的责任？这一问题与初审法院在初审判决中第126段的结论相悖。

46 第一，首先必须指出，条约的起草人以“企业”这一概念统称违反竞争法的所有侵权人。根据《欧共体条约》第81条和第82条的规定，即现行的《欧盟运行条约》第101条或第102条的规定，这些侵权的企业将受到惩罚。（参见判例：Schindler Holding and Others v Commission, C-194/14 P, EU: C: 2015: 717，第54段，2013年7月18日）

47 从欧盟法院的判例法中可以明显看出，欧盟竞争法的适用对象是企业的活动，而且企业的概念涵盖了从事经济活动的任何实体，无论其法律属性和融资方式如何。（参见判例：ETI and Others, C-280/06, EU: C: 2007: 775，第38段，2007年12月11日）

48 欧盟法院还指出，在同一语境下，“企业”一词必须被理解为经济单位，即使在法律上这个经济单位是由几个自然人或者法人组成的。（参见判例：General Quimica and Others v Commission, C-90/09 P, EU: C: 2011: 21，第35段，2011年1月20日）

49 当一个经济实体违反了竞争规则，如果根据规则可以免除个人责任时，该经济实体也应当对违法行为承担责任。（参见判例：ArcelorMittal Luxembourg v Commission和Commission v ArcelorMittal Luxembourg and Others, C-201/09 P and C-216/09 P, EU: C: 2011: 190，第95段，2011年3月29日）

50 In the second place, the infringement of EU competition law must be imputed unequivocally to a legal person on whom fines may be imposed and to whom the statement of objections must be addressed (see, to that effect, judgment of 10 September 2009, Akzo Nobel and Others v Commission, C–97/08 P, EU: C: 2009: 536, paragraph 57).

51 Neither Article 23(2)(a) of Regulation No 1/2003 nor the case–law lays down which legal or natural person the Commission is obliged to hold responsible for the infringement or to punish by the imposition of a fine (see, to that effect, judgment of 11 July 2013, Team Relocations and Others v Commission, C–444/11 P, not published, EU: C: 2013: 464, paragraph 159).

52 By contrast, according to the settled case–law of the Court, the unlawful conduct of a subsidiary may be attributed to the parent company in particular where, although having a separate legal personality, that subsidiary does not determine independently its own conduct on the market, but essentially carries out the instructions given to it by the parent company, having regard especially to the economic, organisational and legal links between those two legal entities (see, to that effect, judgments of 14 July 1972, Imperial Chemical Industries v Commission, 48/69, EU: C: 1972: 70, paragraphs 131 to 133; of 25 October 1983, AEG–Telefunken v Commission, 107/82, EU: C: 1983: 293, paragraphs 49 to 53; of 11 July 2013, Team Relocations and Others v Commission, C–444/11 P, not published, EU: C: 2013: 464, paragraph 157; and of 17 September 2015, Total v Commission, C–597/13 P, EU: C: 2015: 613, paragraph 35).

53 That is the case because, in such a situation, the parent company and its subsidiary form a single economic unit and therefore form a single undertaking for the purposes of EU competition law (judgment of 11 July 2013, Team Relocations and Others v Commission, C–444/11 P, not published, EU: C: 2013: 464, paragraph 157).

54 On that aspect, in the particular case in which a parent company holds all or almost all of the capital in a subsidiary which has committed an infringement of the EU competition rules, there is a rebuttable presumption that that parent company actually exercises a decisive influence over its subsidiary (see, to that effect, judgment of 26 November 2013, Groupe Gascogne v Commission, EU: C: 2013: 770, paragraph 38).

50 第二，针对违反欧盟竞争法的行为，必须明确归因于相关法人，并应对该法人追究责任并进行罚款。（参见判例：Akzo Nobel and Others v Commission，C-97/08 P，EU：C：2009：536，第57段，2009年9月10日）

51 《第1/2003号条例》的第23条第2款a项和相关判例均未规定欧盟委员会有义务对哪一类行为主体（自然人或法人）追究违法责任或作出罚款处罚。（参见判例：Team Relocations and Others v Commission，C-444/11 P，未公开，EU：C：2013：464，第159段，2013年7月11日）

52 相反，根据欧盟法院以往的判例，当子公司的市场行为是基于母公司的指示而不是独立行使时，即使子公司具有独立的法人人格，考虑到母子公司之间经济、组织和法律上的关联，该子公司在市场上的非法行为也应归因于母公司。（参见判例：Imperial Chemical Industries v Commission，48/69，EU：C：1972：70，第131段至第133段，1972年7月14日；AEG-Telefunken v Commission，107/82，EU：C：1983：293，第49段至第53段，1983年10月25日；Team Relocations and Others v Commission，C-444/11 P，未公开，EU：C：2013：464，第157段，2013年7月11日；Total v Commission，C-597/13 P，EU：C：2015：613，第35段，2015年9月17日）

53 在上诉案例中，法院判决的理由是，母公司与其子公司已经组成了一个经济体，进而成为欧盟竞争法规制的一个"企业"。（参见判例：Team Relocations and Others v Commission，C-444/11 P，未公开，EU：C：2013：464，第157段，2013年7月11日）

54 本案中，子公司实施了违反欧盟竞争法的行为，而母公司持有对该子公司全部或绝大部分资本，因此可以作出这样的推论：该母公司实际上对子公司拥有绝对的控制权和影响力。（参见判例：Groupe Gascogne v Commission，EU：C：2013：770，第38段，2013年11月26日）

55 Such a presumption implies, unless it is rebutted, that the actual exercise of decisive influence by the parent company over its subsidiary is established and gives grounds for the Commission to hold the former responsible for the conduct of the latter, without having to produce any further evidence (see, to that effect, judgment of 16 June 2016, Evonik Degussa and AlzChem v Commission, C-155/14 P, EU: C: 2016: 446, paragraph 30).

56 It must be pointed out, in the third place, that, according to the well-established case-law of the Court, the parent company to which the unlawful conduct of its subsidiary is attributed is held individually liable for an infringement of the EU competition rules which it is itself deemed to have infringed, because of the decisive influence which it exercised over the subsidiary and by which it was able to determine the subsidiary's conduct on the market (see, to that effect, judgments of 14 July 1972, Imperial Chemical Industries v Commission, 48/69, EU: C: 1972: 70, paragraphs 140 and 141; of 16 November 2000, Metsä-Serla and Others v Commission, C-294/98 P, EU: C: 2000: 632, paragraphs 28 and 34; of 26 November 2013, Kendrion v Commission, C-50/12 P, EU: C: 2013: 771, paragraph 55; of 10 April 2014, Commission and Others v Siemens Österreich and Others, C-231/11 P to C-233/11 P, EU: C: 2014: 256, paragraph 49; and of 8 May 2014, Bolloré v Commission, C-414/12 P, not published, EU: C: 2014: 301, paragraph 44).

57 As has been observed in paragraph 49 of the present judgment, EU competition law is based on the principle of the personal responsibility of the economic unit which has committed the infringement. Thus, if the parent company is part of that economic unit, it is regarded as personally jointly and severally liable with the other legal persons making up that unit for the infringement committed (see, to that effect, judgment of 10 September 2009, Akzo Nobel and Others v Commission, C-97/08 P, EU: C: 2009: 536, paragraph 77).

58 That is why the joint and several liability as between two companies constituting an economic unit cannot be reduced, as regards the payment of the fine, to a type of security provided by the parent company in order to guarantee payment of the fine imposed on the subsidiary (see, to that effect, judgments of 26 November 2013, Kendrion v Commission, C-50/12 P, EU: C: 2013: 771, paragraphs 55 and 56, and of 19 June 2014, FLS Plast v Commission, C-243/12 P, EU: C: 2014: 2006, paragraph 107).

55 除非有证据对上述推论提出反驳，否则可以认为母公司对其子公司享有决定性的影响力，这足以使欧盟委员会有充分理由认为母公司对子公司的行为应该负责，且无须进一步提供其他证据。（参见判例：Evonik Degussa and AlzChem v Commission，C-155/14 P，EU：C：2016：446，第30段，2016年6月16日）

56 第三，根据欧盟法院的判例，鉴于母公司对子公司具有决定性的影响并能据此决定子公司的市场行为，故子公司违反欧盟竞争法的非法行为应归因于母公司，并由母公司对该行为承担责任。（参见判例：Imperial Chemical Industries v Commission，48/69，EU：C：1972：70，第140段至第141段，1972年7月14日；Metsä-Serla and Others v Commission，C-294/98 P，EU：C：2000：632，第28段至第34段，2000年11月16日；Kendrion v Commission案，C-50/12 P，EU：C：2013：771，第55段，2013年11月26日；Commission and Others v Siemens Österreich and Others，C-231/11 P to C-233/11 P，EU：C：2014：256，第49段，2014年4月10日；Bolloré v Commission，C-414/12 P，未公开，EU：C：2014：301，第44段，2014年5月8日）

57 正如本判决第49段所述，欧盟竞争法的原则之一，是经济单位的个人责任原则，即由实施违法行为的经济单位承担个人责任。因此，如果母公司是该经济单位的一部分，那么母公司应与组成该经济单位的其他法人一起对其违法行为承担连带责任。（参见判例：Akzo Nobel and Others v Commission，C-97/08 P，EU：C：2009：536，第77段，2009年9月10日）

58 由于母公司能为子公司缴纳罚款提供某一种担保，故不能减轻该经济单位中的任意一家公司所承担的连带责任。（参见判例：Kendrion v Commission，C-50/12 P，EU：C：2013：771，第55段至第56段，2013年11月26日；FLS Plast v Commission，C-243/12 P，EU：C：2014：2006，第107段，2014年6月19日）

59 In the fourth place, according to the case−law of the Court, in a situation in which the parent company' s liability results exclusively from the direct participation of its subsidiary in the infringement and the two companies have brought parallel actions having the same object, the General Court may, without ruling ultra petita, take account of the annulment of the finding that the subsidiary committed an infringement for a certain period and make a corresponding reduction in the amount of the fine imposed on the parent company jointly and severally with its subsidiary (see, to that effect, judgment of 22 January 2013, Commission v Tomkins, C−286/11 P, EU: C: 2013: 29, paragraphs 34, 38, 39 and 49).

60 The Court has stated in that respect, first, that, in order to hold any entity within an economic unit liable, it is necessary to prove that one entity at least has committed an infringement of the EU competition rules and that that fact be noted in a decision which has become definitive, and, secondly, that the reason for which it was found that the subsidiary had not acted unlawfully is irrelevant (see, to that effect, judgment of 22 January 2013, Commission v Tomkins, C−286/11 P, EU: C: 2013: 29, paragraphs 37 and 38).

61 It is in that context that the Court referred to the wholly derivative nature of the liability incurred by the parent company solely because of a subsidiary' s direct participation in the infringement (see, to that effect, judgment of 22 January 2013, Commission v Tomkins, C−286/11 P, EU: C: 2013: 29, paragraphs 34, 38, 43 and 49). In that situation, the parent company' s liability arises from its subsidiary' s unlawful conduct, which is attributed to the parent company in view of the economic unit formed by those companies. Consequently, the parent company' s liability necessarily depends on the facts constituting the infringement committed by its subsidiary and to which its liability is inextricably linked.

62 For the same reasons, the Court has made clear that, in a situation in which no factor individually reflects the conduct for which the parent company is held liable, the reduction of the amount of the fine imposed on the subsidiary jointly and severally with its parent company must, in principle, where the necessary procedural requirements are satisfied, be extended to the parent company (see, to that effect, judgment of 17 September 2015, Total v Commission, C−597/13 P, EU: C: 2015: 613, paragraphs 10, 37, 38, 41 and 44).

63 In the fifth place, it is apparent from the case−law of the Court that the Commission' s power to impose penalties can be time−barred vis−à−vis the subsidiary but not the parent company, even though the parent company' s liability may be entirely based on the unlawful conduct of that subsidiary (see, to that effect, judgment of 29 March 2011, ArcelorMittal Luxembourg v Commission and Commission v ArcelorMittal Luxembourgand Others, C−201/09 P and C−216/09 P, EU: C: 2011: 190, paragraphs 102, 103, 148 and 149).

59 第四，根据欧盟法院判例，如果母公司的责任是由其子公司直接参与侵权行为而导致，且母子两家公司已提起相同诉由的上诉理由，则初审法院可在不超出起诉范围的情况下，考虑撤销其对子公司在一定期间内侵权行为的认定，并相应减少对母公司因与其子公司承担连带责任而被罚款的数额。（参见判例：Commission v Tomkins，C-286/11 P，EU：C：2013：29，第34段、第38段、第39段和第49段，2013年1月22日）

60 必须强调的是，其一，为了使经济单位内的任何实体承担责任，有必要证明至少有一个实体实施过违反欧盟竞争法的行为，并且这一事实在欧盟委员会的决定中已经被认定；其二，以子公司未实施违法行动为由的抗辩理与本案的认定关系不大。（参见判例：Commission v Tomkins，C-286/11 P，EU：C：2013：29，第37段和第38段，2013年1月22日）

61 在这种情况下，母公司即使本身未参与实施违法行为，其亦须因子公司独立实施违法行为而承担责任。这种责任的性质是衍生性质的责任。（参见判例：Commission v Tomkins，C-286/11 P，EU：C：2013：29，第34段、第38段、第39段和第49段，2013年1月22日）可见，母公司承担完全衍生性质的责任是因为母子公司已经形成了单一经济实体。因此，母公司所承担的责任与其子公司所实施的违法行为这一事实是密切相关的。

62 基于同样的原因，欧盟法院认为，基于母公司承担完全衍生性质的责任，当欧盟委员会减少了对子公司的罚款金额时，只要原则上符合必要的程序规则，对母公司的罚款金额也应当相应减少。（参见判例：Total v Commission，C-597/13 P，EU：C：2015：613，第10段、第37段、第38段、第41段和第44段，2015年9月17日）

63 第五，欧盟法院在以往的判例里表明，关于时限问题，欧盟委员会对子公司的处罚权力已经丧失时效，但其对母公司的处罚权力不受时限限制，即使母公司的责任是由子公司的违法行为衍生出来的。（参见判例：ArcclorMittal Luxembourg v Commission 和 Commission v ArcelorMittal Luxembourgand Others，C-201/09 P和C-216/09P，EU：C：2011：190，第102段、第103段、第148段和第149段，2011年3月29日）

64 In the present case, it is common ground, as is evident from Article 1 of the decision at issue, that Akzo Nobel Chemicals GmbH and Akzo Nobel Chemicals BV participated directly in the cartels in question, from 24 February 1987 until 28 June 1993, in the case of the former, and from 11 September 1991 until 28 June 1993, in the case of the latter company.

65 It is also common ground that, during the first infringement period, Akzo Nobel indirectly owned the entire share capital of Akzo Nobel Chemicals GmbH and of Akzo Nobel Chemicals BV and exercised decisive influence over them, with the result that, during that infringement period, the three companies formed one and the same undertaking for the purposes of EU competition law.

66 Consequently, in accordance with the case–law referred to in paragraphs 52 to 58 of the present judgment, the unlawful actions taken by Akzo Nobel Chemicals GmbH and Akzo Nobel Chemicals BV during the first infringement period were attributed to Akzo Nobel. Akzo Nobel was thus held individually liable for actions contrary to EU competition rules which it was itself deemed to have taken during that period.

67 Furthermore, it is also undisputed in the present case that Akzo Nobel was held liable because of its participation in the infringements at issue throughout the three infringement periods, that is to say, from 24 February 1987 until 21 March 2000, in the case of the infringement relating to tin stabilisers, and from 11 September 1991 until 22 March 2000, as regards the infringement relating to the ESBO/esters sector, as the ultimate parent company of the Akzo undertaking the various legal entities of which, including Akzo Nobel Chemicals GmbH and Akzo Nobel Chemicals BV, had participated directly in the cartels.

68 It is important to note in this regard that the applicants at first instance had relied, before the General Court, on the expiry of the limitation period provided for in Article 25(1)(b) of Regulation No 1/2003 only with respect to Akzo Nobel Chemicals GmbH and Akzo Nobel Chemicals BV, on the ground that their unlawful conduct had ceased on 28 June 1993.

69 As has been noted in paragraphs 40 and 41 of the present judgment, the General Court accepted the arguments of the applicants at first instance, ruling that the Commission' s power to impose fines on Akzo Nobel Chemicals GmbH and Akzo Nobel Chemicals BV was time–barred.

64 在本案中，处罚决定第1条表明下列事实双方没有争议：阿克苏诺贝尔化学（德国）公司和阿克苏诺贝尔化学（荷兰）公司直接独立参与了相关的卡特尔，其中，阿克苏诺贝尔化学（德国）公司参与卡特尔的时间为1987年2月24日至1993年6月28日；阿克苏诺贝尔化学（荷兰）公司参与卡特尔的时间为1991年9月11日至1993年6月28日。

65 此外，还有一个没有争议的事实是，在第一阶段违法期内，阿克苏诺贝尔公司间接拥有阿克苏诺贝尔化学（德国）公司和阿克苏诺贝尔化学（荷兰）公司的全部股权，并对这两个子公司施加了决定性的影响力。由此导致的结果是，在第一阶段违法期内，这3家公司形成了一个受欧盟竞争法规制的企业。

66 因此，根据本判决第52段至第58段所述的一些判例，阿克苏诺贝尔化学（德国）公司和阿克苏诺贝尔化学（荷兰）公司在第一阶段违法期内实施的违法行动可以归责于阿克苏诺贝尔公司。因此，该期间内子公司的行为，被视为母公司阿克苏诺贝尔公司自身的行为，从而违反了欧盟竞争法，应承担相应的承担。

67 阿克苏集团由诸多法人组成，包括阿克苏诺贝尔化学（德国）公司和阿克苏诺贝尔化学（荷兰）公司，而阿克苏诺贝尔公司是阿克苏集团的最终母公司。在3个阶段违法期内，阿克苏集团具体涉及了以下两个案件：损害锡稳定剂行业案（1987年2月24日至2000年3月21日），以及损害ESBO /酯类行业案（1987年2月24日至2000年3月21日）。阿克苏公司作为最终母公司，因直接参与了卡特尔，而被追究责任。

68 值得注意的是，上诉人在初审程序中提出，依据《第1/2003号条例》的第25条第1款b项关于时限的规定，欧盟委员会无权对阿克苏诺贝尔化学（德国）公司和阿克苏诺贝尔化学（荷兰）公司作出处罚，因为他们在1993年6月28日就已经停止了违法行为。

69 正如本判决第40段和第41段所述，初审法院采纳了上诉人的抗辩，裁定欧盟委员会对阿克苏诺贝尔化学（德国）公司和阿克苏诺贝尔化学（荷兰）公司的罚款权已经丧失了时效。

70 Admittedly, as the General Court in essence underlined in paragraphs 125 and 126 of the judgment under appeal, the fact that the Commission's power to impose penalties is time-barred pursuant to Article 25(1)(b) of Regulation No 1/2003 means that a penalty can no longer be imposed on the companies in respect of which the limitation period has expired.

71 By contrast, the fact that penalties can no longer be imposed on certain companies because the limitation period has expired does not preclude another company, which is considered personally responsible and jointly and severally liable with those companies for the same anticompetitive behaviour, and in respect of which the limitation period has not expired, from having proceedings instituted against it.

72 Contrary to the appellants' contention, the fact that Akzo Nobel's liability in respect of the first infringement period arises exclusively from the direct participation of its subsidiaries in the cartels does not alter that conclusion.

73 First, the anticompetitive activities in relation to the first infringement period are nevertheless regarded as having been carried out by Akzo Nobel itself, since it formed an economic unit, within the meaning of the case-law of the European Union, with Akzo Nobel Chemicals GmbH and Akzo Nobel Chemicals BV.

74 Secondly, as the Advocate General stated, in essence, in points 58 and 59 of his Opinion, it is apparent from the case-law of the Court mentioned in paragraph 62 of the present judgment that factors specific to the parent company may justify assessing the parent company's liability and that of its subsidiary differently, even if the liability of the former is based exclusively on the unlawful conduct of the latter.

75 That is the case here, since, unlike Akzo Nobel Chemicals GmbH and Akzo Nobel Chemicals BV, whose participation in the cartels ended on 28 June 1993, Akzo Nobel, as has been noted in paragraph 67 of the present judgment, was involved in the infringements in question beyond that date, until 21 and 22 March 2000, as regards the infringement concerning the tin stabilisers sector and the infringement concerning the ESBO/esters sector, respectively.

76 Having regard to all of those considerations, it must be concluded that the General Court was fully entitled to find, in paragraph 126 of the judgment under appeal, that the fact that the Commission's power to impose penalties on Akzo Nobel Chemicals GmbH and Akzo Nobel Chemicals BV was time-barred did not preclude Akzo Nobel from being held liable in respect of the first infringement period.

70 在其判决书第125段和第126段中强调，依据《第1/2003号条例》的第25条第1款b项的规定，欧盟委员会的处罚权力已经丧失时效。即只要过了时效，欧盟委员会便没有权利对相关公司进行处罚。

71 但是，需要强调的是，已过时效而丧失处罚权并不意味对其他企业在实施同样违反竞争法的行为进行处罚，无论是个人责任还是母公司的连带责任。况且，对这些公司的处罚权时效并没有过，所以也不影响对些公司提起诉讼。

72 事实上，在第一阶段违法期内阿克苏诺贝尔公司的责任完全源于其子公司直接参与了卡特尔行为，这一事实本身并不能改变阿克苏诺贝尔公司承担责任的结论。

73 首先，在第一阶段违法期内，因为母公司阿克苏诺贝尔公司与子公司阿克苏诺贝尔化学（德国）公司、阿克苏诺贝尔化学（荷兰）公司组成了一个欧盟法意义上的经济单位，因此在这一期间内实施的有关反竞争行为，可以被认为是母公司阿克苏诺贝尔公司实施的行为。

74 其次，正如佐审官在其意见的第58点和第59点所述，基于本判决第62段提到的欧盟法院判例，因母公司独特的性质，我们能够合理地区分母公司和子公司所应承担的责任，即便是母公司基于子公司的违法行为而承担的连带责任。

75 阿克苏诺贝尔化学（德国）公司和阿克苏诺贝尔化学（荷兰）公司于1993年6月28日停止参与卡特尔。与上述2家子公司不同的是，如本判决第67段所述，母公司阿克苏诺贝尔公司在1993年6月28日之后仍然参与实施了违法行为，直至2000年3月21日（损害锡稳定剂行业的违法行为）和2000年3月22日（损害ESBO /酯类行业的违法行为）。

76 基于上述理由，我们可以得出这样的结论：初审法院有权认定欧盟委员会对阿克苏诺贝尔化学（德国）公司和阿克苏诺贝尔化学（荷兰）公司处以惩罚的权力已经丧失时效，但这并非意味着阿克苏诺贝尔公司无须对第一阶段违法期的违法行为承担责任。

77 The single ground of appeal must, therefore, be rejected as being in part inadmissible and in part unfounded.

78 It follows from all of the foregoing that the appeal must be dismissed in its entirety.

Costs

79 In accordance with Article 184(2) of the Rules of Procedure of the Court of Justice, where the appeal is unfounded, the Court is to make a decision as to the costs.

80 Under Article 138(1) of those rules of procedure, which applies to appeal proceedings by virtue of Article 184(1) thereof, the unsuccessful party is to be ordered to pay the costs if they have been applied for in the successful party's pleadings. Since the Commission has applied for costs and the appellants have been unsuccessful as regards their single ground of appeal, the appellants must be ordered to pay the costs of this appeal.

On those grounds, the Court (Fifth Chamber) hereby:

1.Dismisses the appeal;

2.Orders Akzo Nobel NV, Akzo Nobel Chemicals GmbH and Akzo Nobel Chemicals BV to pay the costs.

77 因此，上诉的唯一依据，因部分不予采纳，部分缺乏事实依据，予以驳回。

78 综上所述，上诉人的全部上诉请求予以驳回。

诉讼费用

79 由于上诉缺乏事实根据，本院将根据《欧盟法院程序规则》第184条第2款的规定，对本案的诉讼费用作出如下决定。

80 根据《欧盟法院程序规则》第138条第1款以及第184条第1款的规定，当胜诉方在诉讼请求中要求败诉方承担诉讼费用时，败诉方应承担诉讼费用。由于欧盟委员会曾请求由上诉人承担诉讼费用，且上诉人唯一的上诉依据被驳回，因此上诉人必须承担上诉的费用。

综上，本院（第五法庭）判决如下：

1.驳回上诉；

2.阿克苏诺贝尔公司、阿克苏诺贝尔化学（德国）公司和阿克苏诺贝尔化学（荷兰）公司承担上诉费用。

6

日立乐金数据存储有限公司等诉欧盟委员会

（Hitachi-LG Data Storage，Inc. and others v European Commission）

（*Case T-1/16，2019*）

案例导读*

一、案例基本信息

法　院	初审法院	判决时间	2019年7月12日
案　号	Case T 1/16		
关键词	欧洲光盘驱动器市场；特殊情形；良好行政原则；陈述理由的义务；比例原则和平等待遇原则		
当事人	原　告：日立乐金数据存储有限公司（Hitachi-LG Data Storage, Inc.） 日立乐金数据存储韩国有限公司（Hitachi-LG Data Storage Korea, Inc.） 被　告：欧盟委员会（European Commission）		

二、案例涉及的欧盟法规

（一）《欧共体条约》第81条（现为《欧盟运行条约》第101条）①第1款规定：

"1.下列行为因与内部市场相冲突而应予以禁止：一切可能影响成员国间的贸易且其目标或结果会阻碍、限制或扭曲内部市场竞争的企业之间的协定、企业联合组织的决定和协同行为，特别是：

（1）以直接或间接方式规定收购或销售价格或其他交易条件；

（2）限制或控制生产、市场、技术发展或投资；

（3）分配市场或供货渠道；

（4）对与其他商业伙伴的同等交易适用不同的条件，从而使之在竞争中处于不利地位；

（5）以其他缔约方接受附加义务为条件缔结合同，这些条件从其本

* 作者：胡海龙。

① 程卫东、李靖堃：《欧洲联盟基础条约》，社会科学文献出版社2010年版，第86页。

质上说或者根据商业惯例与此等合同的主题无关。

2.本条所禁止的任何协议或决定应自动无效。

3.但在下列情形下可宣告本条第1款不适用：

——企业之间的任何协议或任何类型的协议；

——企业联合组织的任何决定或任何类型的决定；

——任何协同行为或任何类型的协同行为。

上述措施应有助于改善产品的生产或销售，或有助于推动技术或经济进步，同时保证消费者公平分享由此带来的收益，并且做到：

（1）不对有关企业施加并非为达到这些目标所必不可少的限制；

（2）不为有关企业提供在相关产品的实质部分消除竞争的可能性。”

（二）《欧共体条约》第229条（现为《欧盟运行条约》第261条）①规定：

“欧洲议会和理事会共同或理事会单独，可根据两部条约通过的条例，赋予欧洲联盟法院在这些条例所规定的罚款事宜上的裁量权。”

（三）《2006年罚款指南》第37条规定：

“尽管指南提出了计算罚款数额的一般方法，但如果特定案件存在特殊情形，足以使得欧盟委员会排除适用计算罚款数额的一般方法也具有合法性，则可以排除适用；为了使罚款达到威慑作用，确有必要排除适用第21条规定的罚款上限，也可以排除适用罚款上限。”

三、案件事实和审理过程

本案原告日立乐金数据存储有限公司为日本日立公司与韩国乐金电子公司的合资公司，成立于2000年11月22日，专攻光存储设备代工，为业内大厂之一。2004年7月至2008年11月，飞利浦公司、建兴电子科技股份有限公司、飞利浦建兴数码

① 程卫东、李靖堃：《欧洲联盟基础条约》，社会科学文献出版社2010年版，第141页。

公司（建兴电子科技股份有限公司与飞利浦公司的合资公司）、日立乐金数据存储有限公司、日立乐金数据存储韩国有限公司、东芝三星存储技术、索尼、索尼光领株式会社和广明光电股份有限公司等企业，在戴尔公司与惠普公司光盘驱动器采购招标项目中，通过信息分享，结成价格联盟，哄抬标价。欧盟委员会经调查，认为这些企业通过价格协同行为参与了欧洲经济区光盘驱动器行业的单一、持续的卡特尔，违反了《欧盟运行条约》第101条和《欧洲经济区协定》第53条的规定，并于2015年10月21日对包括本案两原告在内的涉事企业作出第C（2015）7135号最终罚款决定。本案两原告遂于2016年1月4日向初审法院提起诉讼，请求初审法院行使罚款数额裁量权，部分变更欧盟委员会决定，降低罚款数额。初审法院第五法庭于2019年7月12日作出判决，驳回原告的全部诉讼请求。

四、争议焦点和主要法律观点

本案有4个争议焦点。

第一，关于欧盟委员会是否未履行说明理由的义务。原告认为欧盟委员会应考虑本案存在的特殊情形，可以适用《2006年罚款指南》中的例外条款，而排除适用罚款数额计算的一般方法。但欧盟委员会在行政程序或决定中对此未作回应，违反了说明理由的义务。对此，初审法院认为，欧盟委员会说明理由的义务并没有要求其披露在行政程序中处理的所有事实和法律问题。尤其是在确定卡特尔案件当事人的罚款数额时，欧盟委员会在其决定中只要披露确定违法行为严重性及其持续时间的考量因素，即可认为其已经履行了说明理由的义务，而无须披露与罚款计算方法有关的所有数据。本案中，欧盟委员会认为，本案情况并不符合《2006年罚款指南》第37条规定的例外特殊情形，因此选择适用一般方法来计算对原告的罚款数额。所以，欧盟委员会只需在其决定中说明与其计算得出罚款数额的方法相关的因素，而无须说明其在计算中未作考量的因素，特别是欧盟委员会也无须说明其没有适用《2006年罚款指南》第37条规定的例外情形的理由。欧盟委员会没有义务对有关各方所提出的所有主张一一表明其立场。欧盟委员会只要列出所有其在作出决定时考量的事实和法律因素就足够了。

第二，欧盟委员会是否违反良好行政原则。原告指出，欧盟委员会没有就他们关于排除适用计算罚款数额一般方法的申请向咨询委员会或欧盟委员会的委员们征求意见，而征求意见是作出罚款决定前所必经的基本程序。初审法院经审理后认为，本案中，欧盟委员会通过其罚款决定之前，曾于2015年10月5日和15日两次征求咨询委员会的意见。欧盟委员会也已经根据《第1/2003号条例》第14条第3款的规定将一整套本案的相关文件递交给了咨询委员会。所以，咨询委员会已获悉欧盟委员会对该卡特尔进行的查处程序中涉及的主要事实和法律要点，特别是已经了解到相关市场、各相关企业、异议、卡特尔行为持续时间、罚款的计算方法和计算过程以及各相关企业对欧盟委员会异议声明的答复意见。原告提出本案存在特殊情形而向欧盟委员会申请减轻罚款数额，欧盟委员会没有将此申请向咨询委员会征求意见，欧盟委员会的该行为并未违反良好行政原则。事实上，初审法院认为欧盟委员会在查处卡特尔的行政程序中已足够勤勉，因为欧盟委员会：（1）在咨询委员会就罚款决定的初步草案提出书面意见之前，听取并审查了原告的意见；（2）与咨询委员会交流了其依据《第1/2003号条例》第14条第3款计算罚款数额的最重要文件及相关信息。

第三，欧盟委员会在计算罚款数额的时候，未考虑本案的特殊情形，未适用《2006年罚款指南》第37条规定的例外条款，是否构成法律适用错误。初审法院认为，只有当某一案件存在特殊情形，或确有必要使罚款达到威慑性，足以使得欧盟委员会排除适用计算罚款数额的一般方法具备合法性，欧盟委员会才可能依据《2006年罚款指南》第37条的例外规定排除一般计算方法的适用，也就是减少原告的罚款数额。原告声称，本案总共存在3种特殊情形，因此应适用《2006年罚款指南》第37条的例外规则。这3种特殊情形分别是：（1）原告的大部分收入都来自销售单一产品——光盘驱动器；（2）接近销售额10%上限的罚款数额对原告而言打击尤其严重，因为他们是唯一在被罚款之后仍决定继续在光盘驱动器市场上经营的企业，所以他们的总营业额才相对较高；（3）原告声称，鉴于他们依赖母公司，他们的财务状况岌岌可危，不得不进行重组。关于第一点，初审法院认为，原告业务的单一性与评估罚款数额计算方法的合法性无关，欧盟委员会在评估卡特尔行为的严重性时，不必将原告业务的单一性这一因素纳入考量范围；关于第二点，初审法院认为，原告是唯一被罚款后仍决定继续在光盘驱动器市场上经营的企业这一事实，仅与其商业战略有关，而不能成为质疑欧盟委员会罚款数额计算方法合法性的依据；关于第三点，初审法院认为，在确定卡特尔企业的罚款数额时，欧盟委员会没有义务将企业的不良财务状况纳入考量范围，因为如果要求欧盟委员会承担这种义务则意味着给予最不适应市场状况的企业以不正当的竞争优势。另外，尽管原告认为必须对其提出的3种“特殊情形”进行综合评估，以确定是否有理由减少其罚款数额，但鉴于每种情形就其本身而言，都不能证明减少罚款数额具有合理性，所以也无法得出综合这3种情形可以改变初审法院的认定结论。

第四，关于欧盟委员会是否违反了比例原则和平等待遇原则。原告认为，欧盟委员会基于10%罚款上限而减轻了TSST的罚款数额，客观上缩小了原告的罚款数额与TSST罚款数额的差距，使卡特尔成员之间的区分度不足，违反了平等待遇原则和比例原则，为了遵循比例原则应该对原告采取不同于一般的罚款计算方法从而降低罚款数额。初审法院驳回了原告的该项理由。初审法院认为，对TSST适用10%的上限缩小了对TSST的罚款数额与对原告的罚款数额之间的差距，这一事实本身并不能证明降低原告的罚款数额就符合平等待遇原则和比例原则。事实上，这一结果仅是两家企业之间营业额存在的巨大差异造成的，而这正是应用10%上限时所允许考量的因素。初审法院不能以为了更好地对原告的罚款与对其他卡特尔成员企业的罚款作出区分为由，对原告采用不同的罚款计算方法，因为这种区分是没有必要的，并且如果这样做将使罚款的威慑作用减弱，反而赋予了原告不公平的竞争优势。在罚款数额的计算上，不能通过采用不同的计算方法来歧视任何一个违反《欧盟运行条约》第101条第1款规定而参与价格协定或协同行动的卡特尔企业。

五、本案的意义及其启示

本案的意义可以从反垄断执法机构与执法对象两个角度来分析。

从反垄断执法机构的角度来看，应细化执行程序，提高透明度，增强反垄断罚款的确定性。我国《反垄断法》第46条第1款规定：经营者违反本法规定，达成并实施垄断协议的，由反垄断执法机构责令停止违法行为，没收违法所得，并处上一年度销售额1%以上10%以下的罚款；尚未实施所达成的垄断协议的，可以处50万元以下的罚款。但在具体的实施中，据调查，[①]反垄断执法机构在有关“上一年度”“销售额”等确定罚款基数的关键口径上存在较大的不确定性，同时在处罚幅度上，对于“1%以下10%以下”的尺度把握在个案中也存在较大的随意性，未能充分体现平等待遇与比例原则，相关理由表述含糊，自由裁量权行使标准不清，影响罚款决定的可信度与权威性。从本案可以看出，欧盟委员会罚款的设定程序就要完善得多，对于罚款基数的确定方法、理由，相关比例的确定，每一个参与者行为性质、减免因素以及最终罚款数额的确定，均有详细的陈述，值得参考与学习。

就作为反垄断执法对象的经营者而言，则应通过与反垄断执法机构的积极配合，争取豁免。本案中，一方面，原告方试图以自身的业务单一性、受罚之后继续在相关市场经营以及财务困难等因素，请求降低罚款数额，但未得到欧盟欧盟委员会与法院的认可；另一方面，飞利浦公司、建兴电子科技股份有限公司以及其与飞利浦公司的合资公司飞利浦建兴数码公司则因与欧盟委员会的积极配合得以全额免除罚款，原告等公司也因配合时机、对调查的贡献等的不同获得了不同程度的减免。我国《反垄断法》第46条第2款规定：“经营者主动向反垄断执法机构报告达成垄断协议的有关情况并提供重要证据的，反垄断执法机构可以酌情减轻或者免除对该经营者的处罚。”可见，除非经营者有明确的证据可以证明反垄断执法机构存在程序和法律适用上的缺陷或瑕疵，否则以配合换取豁免应是最为明智的出路。

① 王健：《追寻反垄断罚款的确定性》，载《法学》2016年第12期。

表6-1　T 1/16涉及的法律

序号	原文	中文名称	所在段落
1	Treaty on the Functioning of the European Union（TFEU）	《欧盟运行条约》	12、25、37、39、41、49、52、53、54、55、63、65、74、126、151
2	The Agreement on the European Economic Area（EEA）	《欧洲经济区协定》	12、25、35、37、41、70
3	Council Regulation No 1/2003 of 16 December 2002 on the implementation of the rules on competition laid down in Articles 81［EC］and 82［EC］	《关于实施〈欧共体条约〉第81、82条的第1/2003号条例》	17、39、69、73、87、88、89、90、91、95、127、137
4	Guidelines on the method of setting fines imposed pursuant to Article 23（2）（a）of Regulation（EC）No 1/2003	《关于依据〈第1/2003号条例〉第23条第2款a项设定罚款方法的指南》	17、48、51、58、59、61、69、70、71、72、73、77、78、79、80、81、82、93、99、101、103、104、105、107、110、111、116、120、122、124、127、129、132、136、141、142、147、150、152

表6-2　T 1/16涉及的判例

序号	判例名称	案号	所在段落
1	FNICGV v Commission	EU：T：2004：326	53、54、55
2	KME Germany and Others v Commission	EU：C：2011：816	56
3	Telefónica and Telefónica de España v Commission	EU：C：2014：2062	56
4	RWE and RWE Dea v Commission	EU：T：2014：627	56

续表

序号	判例名称	案号	所在段落
5	Sasol and Others v Commission,	EU: T: 2014: 628	56
6	Esso and Others v Commission	EU: T: 2014: 630	56
7	Commission v Edison	EU: C: 2013: 798	63、64、65
8	Volkswagen v Commission	EU: C: 2003: 473	65、74、75
9	AC-Treuhand v Commission	EU: T: 2014: 59	79
10	Printeos and Others v Commission	EU: T: 2016: 722	80
11	La Cinq v Commission	EU: T: 1992: 5	86
12	Limburgse Vinyl Maatschappij and Others v Commission	EU: C: 2002: 582	94
13	Dansk Rørindustri and Others v Commission	EU: C: 2005: 408	104、121
14	Goldfish and Others v Commission	EU: T: 2016: 455	104、121
15	Saint-Gobain Gyproc Belgium v Commission	EU: T: 2008: 252	109、110
16	Musique Diffusion française and Others v Commission	EU: C: 1983: 158	110
17	British Steel v Commission	EU: T: 1999: 52	110
18	Infineon Technologies v Commission	EU: T: 2016: 737	112
19	Kokott in Pilkington Group and Others v Commission	EU: C: 2016: 258	112
20	Pilkington Group and Others v Commission	EU: C: 2016: 631	113

续表

序号	判例名称	案号	所在段落
21	GlaxoSmithKline Services and Others v Commission and Others	EU: C: 2009: 610	126
22	LG Display and LG Display Taiwan v Commission	EU: C: 2015: 258	135
23	Panasonic and MT Picture Display v Commission	EU: T: 2015: 612	143
24	Putters v Commission	EU: T: 2011: 289	150
25	Alliance One International and Standard Commercial Tobacco v Commission and Commission v Alliance One International and Others	EU: C: 2012: 479	151

JUDGMENT OF THE General COURT (Fifth Chamber)

12 July 2019 (*)

(Competition—Agreements, decisions and concerted practices—Market for optical disk drives—Decision finding an infringement of Article 101 TFEU and Article 53 of the EEA Agreement—Collusive agreements relating to procurement events organised by two computer manufacturers—Unlimited jurisdiction — Infringement of the principle of good administration — Obligation to state reasons — Point 37 of the 2006 Guidelines on the method of setting fines — Particular circumstances — Error of law)

In Case T-1/15,

Hitachi-LG Data Storage, Inc., established in Tokyo (Japan),

Hitachi-LG Data Storage Korea, Inc., established in Seoul (South Korea),

represented by L. Gyselen and N. Ersbøll, lawyers,

applicants,

v.

European Commission, represented initially by A. Biolan, M. Farley, C. Giolito and F. van Schaik, and subsequently by A. Biolan, M. Farley and F. van Schaik, acting as Agents,

defendant,

判例正文*

初审法院（第五法庭）
2019年7月12日

（竞争—协议、决定和协同行为—光盘驱动器市场—对违反《欧盟运行条约》第101条和《欧洲经济区协议》第53条的卡特尔作出的决定—关于两个计算机制造商所组织的采购活动的卡特尔协议—罚款数额裁量权—良好行政原则[①]—说明理由的义务—《2006年罚款指南》第37条—特殊情形—法律适用错误）

案号：T-1/15

原告：

日立乐金数据存储有限公司，成立于（日本）东京；

日立乐金数据存储韩国有限公司，成立于（韩国）首尔；

代理律师为L.吉塞伦和N.埃斯伯尔。

被告：

欧盟委员会。

代理人：先是A.彼欧兰、M.费莱、C.吉欧利特和F.范·舍克，后变更为仅有A.彼欧兰、M.费莱和F.范·舍克。

---

* 初译者：胡海龙；校对者：林燕萍、戴娜。

① 良好行政原则是一项欧盟行政法基本原则，其内容多样，无一致定义，如保障相对人知情权、听取意见的权利以及行政机关对其决定说明理由等义务均可被纳入该原则的范围。2000年12月于法国尼斯通过的《欧盟基本权利宪章》将公民获得良好行政的权利纳入公民基本权利之列。根据《欧盟基本权利宪章》第41条之规定，此权利主要包括：在被采取任何不利措施前享有听证的权利；在不妨碍机密、职业秘密和商业秘密的前提下获取个人卷宗的权利；行政机关就其决定应附理由之义务。——译者注

ACTION under Article 263 TFEU seeking a reduction of the amount of the fine imposed by the European Commission on the applicants in its Decision C(2015)7135 final of 21 October 2015 relating to a proceeding under Article 101 TFEU and Article 53 of the EEA Agreement(Case AT.39639—Optical Disk Drives),

原告依据《欧盟运行条约》第263条提起诉讼，请求初审法院减少欧盟委员会依据《欧盟运行条约》第101条和《欧洲经济区协定》第53条于2015年10月21日作出的第C（2005）7135号最终罚款决定（AT.39639—光盘驱动器案）（以下简称欧盟委员会决定）中对原告的罚款数额。

THE GENERAL COURT (Fifth Chamber)

composed of D. Gratsias, President, I. Labucka and I. Ulloa Rubio (Rapporteur), Judges,

Registrar: N. Schall, Administrator,

having regard to the written part of the procedure and further to the hearing on 3 May 2018,

gives the following:

初审法院(第五法庭)

由审判长D.格拉齐亚斯、法官I.拉巴卡和I.乌洛亚·卢比奥(判决书起草人)组成。

书记官:N.沙尔。

本院进行了所有书面程序后,于2018年5月3日开庭审理了本案,经审理作出如下判决:

Judgment

I. Background to the dispute

A. Applicants and relevant market

1 The applicants, Hitachi-LG Data Storage, Inc. and its subsidiary Hitachi-LG Data Storage Korea, Inc., are manufacturers and suppliers of optical disk drives ('ODDs'). In particular, Hitachi-LG Data Storage is a joint venture created by the Japanese company Hitachi, Ltd and by the Korean company LG Electronics Inc. It has operated on the market since 1 July 2001.

2 The infringement concerns ODDs used in personal computers (desktops and notebooks) ('PCs') produced by Dell Inc. and Hewlett Packard ('HP'). ODDs are also used in a wide range of other consumer appliances such as compact disc ('CD') or digital versatile disc ('DVD') players, game consoles and other electronic hardware devices (contested decision, recital 28).

3 ODDs used in PCs differ according to their size, loading mechanisms (slot or tray) and the types of discs that they can read or write. ODDs can be split into two groups: half-height ('HH') drives for desktops and slim drives for notebooks. The slim drive group includes drives that vary by size. Both HH and slim drives differ by type depending on their technical functionality (contested decision, recital 29).

4 Dell and HP are the two most important original equipment manufacturers on the global market for PCs. Those two companies use standard procurement procedures carried out on a global basis which involve, inter alia, quarterly negotiations over a worldwide price and overall purchase volumes with a limited number of pre-qualified ODD suppliers. Generally, regional issues did not play any role in ODD procurement other than that related to forecasted demand from regions affecting overall purchase volumes (contested decision, recital 32).

判 决

I.争议背景

A.原告及相关市场

1 原告日立乐金数据存储有限公司及其子公司日立乐金数据存储韩国有限公司是光盘驱动器的制造商和供应商。尤其是日立乐金数据存储有限公司，它是由日本日立公司和韩国乐金电子公司共同创建的合营企业，自2001年7月1日起即投入市场运营。

2 本案所涉卡特尔是关于在戴尔公司和惠普公司生产的个人电脑（台式机和笔记本电脑）中使用的光盘驱动器。光盘驱动器还广泛应用于其他消费类电子产品中，如CD或DVD播放器、游戏机和其他电子硬件设备（欧盟委员会决定第28段）。

3 个人电脑上使用的光盘驱动器因大小、加载机制（插槽或托盘）以及可读写光盘类型的不同而有所区别。（根据厚度）可以将光盘驱动器分成两大类：用于台式机中的半高光盘驱动器和用于笔记本电脑中的超薄光盘驱动器。超薄光盘驱动器的尺寸很多，有各种大小尺寸。半高光盘驱动器和超薄光盘驱动器又可以根据他们的技术功能分为不同的类型（欧盟委员会决定第29段）。

4 戴尔公司和惠普公司是全球个人电脑市场上最重要的两家设备生产商。这两家企业有着标准化的采购程序，这套程序在全球范围内统一适用。采购程序包括与合格光盘驱动器供应商就全球统一采购价格和采购总量进行季度谈判，合格的供应商数量是有限的。一般而言，除了有些区域的预期需求会影响到采购总量之外，区域问题在光盘驱动器采购中没有任何影响。（欧盟委员会决定第32段）

5 The procurement procedures included requests for quotations, electronic requests for quotations, internet negotiations, e-auctions and bilateral (offline) negotiations. At the close of a procurement event, customers would allocate volumes to participating ODD suppliers (to all or at least most of them, unless there was an exclusion mechanism in place) depending on their quoted prices. For example, the winning bid would receive 35% to 45% of the total market allocation for the relevant quarter, the second best 25% to 30%, the third 20% and so on. These standardised procurement procedures were used by customers' procurement teams with the purpose of achieving efficient procurement at competitive prices. To this end, they used all possible practices to stimulate the price competition between the ODD suppliers (contested decision, recital 33).

6 As regards Dell, it carried out bidding events mainly by internet negotiation. That negotiation could last for a specific period of time or end after a defined period, for example 10 minutes after the last bid, when no ODD supplier continued bidding. In certain circumstances, internet negotiations could last several hours if the bidding was more active or if the duration of the internet negotiation was extended in order to incentivise ODD suppliers to continue bidding. Conversely, even where the length of the internet negotiation was indefinite and depended on the final bid, Dell could announce at some point that the internet negotiation had closed. Dell could decide to change from a 'rank only' to a 'blind' procedure. Dell could cancel the internet negotiation if the bidding or its result were found to be unsatisfactory and run a bilateral negotiation instead. The internet negotiation process was monitored by Dell's responsible Global Commodity Managers (contested decision, recitals 34 and 37).

7 With respect to HP, the main procurement procedures used were requests for quotations and electronic requests for quotations. Both procedures were carried out online using the same platform. As regards (i) the requests for quotations, they were quarterly. They combined online and bilateral offline negotiations spread over a period of time, usually 2 weeks. ODD suppliers were invited to a round of open bidding for a specified period of time to submit their quote to the online platform or by email. Once the first round of bidding had elapsed, HP would meet with each participant and start negotiations based on the ODD supplier's bid to obtain a better bid from each supplier without disclosing the identity or the bid submitted by any other ODD supplier. As regards (ii) the electronic requests for quotations, they were normally run in the format of a reverse auction. In that format, bidders would log onto the online platform at the specified time and the auction would start at a price set by HP. Bidders entering progressively lower bids would be informed of their own rank each time a new bid was submitted. At the end of the allotted time, the ODD supplier having entered the lowest bid would win the auction and other suppliers would be ranked second and third according to their bids (contested decision, recitals 41 to 44).

5 采购程序包括报价邀请、电子报价邀请、互联网谈判、电子拍卖和双边线下谈判等方式。在采购活动结束时，除非依据事先商定的排除规则而排除在外的供应商，客户将根据价格向参与报价的光盘驱动器供应商分配采购量，即所有或至少大多数参与报价的供应商都会获得采购量。例如，最佳报价者将获得本季度总市场采购量35%至45%的份额，次优者将获得25%至30%的份额，第三名获得20%的份额……以此类推。客户的采购团队采取这些标准化采购程序的目的是以有竞争力的价格实现高效采购。为此，他们使用所有可能的做法来促进光盘驱动器供应商之间的价格竞争。（欧盟委员会决定第33段）

6 戴尔公司主要通过互联网谈判的方式进行招标。这种谈判可以持续一个特定时间段，也可以在一个指定的时间点结束。例如，在最后一个光盘驱动器供应商投标完毕的10分钟后结束。在一些特定情况下，比如，竞标活跃的时候，或者为了激励光盘驱动器供应商持续竞标而延长时间的情况下，互联网谈判可能会持续几个小时。相反，即使互联网谈判的时长并不确定且取决于最后一次投标的时间，戴尔公司也可以在某个时点宣布互联网谈判提前结束。戴尔公司有权决定将评出中标者的程序从“仅靠竞价排名”变更为“盲评”，也可以在觉得招投标过程或其结果不令人满意时，取消互联网谈判，改为进行双边谈判。互联网谈判过程由戴尔公司的全球产品经理们负责监督。（欧盟委员会决定第34段和第37段）

7 惠普公司主要采用的采购程序是报价邀请和电子报价邀请。这两个程序都是使用同一个平台在线执行的。（1）报价邀请程序，该采购程序以季度为单位进行，结合线上和线下双边谈判，持续时间通常是两周。光盘驱动器供应商们受邀在指定时间内通过在线平台或电子邮件提交报价，公开投标。第一轮投标结束后，惠普公司将与每一位参与者会面，并根据供应商的报价开始谈判，以便在不披露任何其他供应商的身份及报价的情况下，从每一位供应商处获得更好的报价。（2）电子报价邀请程序，该采购程序通常以反向拍卖的形式进行。在这种模式下，竞拍者在指定时间登录在线平台，以惠普公司设定的初始价格开始拍卖。渐次降低出价的竞拍者们将在每一次出价时知悉他们的排名。拍卖时间截止时，出价最低的供应商将赢得拍卖，其他供应商亦将根据各自的出价获得相应排名（欧盟委员会决定第41段至第44段）。

B. Administrative procedure

8 On 14 January 2009, the European Commission received a request for immunity under its Notice on Immunity from fines and reduction of fines in cartel cases (OJ 2006 C 298, p. 17)('the Leniency Notice') from Koninklijke Philips NV ('Philips'). On 29 January and 2 March 2009, that request was supplemented in order to include, alongside Philips, Lite-On IT Corporation and their joint venture Philips & Lite-On Digital Solutions Corporation ('PLDS').7 By the judgment under appeal, the General Court dismissed the action in its entirety.

9 On 29 June 2009, the Commission sent a request for information to undertakings active in the ODD sector.

10 On 30 June 2009, the Commission granted conditional immunity to Philips, Lite-On IT and PLDS.

11 On 4 and 6 August 2009, the applicants submitted an application to the Commission for a reduction of the amount of the fine under the Leniency Notice.

12 On 18 July 2012, the Commission initiated a proceeding and adopted a statement of objections against 13 ODD suppliers, including the applicants. In that statement of objections, the Commission stated, in essence, that those companies had infringed Article 101 TFEU and Article 53 of the Agreement on the European Economic Area (EEA) by participating in a cartel on ODDs from 5 February 2004 until 29 June 2009, consisting in orchestrating their conduct with respect to invitations to tender organised by two computer manufacturers, Dell and HP.

13 On the same day the Commission granted conditional immunity to the applicants.

14 On 29 and 30 November 2012, all the addressees of the statement of objections took part in a hearing before the Commission.

15 On 14 December 2012, the Commission requested all the parties to provide the relevant documents received from Dell and HP during the infringement period. All the parties replied to those requests and each was granted access to the replies provided by the other ODD suppliers.

16 On 18 February 2014, the Commission adopted two supplementary statements of objections to supplement, amend and clarify the objections addressed to certain addressees of the statement of objections as regards their liability for the alleged infringement.

B. 行政程序[①]

8 2009年1月14日，飞利浦公司根据《关于卡特尔案件罚款豁免和减轻公告》(OJ 2006 C 298，p. 17，以下简称《宽恕公告》)向欧盟委员会提出豁免申请。2009年1月29日和3月2日，欧盟委员会又收到了飞利浦公司提交的上述豁免申请的补充材料，目的是将建兴电子科技股份有限公司以及飞利浦与其成立的合资公司飞利浦建兴数码公司一并纳入豁免申请中。

9 2009年6月29日，欧盟委员会向活跃在光盘驱动器行业的各企业发征询函，要求其提供相关信息。

10 2009年6月30日，欧盟委员会给予飞利浦公司、建兴电子科技股份有限公司和飞利浦建兴数码公司附条件件的豁免。

11 2009年8月4日和6日，原告根据《宽恕公告》向欧盟委员会提交了减少罚款数额的申请。

12 2012年7月18日，欧盟委员会启动调查程序，并通过了一项针对包括原告在内的13家光盘驱动器供应商的异议声明。欧盟委员会在异议声明中表示，这些企业在2004年2月5日至2009年6月29日，参与了一个关于光盘驱动器的卡特尔，在戴尔公司和惠普公司组织的招标活动中协同行动，违反了《欧盟运行条约》第101条和《欧洲经济区协定》第53条的规定。

13 同日，欧盟委员会给予原告以附条件的豁免。

14 2012年11月29日和30日，收到异议声明的所有企业都参加了欧盟委员会组织的听证会。

15 2012年12月14日，欧盟委员会要求各企业提供其参与卡特尔期间从戴尔公司和惠普公司处收到的相关文件。各企业对此要求都作出了回复，并且每一当事方都被授权查阅其他各方提供的回复。

16 2014年2月18日，欧盟委员会通过了两份补充异议声明，以补充、修订和澄清前述异议声明中针对某些企业实施卡特尔行为应承担责任而作的陈述。

① 即欧盟委员会进行的查处该卡特尔的行政程序。——译者注

17 On 26 February 2015, the applicants requested the Commission to reduce the amount of the fine because of the 'particular circumstances' for the purpose of point 37 of the Guidelines on the method of setting fines imposed pursuant to Article 23(2)(a) of Commission Regulation (EC) No 1/2003 (OJ 2006 C 210, p. 2) ('the Guidelines').

18 On 5 March 2015, the applicants and their outside counsel met the Commission in order to present their request for a reduction of the amount of the fine.

19 On 1 June 2015, the Commission adopted another supplementary statement of objections. The purpose of this new statement of objections was to supplement the earlier statements of objections by addressing the objections set out in those statements to additional legal entities belonging to the groups of undertakings (parent companies or predecessors) which had already been addressees of the original statement of objections.

20 The addressees of the statements of objections of 18 February 2014 and 1 June 2015 made known their views to the Commission in writing but did not request a hearing.

21 On 3 June 2015, the Commission issued a letter of facts to all the parties. The addressees of the letter of facts made known their views to the Commission in writing.

22 On 14 September 2015, the applicants submitted a second request to the Commission for a reduction of the amount of the fine. The purpose of this request was to provide an update of certain data presented in their request of 26 February 2015.

23 On 18 September 2015, the applicants and their outside counsel took part in a second meeting with the Commission concerning the state of the file.

24 On 5 and 15 October 2015, the Advisory Committee on Restrictive Practices and Dominant Positions ('the Advisory Committee') was consulted by the Commission.

25 On 21 October 2015, the Commission adopted Decision C(2015) 7135 final relating to a proceeding pursuant to Article 101 TFEU and Article 53 of the EEA Agreement (Case AT.39639—Optical Disk Drives) ('the contested decision').

17 2015年2月26日，原告以其符合《2006年罚款指南》第37条规定的特殊情形为由，请求欧盟委员会减少罚款数额。

18 2015年3月5日，原告及其外部律师会见了欧盟委员会，提出了减少罚款数额的申请。

19 2015年6月1日，欧盟委员会通过了另一份补充异议声明，是对前一份异议声明的补充，这份补充异议声明发送的对象是先前一份异议声明中已列入的当事方所在集团的其他法律实体，比如，其母公司或前身。

20 收到2014年2月18日和2015年6月1日异议声明的企业以书面形式向欧盟委员会表明了他们的意见，但没有要求举行听证会。

21 2015年6月3日，欧盟委员会向所有当事方发送了一份事实征询函。事实征询函的收件人以书面形式向欧盟委员会表明了他们的意见。

22 2015年9月14日，原告向欧盟委员会提交了第二份要求减少罚款数额的申请。这份申请的目的是更新他们在2015年2月26日的豁免申请中陈述的某些数据。

23 2015年9月18日，原告及其外部律师参加了欧盟委员会就本案举行的第二次会议。

24 2015年10月5日和15日，欧盟委员会向限制竞争行为及滥用支配地位咨询委员会（以下简称咨询委员会）征询了意见。

25 2015年10月21日，欧盟委员会依据《欧盟运行条约》第101条和《欧洲经济区协定》第53条作出第C（2015）7135号最终罚款决定（AT.39639—光盘驱动器案）（以下简称欧盟委员会决定）。

C. Contested decision

1. The infringement at issue

26 In the contested decision, the Commission considered that the cartel participants had coordinated their competitive behaviour, at least between 23 June 2004 and 25 November 2008. It specified that that coordination took place through a network of parallel bilateral contacts. It stated that the cartel participants sought to accommodate their volumes on the market and ensure that the prices remained at levels higher than they would have been in the absence of those bilateral contacts (contested decision, recital 67).

27 The Commission specified, in the contested decision, that the coordination between the cartel participants concerned the customer accounts of Dell and HP, the two most important original equipment manufacturers on the global market for PCs. According to the Commission, in addition to bilateral negotiations with their ODD suppliers, Dell and HP applied standardised procurement procedures, which took place at least on a quarterly basis. The Commission stated that the cartel members used their network of bilateral contacts to manipulate those procurement procedures, thus thwarting their customers' attempts to stimulate price competition (contested decision, recital 68).

28 According to the Commission, regular exchanges of information in particular enabled the cartel members to possess a very complex knowledge of their competitors' intentions even before they had entered the procurement procedure, and therefore to foresee their competitive strategy (contested decision, recital 69).

29 The Commission added that, on a regular basis, the cartel members exchanged pricing information regarding specific customer accounts as well as information unrelated to pricing, such as existing production and supply capacity, inventory status, the qualification status, and timing of the introduction of new products or upgrades. The Commission stated that, in addition, the ODD suppliers monitored the final results of closed procurement events, that is the rank, the price and the volume obtained (contested decision, recital 70).

C.欧盟委员会作出的决定

1. 争议事项

26 欧盟委员会在其决定中认为，卡特尔成员企业至少在2004年6月23日至2008年11月25日实施了协同行为。欧盟委员会特别指出，这种协同行为是通过平行的双边联系网进行的。卡特尔成员企业设法协调各自产品的市场交易量，以确保产品价格保持在比没有这些双边联系时更高的水平上（欧盟委员会决定第67段）。

27 欧盟委员会在其决定中明确指出，卡特尔成员之间的协同行为涉及戴尔公司和惠普公司的采购账户，这两家是全球个人电脑市场上最重要的设备厂商。据欧盟委员会称，除了与光盘驱动器供应商进行双边谈判外，戴尔公司和惠普公司还采用标准化的采购程序，来完成每季度至少一次的采购。卡特尔成员利用其双边联系网操纵这些采购程序，从而挫败其客户激励供应商们竞价夺标的意图（欧盟委员会决定第68段）。

28 欧盟委员会认为，协同行为，尤其是定期信息交换使卡特尔成员能够在进入采购程序之前就对竞争对手的意图有非常深入的了解，从而预见其竞争策略（欧盟委员会决定第69段）。

29 欧盟委员会补充说明，卡特尔成员之间的定期交换的信息包括特定采购商的产品定价信息，还有一些与定价无关的信息，如现有生产和供应能力、库存状况、准入状态以及推出新产品或产品升级的时机等。此外，光盘驱动器供应商们还监测与已经结束的采购活动的最终结果相关的信息，即排名、出价和获得的采购量等（欧盟委员会决定第70段）。

30 The Commission further stated that, whilst taking into account that the cartel members must keep their contacts secret from customers, to contact each other suppliers used the means they deemed sufficiently appropriate to achieve the desired result. The Commission specified that in fact an attempt to convene a kick-off meeting to hold regular multilateral meetings between ODD suppliers had failed in 2003 after having been revealed to a customer. According to the Commission, instead, there were bilateral contacts, mostly via phone calls and, from time to time, via emails, including private (hotmail) addresses and instant messaging services, or meetings, mostly at the level of global account managers (contested decision, recital 71).

31 The Commission found that the cartel participants contacted each other regularly and that the contacts, mainly by telephone, became more frequent around the procurement events, amounting to several calls per day between some pairs of cartel participants. It stated that, generally, contacts between some pairs of cartel participants were significantly higher than between other pairs (contested decision, recital 72).

2. The applicants' liability

32 The applicants' liability was established owing to their direct participation in the cartel from 23 June 2004 until 25 November 2008, in particular for their coordination with other competitors with regard to Dell and HP (contested decision, recital 494).

3. The fine imposed on the applicants

33 As regards the calculation of the amount of the fine imposed on the applicants, the Commission relied on the Guidelines.

34 First of all, in order to determine the basic amount of the fine, the Commission considered that, in view of the considerable differences in the duration of the suppliers' participation and in order better to reflect the actual impact of the cartel, it was appropriate to use an annual average calculated on the basis of the actual value of sales made by the undertakings during the full calendar months of their respective participation in the infringement (contested decision, recital 527).

35 The Commission thus explained that the value of sales was calculated on the basis of sales of ODDs for PCs and invoiced to HP and Dell entities located in the EEA (contested decision, recital 528).

30 欧盟委员会进一步指出，考虑到必须将相互之间的联络对客户[①]保密，卡特尔成员采取了他们认为足够适当的手段来实现预期的目的。事实上，2003年光盘驱动器供应商们就企图召开一次启动会议，以建立相互间的定期多方会议机制。但这一企图因客户事先知悉相关信息而未能得逞。根据欧盟委员会的说法，此后，双边联系取代了多边联系，双边联系成为供应商们沟通信息的途径。供应商们主要通过电话，有时也通过电子邮件（包括私人hotmail邮件）、即时通信服务或者召开会议来互相交换信息，这些沟通大多在供应商的全球客户经理这一级别的员工之间进行（欧盟委员会决定第71段）。

31 欧盟委员会发现，卡特尔成员之间主要通过电话进行定期联系。这种联系在采购活动进行期间变得尤其频繁，部分卡特尔成员之间每天都有几次电话。欧盟委员会指出，总体而言，部分卡特尔成员之间的相互联系明显高于其他成员（欧盟委员会决定第72段）。

2. 原告应承担的责任

32 原告因其在2004年6月23日至2008年11月25日直接参与了卡特尔而需承担相应的法律责任，特别是原告与其他竞争对手就戴尔公司和惠普公司的采购实施了协同行为。（欧盟委员会决定第494段）

3. 对原告的罚款

33 欧盟委员会依据《2006年罚款指南》计算对原告的罚款数额。

34 首先，为了确定罚款基数，欧盟委员会认为，鉴于供应商们参与卡特尔的持续时间存在显著差异，为了能更好地反映卡特尔的实际影响，以各卡特尔成员在各自参与卡特尔期间整个日历月中的实际销售额为基础计算出各企业的平均年销售额是恰当的（欧盟委员会决定第527段）。

35 欧盟委员会进一步解释，作为计算销售额基础的光盘驱动器，必须是用于个人电脑、并向位于欧洲经济区的惠普公司和戴尔公司开具过发票的光盘驱动器（欧盟委员会决定第528段）。

---

① 此处的客户就是指戴尔公司和惠普公司，他们是本案卡特尔成员的客户。——译者注

36 The Commission further considered that, since the anticompetitive conduct with regard to HP had begun later and in order to take the evolution of the cartel into account, the relevant value of sales would be calculated separately for HP and for Dell, and that two duration multipliers would be applied (contested decision, recital 530).

37 Next, the Commission decided that, since price coordination agreements are by their very nature among the worst kind of infringements of Article 101 TFEU and Article 53 of the EEA Agreement, and since the cartel covered at least the whole of the EEA, the percentage for gravity used in this case would be 16% for all addressees of the contested decision (contested decision, recital 544).

38 Furthermore, the Commission stated that, given the circumstances of the case, it was necessary to add an amount of 16% for deterrence (contested decision, recitals 554 and 555).

39 Moreover, since the adjusted basic amount of the fine imposed on the applicants did not reach the cap of 10% of their turnover, the Commission was not required to make a fresh adjustment on the basis of Article 23 (2) of Council Regulation (EC) No 1/2003 of 16 December 2002 on the implementation of the rules on competition laid down in Articles [101] and [102 TFEU] (OJ 2003 L 1, p. 1). The adjusted basic amount of the fine imposed on the applicants, calculated according to the methodology described above, came to 8.45% of their total turnover in 2014, the business year preceding the adoption of the contested decision (contested decision, recitals 570 to 572).

40 Lastly, the applicants received a reduction of 50% of the amount of their fine for having cooperated in the investigation in the context of the Commission's leniency programme, and also partial immunity for having enabled the Commission to establish that the cartel was of longer duration (contested decision, recitals 575 and 582 to 592).

41 The operative part of the contested decision, in so far as it concerns the applicants, reads as follows:

'Article 1

The following undertakings infringed Article 101 TFEU and Article 53 of the EEA Agreement by participating, during the periods indicated, in a single and continuous infringement, which consisted of several separate infringements, in the optical disk drives sector covering the whole of the EEA, which consisted of price coordination arrangements:

...

36 欧盟委员会还指出，由于与惠普公司相关的限制竞争行为开始较晚，同时为了将卡特尔行为存在演变这一因素纳入考量范围，对惠普公司和戴尔公司的光盘驱动器销售额将分别计算，并将采用两个（不同的）持续时间乘数（欧盟委员会决定第530段）。

37 其次，欧盟委员会决定，由于价格协定性质上属于《欧盟运行条约》第101条和《欧洲经济区协定》第53条规定的最严重的违法行为，而且此卡特尔行为至少涵盖了整个欧洲经济区，所以本案中将对所有处罚对象适用重罚16%的比例（欧盟委员会决定第544段）。

38 此外，欧盟委员会指出，鉴于本案的情况，为了使罚款达到威慑作用，有必要再附加16%（欧盟委员会决定第554段和第555段）。

39 根据前述方法计算的对原告的罚款基数为2014年（欧盟委员会决定作出前一营业年度）总营业额的8.45%（欧盟委员会决定第570段至第572段）。由于调整后对原告的罚款基数未达到其总销售额10%的上限，欧盟委员会无须依据2002年12月16日《关于实施〈欧共体条约〉第81条和第82条的第1/2003号条例》（(OJ 2003 L 1, p. 1, 以下简称《第1/2003号条例》）第23条第2款作出新的调整。

40 最后，由于原告基于《宽恕公告》向欧盟委员会提出豁免，并配合欧盟委员会的调查，从而获得了罚款数额50%的减免。同时，并因其使欧盟委员会能够查实该卡特尔持续期间更长而再获得部分豁免（欧盟委员会决定第575段、第582段至第592段）。

41 欧盟委员会决定中关于原告的可执行部分如下：

“第1条

下列企业在一定期间内参与了覆盖整个欧洲经济区的光盘驱动器市场卡特尔，实施了包括价格协定在内的一系列单独和持续的卡特尔行为，违反了《欧盟运行条约》第101条第3款和《欧洲经济区协定》第53条：

……

(d)[the applicants] from 23 June 2004 to 25 November 2008, for their coordination with regards to Dell and HP.

...

Article 2

For the infringement referred to in Article 1, the following fines are imposed:

...

(d)[the applicants], jointly and severally liable: EUR 37 121 000.'

Ⅱ. Procedure and forms of order sought

42 By application lodged at the Court Registry on 4 January 2016, the applicants brought the present action.

43 The Commission lodged the defence on 29 April 2016.

44 On a proposal from the Judge-Rapporteur, the Court (Fifth Chamber) decided to open the oral part of the procedure and, by way of measures of organisation of procedure provided for in Article 89 of its Rules of Procedure, requested the applicants to lodge a document and to make written submissions on certain aspects of the dispute. The applicants complied with those requests within the prescribed period.

45 The parties presented oral argument and answered the questions put to them by the Court at the hearing on 3 May 2018.

46 The applicants claim that the Court should:

–reduce the amount of the fine imposed on them in Article 2(d) of the contested decision to take account of the particularities of the case;

–order the Commission to pay the costs.

47 The Commission contends that the Court should:

–dismiss the action;

–order the applicants to pay the costs.

（d）[原告]自2004年6月23日至2008年11月25日，实施了与戴尔公司和惠普公司相关的价格协定行为。

……

第2条

对第一条所指的违法行为，处以下列罚款：

……

（d）对[原告]处以连带罚款37 121 000欧元。”

Ⅱ.诉讼程序及双方当事人的观点

42 2016年1月4日，原告向初审法院起诉。

43 2016年4月29日，欧盟委员会提交答辩意见。

44 根据本案审理法官及判决书起草人的提议，本院第五法庭决定先启动本案口头审理程序。根据《欧盟法院程序规则》第89条的规定，先由原告向本院提交一份文件，就争议的某些方面提出书面意见。原告在规定期限内提交了相关文件和书面意见。

45 在2018年5月3日的口头审理程序中，双方进行了口头辩论，并回答了本院在审理中提出的问题。

46 原告向本院提出的诉讼请求：

——考虑到本案的特殊情形，降低欧盟委员会决定第2条d款对原告作出的罚款数额；

——由欧盟委员会承担诉讼费用。

47 欧盟委员会向本院答辩要求：

——驳回起诉；

——由原告承担诉讼费用。

Ⅲ. LAW

A. The scope of the dispute

48 In support of the action, the applicants raise two pleas in law. First, they claim that the Commission breached the principle of good administration and its obligation to state reasons by not responding to their request under point 37 of the Guidelines. Second, they submit that the Commission erred in law in not derogating from the general method set out in the Guidelines in order to reduce the amount of the fine imposed on them in the light of the particular characteristics of the case and the applicants' role in the market for ODDs.

49 By their first head of claim, and as is apparent from paragraphs 3, 7, 41 and 43 of the application and paragraphs 11 to 18 of the reply, the applicants request the Court to exercise its unlimited jurisdiction under Article 261 TFEU and reduce the amount of the fine imposed on them. They state, moreover, that they do not seek annulment of the contested decision in the event that the Court should find that there has been a breach by the Commission of the obligation to state reasons or of the principle of good administration.

50 The Court, by way of measures of organisation of procedure under Article 89 of the Rules of Procedure, invited the applicants to clarify whether, as the application and reply appear to indicate, they did not intend to submit, in the context of their application, a claim for annulment, but only a claim for reduction of the amount of the fine.

51 In their reply to the measures of organisation of procedure of the Court, the applicants stated that they were requesting the Court to exercise its unlimited jurisdiction by reviewing the Commission's implicit decision to reject their request for a reduction of the amount of the fine under point 37 of the Guidelines and by reviewing the substance of that request.

52 Nevertheless, in that reply to the measures of organisation of procedure, the applicants also stated that they were aware of the fact that to ask the Court to exercise its unlimited jurisdiction with regard to the fine under Article 261 TFEU 'necessarily comprises or includes a request for the annulment, in whole or in part, of that decision' and that, if, in its review of legality under Article 263 TFEU, the Court concluded that the Commission made no error of law, it could carry out a full review of the amount of the fine in accordance with Article 261 TFEU.

Ⅲ. 法律问题

A.争议范围

48 原告提出了两项理由支持其诉请。第一项理由是，原告声称，欧盟委员会对原告根据《2006年罚款指南》第37条提出的减轻罚款的申请未作任何回应，违反了良好行政原则和说明理由的义务。第二项理由是，原告认为，欧盟委员会未能考虑到本案存在特殊情形从而排除适用《2006年罚款指南》设定的罚款计算一般方法，以及根据原告在卡特尔中所起的作用而减少对原告罚款数额，属于法律适用错误。

49 原告提出的第一项诉请，即起诉状第3段、第7段、第41段和第43段以及书面答复函第11段至第18段所述，原告是在请求本院依据《欧盟运行条约》第261条赋予的罚款数额裁量权来减少对其的罚款数额。此外，原告表示，即使初审法院认定欧盟委员会确实违反了良好行政原则或违反了说明理由的义务，原告也并不请求本院撤销欧盟委员会决定。

50 本院根据《欧盟法院程序规则》第89条的程序性规定，请原告明确诉请：原告是否确如起诉状和书面答复函所表明的那样，不提出撤销欧盟委员会决定的诉请，而仅请求减少罚款数额？

51 对于本院根据程序规则提出的问题，原告答复如下：原告根据《2006年罚款指南》第37条向欧盟委员会申请减轻罚款，但欧盟委员会无视原告的申请，也就是拒绝了原告，故原告请求初审法院行使罚款数额决定权，审查欧盟委员会这一决定的合理性，以及审查原告该减轻罚款申请的实质合理性。

52 然而，原告在答复中还说，他们清楚，请求初审法院行使《欧盟运行条约》第261条赋予的罚款数额裁量权，则“必然包括了请求全部或部分撤销欧盟委员会的决定”，而且，即使初审法院依据《欧盟运行条约》第263条对欧盟委员会决定进行合法性审查后，得出欧盟委员会不存在法律适用错误的结论，初审法院仍然可以根据《欧盟运行条约》第261条对罚款数额进行全面审查。

53 In that connection, it must be borne in mind that the Treaty does not recognise the 'action under the Court's unlimited jurisdiction' as an autonomous remedy. Article 261 TFEU confines itself to providing that regulations adopted pursuant to the provisions of the Treaties may give the European Union judicature unlimited jurisdiction with regard to the penalties provided for in those regulations (order of 9 November 2004, FNICGV v Commission, T 252/03, EU: T: 2004: 326, paragraph 22).

54 Furthermore, that unlimited jurisdiction can be exercised by the EU judicature only in the context of the review of acts of the institutions, more particularly in actions for annulment. The sole effect of Article 261 TFEU is to enlarge the extent of the powers the EU judicature has in the context of the action referred to in Article 263 TFEU (see, to that effect, order of 9 November 2004, FNICGV v Commission, T 252/03, EU: T: 2004: 326, paragraphs 24 and 25).

55 Consequently, an action in which the EU judicature is asked to exercise its unlimited jurisdiction with respect to a decision imposing a penalty, a jurisdiction conferred by Article 261 TFEU, but exercised pursuant to Article 263 TFEU, necessarily comprises or includes a request for the annulment, in whole or in part, of that decision (see, to that effect, order of 9 November 2004, FNICGV v Commission, T 252/03, EU: T: 2004: 326, paragraph 25).

56 It is therefore only after the Court has finished reviewing the legality of the decision referred to it, in the light of the pleas in law submitted to it and of grounds which, where applicable, it has raised of its own motion, that, in the event that it does not annul the decision in full, it is to exercise its unlimited jurisdiction in order, first, to draw the appropriate conclusions from its findings with respect to the lawfulness of that decision and, secondly, to establish, according to the information which has been brought to its attention (see, to that effect, judgments of 8 December 2011, KME Germany and Others v Commission, C 389/10 P, EU: C: 2011: 816, paragraph 131, and of 10 July 2014, Telefónica and Telefónica de España v Commission, C 295/12 P, EU: C: 2014: 2062, paragraph 213), whether it is appropriate, on the date on which it adopts its decision (judgments of 11 July 2014, RWE and RWE Dea v Commission, T 543/08, EU: T: 2014: 627, paragraph 257; of 11 July 2014, Sasol and Others v Commission, T 541/08, EU: T: 2014: 628, paragraph 438; and of 11 July 2014, Esso and Others v Commission, T 540/08, EU: T: 2014: 630, paragraph 133), to substitute its own assessment for that of the Commission, so that the amount of the fine is appropriate.

53 对此，本院认为，必须强调《欧盟运行条约》并未将“欧盟司法机关行使罚款数额裁量权”定义为一种真正可以“自由”行使的救济权。根据《欧盟运行条约》第261条的规定，欧盟司法机关行使罚款数额裁量权必须遵照欧盟各条约通过的条例中的明文规定（参见判例：2004年11月9日，FNICGV v Commission，T 252/03，EU：T：2004：326，第22段）。

54 不仅如此，“罚款数额裁量权”只能由欧盟司法机关在对相关机构的决定进行合法性审查时行使，特别是在撤销之诉[①]中行使。《欧盟运行条约》第261条仅有的意义就是扩大《欧盟运行条约》第263条赋予欧盟司法机关的权限范围。（参见判例：2004年11月9日，FNICGV v Commission，T 252/03，EU：T：2004：326，第24段和第25段）

55 因此，当事人在诉讼程序中请求欧盟司法机关对某一罚款决定行使其依据《欧盟运行条约》第261条享有的罚款数额裁量权，则必然包括行使全部或部分撤销这一罚款决定的权力。这一权限，是《欧盟运行条约》第263条赋予的。（参见判例：2004年11月9日，FNICGV v Commission，T 252/03，EU：T：2004：326，第25段）

56 所以，初审法院根据原告提出的诉请及理由对争议决定进行合法性审查，经审查后，只有在认定该决定是合法的，无须全部撤销的情况下，才能行使罚款数额裁量权。[②]具体而言，首先，初审法院依据其查明的事实得出争议决定具有合法性的结论；其次，初审法院根据本案关键信息及各种数据（认可该争议决定具备合法性所依据的各种数据）来确定是否以其自己的评估代替欧盟委员会的评估，从而使罚款数额更加合理（参见判例：2011年12月8日，KME Germany and Others v Commission，C 389/10 P，EU：C：2011：816，第131段，以及2014年7月10日，Telefónica and Telefónica de España v Commission，C 295/12 P，EU：C：2014：2062，第213段。参见判例：2014年7月11日，RWE and RWE Dea v Commission，T 543/08，EU：T：2014：627，第257段；2014年7月11日，Sasol and Others v Commission，T 541/08，EU：T：2014：628，第438段；以及2014年7月11日，Esso and Others v Commission，T 540/08，EU：T：2014：630，第133段）。

---

① 例如，请求撤销欧盟委员会决定的诉讼程序。——译者注

② 如果初审法院审查后认定欧盟委员会的决定不具有合法性，那么将导致该决定被全部撤销，这样就不存在罚款数额合适与否的问题了，也就不需要初审法院行使其罚款数额裁量权。——译者注

57 In the present case, although, in the application, the applicants submitted a claim only for variation and have indicated that they do not seek annulment of the contested decision, it is apparent from their subsequent explanations that they do not object to the Court reclassifying their claim in accordance with the case-law referred to in paragraphs 53 to 56 above.

58 It must therefore be held that the present action consists of (i) a claim for annulment in part of the contested decision, in so far as the Commission rejected the applicants' request for a reduction, under point 37 of the Guidelines, of the amount of the fine imposed on them in Article 2 (d) of the contested decision and (ii) a claim for variation of that decision asking the Court to uphold that request itself and, consequently, to reduce that amount.

B. The claim for annulment

59 The applicants put forward two pleas. First, they claim that the Commission breached the principle of good administration and its obligation to state reasons by not responding to their request under point 37 of the Guidelines. Second, they submit that the Commission erred in law in not derogating from the general method set out in the Guidelines in order to reduce the amount of the fine imposed, in the light of the particular characteristics of the case and the applicants' role in the market for ODDs.

1. First plea: breach of the principle of good administration and of the obligation to state reasons

60 In essence, this plea in law is made up of two parts. The first alleges breach of the obligation to state reasons. The second alleges breach of the principle of good administration.

(a) The first part: alleging breach of the obligation to state reasons

61 The applicants take issue with the Commission for having failed to respond to their request that the 'particularities' should be taken into account in the calculation of the amount of the fines, under point 37 of the Guidelines, during the administrative procedure or in the contested decision. They maintain that the Commission's discretion to apply point 37 of the Guidelines does not exempt it from taking their request into consideration in its internal decision-making process or in the contested decision.

62 The Commission disputes the arguments put forward by the applicants.

57 本案中，尽管原告的诉请只提出了变更罚款数额的请求，并表示不请求初审法院撤销欧盟委员会决定。但从原告随后的解释中可以明显看出，他们不反对初审法院根据上文第53段至第56段提到的以往判例来重新明确其诉请。

58 因此，本院认为，原告提出的诉请应归纳如下：（1）请求部分撤销欧盟委员会的决定，该决定第2条d款对原告处以罚款，原告基于《2006年罚款指南》第37条申请欧盟委员会减少罚款金额，但遭到欧盟委员会拒绝；（2）请求初审法院支持原告减轻罚款的申请，减少对原告的罚款数额。

B.请求撤销欧盟委员会的决定

59 为支持其诉请，原告提出了两项理由。第一，原告声称，欧盟委员会没有对原告根据《2006年罚款指南》第37条提出的减轻罚款申请作出任何回应，违反了良好行政原则和说明理由的义务；第二，原告认为，欧盟委员会未能考虑到本案存在特殊情形，该特殊情形可以排除适用《2006年罚款指南》设定的罚款数额计算的一般方法，所以欧盟委员会未能根据本案的特殊情形和原告在卡特尔中所起的作用而减少对原告罚款数额，属于法律适用错误。

1. 第一项理由：欧盟委员会违反了良好行政原则和说明理由的义务

60 原告提出的第一项理由实质上由两部分组成：一、欧盟委员会未履行说明理由的义务；二、欧盟委员会违反了良好行政原则。

（a）第一部分：欧盟委员会未履行说明理由的义务

61 原告请求欧盟委员会在查处卡特尔的行政程序中计算罚款数额时，按照《2006年罚款指南》第37条的规定考虑本案特殊情形的存在，而非仅适用罚款数额计算的一般方法。但欧盟委员会对于原告的该项请求未作任何回应，原告对此有异议。原告认为，虽然欧盟委员会对是否适用《2006年罚款指南》第37条有自由裁量权，但这并不意味着欧盟委员会可以无视原告的请求，欧盟委员会应当在作出决策的过程中或在争议决定中将原告的请求纳入考虑范围。

62 欧盟委员会对原告的主张不予认可。

63 As regards the obligation to state reasons, it should be borne in mind that the statement of reasons required under Article 296 TFEU must be appropriate to the measure in question and must disclose in a clear and unequivocal fashion the reasoning followed by the institution which adopted that measure, in such a way as to enable the persons concerned to ascertain the reasons for the measure and to enable the competent court to carry out its review (judgment of 5 December 2013, Commission v Edison, C 446/11 P, not published, EU: C: 2013: 798, paragraph 21).

64 Thus, it is settled case-law that the purpose of the obligation to state the reasons on which an individual decision is based is, in addition to permitting review by the Courts, to provide the person concerned with sufficient information to know whether the decision may be vitiated by an error enabling its validity to be challenged (see judgment of 5 December 2013, Commission v Edison, C 446/11 P, not published, EU: C: 2013: 798, paragraph 22 and the case-law cited).

65 Although the Commission is required under Article 296 TFEU to set out all the circumstances of fact and law justifying the adoption of a decision and the legal considerations which led the Commission to adopt it, that article does not require the Commission to discuss all the matters of fact and of law which may have been dealt with during the administrative proceedings (see, by analogy, judgment of 18 September 2003, Volkswagen v Commission, C 338/00 P, EU: C: 2003: 473, paragraph 127 and the case-law cited). The requirements to be satisfied by the statement of reasons depend on the circumstances of each case, in particular the content of the measure in question, the nature of the reasons given and the interest which the addressees of the measure, or other parties to whom it is of direct and individual concern, may have in obtaining explanations (judgment of 5 December 2013, Commission v Edison, C 446/11 P, not published, EU: C: 2013: 798, paragraph 23).

66 Furthermore, it must be pointed out that, in the determination of the amount of the fine in a case of infringement of the competition rules, the Commission fulfils its obligation to state reasons when it indicates in its decision the factors which enabled it to determine the gravity of the infringement and its duration, and it is not required to indicate the figures relating to the method of calculating the fine (see, to that effect, judgment of 22 October 2015, AC-Treuhand AG v Commission, C 194/14 P, EU: C: 2015: 717, paragraph 68).

67 It is appropriate to examine (i) whether the Commission identified with sufficient clarity the factors it took into account for calculating the amount of the fine imposed on the applicants and (ii) whether the Commission was required to state, in the grounds of the contested decision, the reasons as to why it did not take into account the particular circumstances alleged by the applicants.

63 本院认为，关于说明理由的义务，《欧盟运行条约》第296条所规定的“说明理由的义务”是指欧盟委员会必须说明其采取相关措施[①]的理由。欧盟委员会必须清晰明确地说明其为何采取某一措施，以使相关人员能够清楚明白，并使有管辖权的法院能够对此进行合法性审查（参见判例：2013年12月5日，Commission v Edison，C 446/11 P，未公布，EU：C：2013：798，第21段）。

64 因此，根据以往判例，之所以要求欧盟委员会说明其作出的某一决定所依据的理由：一方面，使法院能够进行司法审查；另一方面，向相关人员提供足够的信息，以便其了解该决定是否会因为法律适用错误而无效（参见判例：2013年12月5日，Commission v Edison，C 446/11 P，未公布，EU：C：2013：798，第22段和引用的判例法）。

65 尽管《欧盟运行条约》第296条要求欧盟委员会列出所有可以证明其所作决定具有正当性的事实和法律基础，以及所有导致其作出该决定的法律上的考量因素，但并不要求欧盟委员会解释其在行政程序中遇到的所有事实和法律问题（参见判例：2003年9月18日，Volkswagen v Commission，C 338/00 P，EU：C：2003：473，第127段和所援引的判例法）。判断欧盟委员会是否履行了“说明理由的义务”，需要结合每一案件的具体情况，特别是其所作措施的内容、所述理由的性质、该措施关系的人员的利益，或者那些与该措施直接相关且可能需要对其说明理由的其他当事方的利益（参见判例：2013年12月5日，Commission v Edison，C 446/11 P，未公布，EU：C：2013：798，第23段）。

66 此外，必须指出，在确定卡特尔案件当事人的罚款数额时，欧盟委员会在其决定中只要披露确定违法行为严重性及其持续时间的考量因素，即可认为其已经履行了说明理由的义务，而无须要求其披露与罚款计算方法有关的所有数据（参见判例：2015年10月22日，AC Treuhand AG v Commission，C 194/14 P，EU：C：2015：717，第68段）。

67 本案中应当考虑：（1）欧盟委员会是否足够清楚地阐明了其计算与原告罚款数额相关的考量因素；（2）如本案所示的欧盟委员会所作的罚款决定，是否有义务说明其没有考虑原告主张的“特殊情形”的理由。

① 欧盟委员会作出罚款决定，就是“措施”的一种。——译者注

(1) The statement of reasons for the fine imposed on the applicants

68 In the present case, it must be pointed out that recitals 527 to 593 of the contested decision set out the factors which the Commission took into account in order to calculate the fines imposed on the members of the cartel, in particular the factors relating to the gravity and duration of the infringements committed by the applicants. Those factors are such as to enable the applicants to understand the matters which enabled the Commission to carry out its assessment as to the final amount of the fine imposed.

69 Article 23(3) of Regulation No 1/2003 provides that in fixing the amount of the fine the Commission must have regard both to the gravity and to the duration of the infringement. Point 19 of the Guidelines provides that the basic amount of the fine is related to a proportion of the value of sales, depending on the degree of gravity of the infringement, multiplied by the number of years of infringement. In the present case, the Commission stated, in recitals 527 to 540 of the contested decision, that, in view of the considerable differences in the duration of the involvement of the different cartel participants and in order better to reflect the actual impact of the cartel, a proxy for the annual value of sales (an annual average calculated on the basis of the actual value of sales made by the undertakings during the months of their respective participation in the infringement) served as the basis for the calculation of the basic amount of the fines.

70 More specifically, with regard to taking into account the gravity of the infringement, according to points 21 to 23 of the Guidelines, the proportion of the value of sales taken into account will be set at a level of up to 30%, on the basis of a number of factors, such as the nature of the infringement, the combined market share of all the undertakings concerned, the geographic scope of the infringement and whether or not the infringement has been implemented, since price-fixing, market-sharing and output-limitation agreements are, by their very nature, among the most harmful restrictions of competition. Point 25 of the Guidelines states that, as a deterrent, the Commission includes in the basic amount of the fine a proportion, used to calculate an additional amount, of between 15% and 25% of the value of sales, taking the above factors into account. In the present case, having regard to the nature of the cartel and the territory in which it produced its effects, namely collusive agreements relating to procurement events concerning optical disk drives for PCs covering the entire EEA territory concerning price increases, the multiplier for the gravity of the infringement and the multiplier for an additional amount were both fixed at 16%. Those considerations were analysed and developed by the Commission in recitals 541 to 551 and 554 to 557 of the contested decision.

（1） 欧盟委员会是否已说明与原告罚款相关的理由

68 本案中，欧盟委员会决定第527段至第593段列明了欧盟委员会在计算罚款数额时的考量因素，特别是与卡特尔行为的严重性和持续时间相关的因素。欧盟委员会披露的这些考量因素可使原告了解欧盟委员会是如何评估从而最终得出罚款数额的。

69 《第1/2003号条例》第23条第3款规定，在确定罚款数额时，欧盟委员会必须考虑违法行为的严重性和持续时间。《2006年罚款指南》第19条规定，罚款基数与卡特尔成员销售额的一定比例相关，具体取决于卡特尔行为的严重性和持续时间。在本案中，欧盟委员会在其决定第527段至第540段中指出，鉴于本案不同卡特尔成员参与该卡特尔的期间段存在显著差异，为了能更好地反映卡特尔的实际影响，以各卡特尔成员在各自参与卡特尔期间整个日历月中的实际销售额为基础计算出各卡特尔成员的平均年销售额，以此平均年销售额作为计算罚款基数的基础。

70 具体来说，就卡特尔行为的严重性对罚款基数的影响而言，《2006年罚款指南》第21条至第23条规定，应根据卡特尔行为的性质、所有卡特尔成员的市场份额总数、卡特尔涉及的地域范围以及卡特尔行为是否已经实施（就卡特尔的性质而言，价格垄断、市场分割和产量限制协议是最严重的卡特尔行为）等诸多因素，以销售额的30%为上限封顶，在该比例范围内确定罚款基数。《2006年罚款指南》第25条规定，为了使罚款达到威慑作用，欧盟委员会将衡量上述因素的影响，再附加销售额的15%至25%计入罚款基数。在本案中，考虑到卡特尔的性质及其影响到的区域，卡特尔成员们实施的价格协定行为影响到整个欧洲经济区的个人台式电脑光盘驱动器价格，基于该卡特尔行为的严重性，罚款基数比例以及附加比例都确定为16%（参见欧盟委员会决定第541段至第551段、第554段至第557段）。

71 Moreover, with respect to taking into account of the duration of the infringement, point 24 of the Guidelines provides (i) that the amount determined on the basis of the value of sales is multiplied by the number of years of participation in the infringement and (ii) that periods of less than 6 months are counted as half a year and periods longer than 6 months but shorter than 1 year are counted as a full year. The applicants made sales to Dell from 23 June 2004 to 25 November 2008 and to HP from 30 November 2005 to 25 November 2008. The value of the sales made was EUR 49 219 825 and EUR 52 588 024 respectively. Those considerations were also analysed and developed by the Commission in recitals 552 and 553 of the contested decision.

72 Under points 27 to 31 of the Guidelines, the basic amount may then be adjusted in order to take into account aggravating and mitigating circumstances and to ensure that fines have a sufficiently deterrent effect. According to point 34 of those guidelines, it may also be reduced to take into account the Leniency Notice. In the present case, the Commission did not apply any aggravating circumstances. Those considerations were analysed and developed by the Commission in recitals 559 to 569 of the contested decision.

73 Lastly, it is also stated in point 32 of the Guidelines that, as laid down in Article 23 (2) of Regulation No 1/2003, for each undertaking or association of undertakings participating in the infringement, the final amount of the fine must not, in any event, exceed 10% of the total turnover in the preceding business year. In the present case, given that the adjusted basic amount of the fine imposed on the applicants did not reach the cap of 10% of their turnover, the Commission was not required to make a fresh adjustment. Those considerations were analysed and developed by the Commission in recitals 570 to 572 of the contested decision.

74 It follows from the foregoing that the statement of reasons for the contested decision showed, in accordance with Article 296 TFEU, in a clear and unequivocal fashion the Commission's reasoning and so enabled the applicants to ascertain the reasons for that decision in order to defend their rights, and the Court to review the correctness of the decision (see, to that effect, judgment of 18 September 2003, Volkswagen v Commission, C 338/00 P, EU: C: 2003: 473, paragraph 124 and the case-law cited).

71 至于违法行为持续时间对罚款基数的影响，根据《2006年罚款指南》第24条的规定，即（1）以卡特尔成员的销售额乘以参与卡特尔行为的年数计算罚款基数；（2）不足六个月的按半年计算，六个月以上不满一年的按一年计算。原告于2004年6月23日至2008年11月25日向戴尔公司出售光盘驱动器，并于2005年11月30日至2008年11月25日向惠普公司出售光盘驱动器。针对两公司的销售额分别为49 219 825欧元和52 588 024欧元。欧盟委员会决定的第552段和第553段对此有详细分析和阐述。

72 根据《2006年罚款指南》第27条至第31条的规定，如果存在从轻或加重情节，则罚款基数相应调整，以确保罚款具有足够的威慑作用。根据《2006年罚款指南》第34条的规定，罚款数额还可依据宽恕政策而予以豁免减轻。在本案中，欧盟委员会未适用任何加重情节。欧盟委员会决定的第559段至第569段对此有详细分析和阐述。

73 最后，《2006年罚款指南》第32条还指明，根据《第1/2003号条例》第23条第2款的规定，对于参与违法行为的每个企业或企业联合体而言，罚款的最终数额无论如何不得超过其上一个营业年度总营业额的10%。在本案中，调整后对原告的罚款数额并未达到其上一个营业年度总营业额10%的上限，故欧盟委员会无须再次作出调整。欧盟委员会决定的第570段至第572段对此有详细分析和阐述。

74 综上所述，欧盟委员会决定已根据《欧盟运行条约》第296条的规定，清晰、明确地载明了欧盟委员会作出该决定的理由，从而使原告能够清楚地明白自己被罚款的理由，维护了原告应有的权利，也达到了使法院得以审查该决定是否具有合法性这一目的。（参见判例：2003年9月18日，Volkswagen v Commission，C 338/00 P，EU：C：2003：473，第124段和所援引的判例法）

75 As to the remainder, in the contested decision, more specifically in recitals 532 to 540 and 547 to 549 thereof, the Commission expressly replied to some of the points made by the applicants in response to the statement of objections. In that regard, it should be made clear that, although the Commission is required to set out all the circumstances of fact and law justifying the adoption of a decision and the legal considerations which led the Commission to adopt it, the Commission is not required to discuss all the matters of fact and law which may have been dealt with during the administrative procedure (see judgment of 18 September 2003, Volkswagen v Commission, C 338/00 P, EU: C: 2003: 473, paragraph 127 and the case-law cited). All that was required of the Commission was to explain clearly and unequivocally, as it did in recitals 527 to 593 of the contested decision, the most relevant factors, in particular those relating to the gravity and duration of the infringements committed by the applicants, which were taken into account to calculate the amount of the fine imposed.

76 It must therefore be held that the Commission gave sufficient reasons in the contested decision concerning the factors taken into consideration to calculate the amount of the fine imposed on the applicants.

(2) The Commission's obligation to state the reasons for not taking into account the particular circumstances alleged by the applicants

77 As regards the applicants' argument that the Commission breached its obligation to state reasons by not indicating, in the contested decision, the reasons for which it did not depart, following their request and pursuant to point 37 of the Guidelines, from the general methodology for calculating the amount of the fine, it should be noted that, as is apparent from the case-law cited in paragraphs 65 and 75 above, the Commission has no obligation to highlight in its decision all the matters of fact and of law which may have been dealt with during the administrative procedure and those which it did not take into account when calculating the amount of the fine imposed.

78 In addition, it should be noted that the applicable rules provide that the Commission may depart from the general methodology for setting the amount of the fine, on a purely exceptional basis, in two circumstances. First, pursuant to point 35 of the Guidelines, the Commission may take into account, for the purposes of setting the amount of the fine, an undertaking's inability to pay. In the present case, it should be noted that, during the informal meeting of 5 March 2015, the Commission explicitly asked the applicants to confirm that they were not claiming an inability to pay the fine under point 35 of the Guidelines, and that the applicants confirmed that they were not requesting that that procedure be applied. Second, pursuant to point 37 of the Guidelines, it is foreseen that the particularities of a case or the need to achieve deterrence in a particular case may justify the Commission departing from the methodology set out in those guidelines.

75 至于其余事项，在欧盟委员会决定中，具体在该决定第532段至第540段、第547段至第549段中，欧盟委员会明确答复了原告对欧盟委员会出具的异议声明提出的质疑。需再次强调的是，尽管《欧盟运行条约》第296条要求欧盟委员会列出所有可以证明其所作决定具有正当性的事实和法律基础，以及所有导致其作出该决定的法律上的考量因素，但并不要求欧盟委员会解释其在行政程序中遇到的所有事实和法律问题（参见判例：2003年9月18日，Volkswagen v Commission，C 338/00 P，EU：C：2003：473，第127段和所援引的判例法）。所以，欧盟委员会需要做的就是清楚、毫不含糊地解释与作出决定相关的最关键的因素，特别是那些作为计算罚款数额的考量因素，以及与卡特尔行为的严重性和持续时间有关的因素。在本案中，欧盟委员会在其决定第527段至第593段已经说得很清楚了。

76 因此，本院认为，欧盟委员会在其决定中已经充分说明了在计算对原告罚款数额时所考虑的各种相关因素。

（2）原告提出欧盟委员会应考虑本案具有“特殊情形”，欧盟委员会却未将该观点纳入计算罚款的考量范围，那么欧盟委员会对此是否有说明理由的义务？

77 原告又称，原告请求欧盟委员会在计算罚款金额时应该适用《2006年罚款指南》第37条，考虑本案特殊情形的存在，排除适用罚款数额计算的一般方法，但欧盟委员会没有理睬原告的请求，欧盟委员会也未阐明其不这么做的理由，违反了说明理由的义务。对原告的该项主张，本院认为，从上文第65段和第75段引述的判例法可以明显看出，欧盟委员会没有义务在决定中解释其在行政程序中遇到的所有事实和法律问题，也没有义务阐明其在计算罚款数额时未作考虑的事项。

78 此外，应当指出，根据相关法律的规定，只有在两种情况下（纯粹是特例），欧盟委员会才能排除适用罚款数额计算的一般方法：第一，根据《2006年罚款指南》第35条的规定，在对没有支付能力的企业设定罚款时可以排除适用罚款数额计算的一般方法。本案中，在2015年3月5日的非正式会议上，欧盟委员会已要求原告明确其是否主张存在《2006年罚款指南》第35条规定的无力支付罚款的法定事由，而原告也确认了其不存在无力支付罚款的事由，故该情况不适用于本案情形。第二，根据《2006年罚款指南》第37条的规定，如果可以预见到，某一案件非常特殊，足以使欧盟委员会排除适用计算罚款数额的一般方法也具有合法性，则可以排除适用；或者，为了使罚款达到威慑作用，确有必要排除适用罚款上限。

79 However, according to the case-law, it must be held that the discretion conferred on the Commission in the Guidelines does not extend to exempting it from the obligation to justify recourse to this exception. The Commission must specify the particularities of the case or the need to achieve a particular level of deterrence justifying recourse to this exception (see, to that effect, judgment of 6 February 2014, AC-Treuhand v Commission, T 27/10, EU: T: 2014: 59, paragraph 306).

80 In particular, when the Commission decides to depart from the general methodology set out in the Guidelines, by which it limited the discretion it may itself exercise in setting the amount of fines, and relies on point 37 of those guidelines, the requirements relating to the duty to state reasons must be complied with all the more rigorously. In that regard, it is appropriate to refer to the settled case-law to the effect that those guidelines lay down a rule of conduct indicating the approach to be adopted from which the Commission cannot depart, in an individual case, without giving reasons which are compatible with, inter alia, the principle of equal treatment. Those reasons must be all the more specific because point 37 of the Guidelines simply makes a vague reference to 'the particularities of a given case' and thus leaves the Commission a broad discretion where it decides to make an exceptional adjustment of the basic amount of the fines to be imposed on the undertakings concerned. In such a case, the Commission's respect for the rights guaranteed by the EU legal order in administrative procedures, including the obligation to state reasons, is of even more fundamental importance (see judgment of 13 December 2016, Printeos and Others v Commission, T 95/15, EU: T: 2016: 722, paragraph 48 and the case-law cited).

81 By contrast, in the present case, the Commission took the view that the particular circumstances provided for in point 37 of the Guidelines were not met and, consequently, opted for the application of the general methodology in order to calculate the amount of the fine imposed on the applicants. Accordingly, and as is clear from the case-law cited in paragraphs 65 and 75 above, the Commission was required only to state the reasons, in the contested decision, relating to the methodology applied to calculate the amount of the fine and not the factors that it did not take into account in that calculation and, in particular, the reasons for which it did not have recourse to the exception laid down in point 37 of the Guidelines. As has already been noted (see paragraph 77 above), the Commission is not obliged to adopt a position on all of the arguments relied on by the parties concerned. It is sufficient if it sets out the facts and the legal considerations having decisive importance in the context of the decision.

79 但是，根据以往判例，《2006年罚款指南》赋予欧盟委员会在计算罚款数额的裁量权并不包括免除欧盟委员会在适用上述两种特例情形之时的证明义务。如果欧盟委员会排除适用罚款数额计算的一般方法，则欧盟委员会必须证明，该案件非常特殊，足以使欧盟委员会的排除适用具备合法性；或者，如果排除适用罚款上限，则必须证明是为了达到威慑作用，确有必要排除适用的。（参见判例：2014年2月6日，AC Treuhand v Commission，T 27/10，EU：T：2014：59，第306段）

80 特别是，当欧盟委员会决定依据《2006年罚款指南》第37条而排除适用罚款数额计算的一般方法时，欧盟委员会必须更加严格地履行说明理由的义务，必须满足履行该义务的所有要求。具体而言，根据以往判例，《2006年罚款指南》规定了欧盟委员会在一般个案中不能排除适用罚款数额计算的一般方法，除非其能给出充足理由，这些理由包括其行为符合平等待遇原则。这些理由必须很具体，因为《2006年罚款指南》第37条只是含糊其辞地提到“特定案件的特殊情形”，从而使欧盟委员会在决定对有关企业所处的罚款基数作出例外调整时拥有广泛的自由裁量权。在这种情况下，欧盟委员会在行政程序中应尊重欧盟法律所保障的当事人权利，包括其需严格履行说明理由的义务。这一点显得尤其重要，这是最基本的义务。（参见判例：2016年12月13日，Printeos and Others v Commission，T 95/15，EU：T：2016：722，第48段和引用的判例法）

81 相比之下，本案中，欧盟委员会认为本案并不符合《2006年罚款指南》第37条规定的特殊情形，因此选择适用一般方法来计算对原告的罚款数额。所以，正如上文第65段和第75段引述的判例所明确指出的，欧盟委员会只需在其决定中说明与其计算得出罚款数额的方法相关的因素，而无须说明其在计算中未作考量的因素。特别是欧盟委员会也无须说明其没有适用《2006年罚款指南》第37条规定的例外情形的理由。正如上文第77段所指出的，欧盟委员会没有义务对有关各方所提出的所有主张一一表明其立场。欧盟委员会只要列出所有其在作出决定时考量的事实和法律因素就足够了。

82 In those circumstances, it is necessary to reject the applicants' arguments that the Commission did not comply with its obligation to state reasons in the contested decision on account of not having given reasons in that decision for the failure to apply the exception provided for in point 37 of the Guidelines following the applicants' request. The first part of the first plea must therefore be rejected.

(b) Second part: breach of the principle of good administration

83 The applicants observe that the Commission did not consult, concerning their request for a derogation from the general rule on the setting of fines, either the Advisory Committee or the College of Commissioners, such a consultation being an essential procedural requirement for imposing a fine on them. In particular, they maintain that the fine might have been lower if the draft decision had taken account of their request and if, consequently, the Advisory Committee and the College of Commissioners had been consulted in that regard.

84 The Commission disputes the applicants' arguments.

85 Under Article 41(1) of the Charter of Fundamental Rights of the European Union, relating to the right to good administration, every person has the right to have his or her affairs handled impartially, fairly and within a reasonable time by the institutions, bodies, offices and agencies of the Union.

86 According to the case-law, the principle of sound administration consists in the duty of the competent institution to examine carefully and impartially all the relevant aspects in the individual case (judgment of 24 January 1992, La Cinq v Commission, T 44/90, EU: T: 1992: 5, paragraph 86).

87 Furthermore, Article 14 of Regulation No 1/2003 provides:

'1. The Commission shall consult an Advisory Committee on Restrictive Practices and Dominant Positions prior to the taking of any decision under Articles 7, 8, 9, 10, 23, Article 24(2) and Article 29(1).

...

82 综上所述，原告的第一项理由——欧盟委员会拒绝了原告提出的应依据《2006年罚款指南》第37条考虑本案存在特殊情况，但欧盟委员会未能说明拒绝的理由，违反了说明理由的义务——本院对该项理由予以驳回。

（b） 第二部分：欧盟委员会违反了良好行政原则

83 原告指出，欧盟委员会没有就他们关于排除适用罚款数额计算的一般方法的申请向咨询委员会或欧盟委员会的委员们[①]征求意见，而征求意见是对原告处以罚款前所必经的基本程序。特别是原告认为，如果欧盟委员会罚款决定的草案将原告的申请全部加以考虑了，且征求了咨询委员会和欧盟委员会委员们的意见，则罚款可能会低于现在的数额。

84 欧盟委员会不认可原告的主张。

85 首先，根据《欧洲联盟基本权利宪章》第41条第1项关于良好行政管理权利的规定，人人有权在合理时间内使其事务获得欧盟各机构、团体、办事处和机关的公平、公正处理。

86 根据以往判例，良好行政原则要求行政主管机构认真、公正地审查个案相关的所有因素。（参见判例：1992年1月24日，La Cinq v Commission，T 44/90，EU：T：1992：5，第86段）

87 其次，《第1/2003号条例》第14条规定：

“1.欧盟委员会在根据第7条、第8条、第9条、第10条、第23条、第24条第2款和第29条第1款作出任何决定之前，应征询‘限制竞争行为及滥用支配地位咨询委员会’的意见。

……

① 欧盟委员会由27名委员组成，其中一名担任欧盟委员会主席领导整个委员会，非主席的那些委员也根据其职责领域被称为欧盟某某（比如外交）事务专员。自2003年2月《尼斯条约》开始生效后，欧盟各成员国都选派一名委员。委员会的成员之间互相平等，共同制定政策。欧盟委员会和欧洲议会一样，每届任期五年。——译者注

3. The consultation may take place at a meeting convened and chaired by the Commission, held not earlier than 14 days after dispatch of the notice convening it, together with a summary of the case, an indication of the most important documents and a preliminary draft decision. ... The Advisory Committee shall deliver a written opinion on the Commission's preliminary draft decision. ...

...

5. The Commission shall take the utmost account of the opinion delivered by the Advisory Committee. It shall inform the Committee of the manner in which its opinion has been taken into account.

...'

88 Lastly, as set out in Article 33 of Regulation No 1/2003, 'before publishing a draft measure and before adopting it, the Commission shall consult the Advisory Committee on Restrictive Practices and Dominant Positions'.

89 In the present case, it is apparent from the case file (i) that the Advisory Committee was consulted twice, on 5 and 15 October 2015, before the adoption of the contested decision and (ii) that a whole set of documents on this case was sent to the members of that committee in accordance with Article 14(3) of Regulation No 1/2003. Among those documents, the Commission asserts that it provided: a summary of the case file, its letter of facts dated 3 June 2015, the replies to that letter by the companies affected by the fine, including the applicants' reply of 26 June 2015, the draft decision including the annexes, a fines table with a detailed overview of how they would be calculated, the statement of objections and the replies thereto.

90 In the first place, it should be noted that the Advisory Committee had been informed of the main points of fact and law of the proceedings, in particular, the market, the addressees, the objections, the duration of the infringement, the methodology and calculation of the fines and the views expressed by the addressees in response to the objections raised by the Commission. Those documents could therefore be considered 'the most important documents' within the meaning of Article 14(3) of Regulation No 1/2003.

91 In the second place, it should be noted that Article 14 of Regulation No 1/2003 does not require that the applicants' requests be attached to those documents. Indeed, under Article 14(3) of Regulation No 1/2003, the dispatch of the notice convening the Advisory Committee is accompanied by 'a summary of the case, an indication of the most important documents and a preliminary draft decision'. The expression 'an indication of the most important documents' cannot mean that the Commission is required to forward to the Advisory Committee all the documentation exchanged with the companies concerned.

3. 征询意见可在欧盟委员会召集和主持的会议上进行，该会议应在发出咨询通知后的14天内举行，咨询通知应附有案件摘要、最重要文件的说明和罚款决定的初步草案……咨询委员会应就欧盟委员会的初步草案提出书面意见……

……

5. 欧盟委员会应充分考虑咨询委员会提出的意见，并告知咨询委员会他们对这些意见作何考虑。”

88 最后，根据《第1/2003号条例》第33条的规定，“在公布一项决定的草案和通过该草案之前，欧盟委员会应向咨询委员会征询意见”。

89 在本案中，从案卷中可见：(1)在欧盟委员会通过其罚款决定之前，曾于2015年10月5日和15日两次征求咨询委员会的意见；(2)根据《第1/2003号条例》第14条第3款的规定，欧盟委员会已经将一整套本案的相关文件递交给了咨询委员会的委员们。欧盟委员会称，递交的这些文件包括：案卷摘要、欧盟委员会于2015年6月3日向各相关企业出具的事实征询函、各相关企业对该事实征询函的答复（其中包括原告于2015年6月26日作出的答复）以及罚款决定的草案（该草案包括附件、一份详细阐明罚款计算方式的表格、欧盟委员会向各相关企业出具的异议声明以及他们的答复）。

90 本院认为，第一，应当指出，咨询委员会已获悉欧盟委员会对该卡特尔进行的查处程序中涉及的主要事实和法律要点，特别是已经了解到相关市场、各相关企业、异议、卡特尔行为持续时间、罚款的计算方法和计算过程以及各相关企业对欧盟委员会异议声明的答复意见。因此，涵盖此等信息的这些文件可以被认为是《第1/2003号条例》第14条第3款所指的“最重要文件”。

91 第二，《第1/2003号条例》第14条并不要求欧盟委员会必须将原告的申请也附在这些文件上。实际上，根据《第1/2003号条例》第14条第3款，欧盟委员会向咨询委员会发出的咨询通知书应附有“案件摘要、最重要文件的说明和罚款决定的初步草案”。此处的“最重要文件”并不意味着欧盟委员会必须将与相关企业交换的所有文件皆附在咨询通知书上递交给咨询委员会。

92 In the third place, it should be noted that the Commission sent to the Advisory Committee a letter of facts dated 3 June 2015 as well as the applicants' reply to that letter dated 26 June 2015. It should therefore be observed that the applicants had the opportunity (i) to acquaint themselves with the most important facts to be taken into consideration by the Commission for calculating the amount of the fine and (ii) to submit their observations on those facts set out by the Commission. Those observations were, moreover, communicated to the Advisory Committee.

93 Therefore, to the extent that the applicants' first request — seeking a reduction in the amount of the fine due to 'particular circumstances' specific to them for the purpose of point 37 of the Guidelines — was made on 26 February 2015, namely well before the date that the letter of facts was communicated by the Commission to the applicants, they cannot criticise the Commission for not having communicated that information to the Advisory Committee. Even though the Commission did not include that information in the statement of facts or in the indication of the most important documents, the applicants had the opportunity to describe the importance that that information had for the calculation of the amount of the fine in their observations of 26 June 2015.

94 Moreover, in so far as the information adduced by the applicants as part of their second request of 14 September 2015 does not contain substantial amendments as compared with the first request, since it is an update of the facts already set out, the Commission, which was not required to hear the applicants again before adopting the contested decision, was not required to carry out a fresh consultation of the Advisory Committee (see, to that effect, judgment of 15 October 2002, Limburgse Vinyl Maatschappij and Others v Commission, C 238/99 P, C 244/99 P, C 245/99 P, C 247/99 P, C 250/99 P to C 252/99 P and C 254/99 P, EU: C: 2002: 582, paragraph 118). Nevertheless, it should be noted that the Commission had another informal meeting with the applicants, on 18 September 2015, in which they were given the opportunity to comment on the new facts and that, subsequently, on 15 October 2015 the Advisory Committee was consulted again. However, the Commission considered that those facts were not decisive for the calculation of the amount of the fine imposed on the applicants, which is why they were not brought to the attention of the Advisory Committee.

95 It follows from all of the foregoing that the Commission did not breach the principle of good administration on the ground that it did not consult the Advisory Committee on the particular circumstances relied on by the applicants. Indeed, the Commission was diligent during the administrative procedure since it (i) heard the applicants and examined their observations before the Advisory Committee delivered a written opinion on the preliminary draft decision and (ii) communicated to that committee the most important information for the calculation of the amount of the fine under Article 14(3) of Regulation No 1/2003.

92 第三，欧盟委员会向咨询委员会发送的资料中包含一封其于2015年6月3日发出的事实征询函，以及原告于2015年6月26日对该征询函的答复。在此应当指出，原告有机会（1）了解欧盟委员会在计算罚款数额时考虑的最重要事实是哪些，以及（2）对于欧盟委员会正在考虑的事实问题提出自己的意见。而这些信息都已递交给咨询委员会。

93 因此，就原告的第一项申请，即原告认为本案存在《2006年罚款指南》第37条规定的特殊情形，从而申请减少罚款数额。该申请在2015年2月26日就已经提出，也就是说，早在欧盟委员会向原告发出事实征询函之前，原告就已经提出该项诉请，因此他们不能批评欧盟委员会没有将该诉请告知咨询委员会。因为即使欧盟委员会在递交给咨询委员会的事实陈述或最重要文件的说明中没有列入原告的这一申请，原告仍有机会在2015年6月26日的答复函中强调这一申请对于计算罚款数额的重要性。

94 此外，原告在2015年9月14日第二次申请中引用的信息与第一次申请相比，并没有实质性修改，仅是陈述事实的更新。因此，欧盟委员会在通过最终罚款决定之前，不需要再次听取原告的意见，也不需要重新征求咨询委员会的意见（参见判例：2002年10月15日，, Limburgse Vinyl Maatschappij and Others v Commission, C 238/99 P, C 244/99 P, C 245/99 P, C 247/99 P, C 250/99 P至C 252/99 P和C 254/99 P, EU: C: 2002: 582，第118段）。而且，应当指出，欧盟委员会于2015年9月18日以非正式的方式会见了原告，让他们有机会对新的事实发表意见。欧盟委员会随后于2015年10月15日再次征求了咨询委员会的意见。然而，欧盟委员会认为，这些事实对计算罚款数额没有决定性的影响，因此没有必要特别提示咨询委员会注意这些事实。

95 综上所述，原告提出本案存在特殊情形而向欧盟委员会申请减轻罚款数额，欧盟委员会没有将此申请向咨询委员会征求意见。本院认为，欧盟委员会的该行为并未违反良好行政原则。事实上，欧盟委员会在查处卡特尔的行政程序中已足够勤勉，因为欧盟委员会：（1）在咨询委员会就罚款决定的初步草案提出书面意见之前，听取并审查了原告的意见，以及（2）与咨询委员会交流了其依据《第1/2003号条例》第14条第3款计算罚款数额的最重要文件及相关信息。

96 Considerations similar to those set out in paragraphs 89 to 95 above are applicable to the applicants' arguments concerning the consultation of the College of Commissioners. In that regard, it is apparent from the case file that, before adopting the contested decision, essential components of the draft decision, namely the draft and its annexes, the opinion of the Advisory Committee and the final report of the Hearing Officer, were submitted for final approval to the College of Commissioners.

97 Lastly, in so far as the applicants claim, in the context of the present complaint, that the amount of the fine could have been lower if the Advisory Committee and the College of Commissioners had been consulted on that information, it is sufficient to state that it follows from the considerations set out in paragraphs 108 to 129 below that the Commission did not err in law in finding that it was not necessary to take into account the information supporting the applicants' request for a derogation from the general rule on the setting of fines, and from paragraphs 145 to 148 below that the principles of equality and proportionality did not justify such account being taken.

98 In the light of the foregoing considerations, the second part of the first plea must be rejected, as must the first plea in its entirety.

2. Second plea: error of law

99 The applicants claim that the Commission erred in law in not applying, when calculating the amount of the fine, in the light of the particularities of the case, the exception provided for in point 37 of the Guidelines.

100 In the context of that plea, the applicants put forward two complaints, alleging, first, an error of assessment of the particular circumstances alleged by the applicants and, secondly, breach of the principle of equality and proportionality of penalties.

(a) First complaint: error of assessment of the particular circumstances alleged by the applicants

101 The applicants claim, in essence, that the particularities of the present case, on account of which the exception to the general methodology for calculating the amount of the fine provided for in point 37 of the Guidelines should be applied, are to be found in the combination of three circumstances. The applicants assert, first, that they derive the bulk of their revenue from a single product, namely ODDs. They maintain, second, that the fine imposed, which is close to the 10% cap, hit them particularly hard because they are the only companies that were fined that decided to continue to operate on the ODD market, as a result of which their total turnover is relatively high. The applicants assert, third, that they were in a precarious financial situation that obliged them to restructure, given that they are dependent on their parent companies.

96 上文第89段至第95段的论证，可同样适用于原告关于欧盟委员会未向欧盟委员会委员们征求意见而违反良好行政原则的这一主张。在这方面，从案卷中可以明显看出，在通过罚款决定之前，欧盟委员会已经将其起草的罚款决定草案的基本组成部分——草案及其附件、咨询委员会的意见和听证官的最后报告，提交给欧盟委员会的委员们进行最后核准。

97 最后，就原告在本项理由中主张"如果欧盟委员会就那些信息向咨询委员会和欧盟委员会委员们征求了意见，则罚款数额可能会更低"。下文第108段至第129段的论证可以说明：欧盟委员会认为没有必要考虑原告主张的"有理由在本案中排除适用计算罚款的一般规则"，在法律适用上也没有错误。同时，第145段至第148段的论证也足以说明，平等待遇和比例原则并没有要求欧盟委员会必须考虑原告的所有主张。换言之，欧盟委员会不考虑原告的该项主张，并不违反平等待遇原则和比例原则。

98 综上所述，原告第一项理由的第二部分应予驳回。因此，本院原告的第一项理由全部驳回。

2. 第二项理由：欧盟委员会适用法律错误

99 原告声称，欧盟委员会未能基于本案存在特殊情形而依据《2006年罚款指南》的例外规定排除适用罚款数额计算的一般方法，在这一点上欧盟委员会适用法律错误。

100 在该项理由中，原告提出了两项主张：一是欧盟委员会对原告所称的"本案特殊情形"评估有误；二是欧盟委员会违反了平等待遇和比例原则。

（a） 第一项主张：欧盟委员会对原告所称的"本案特殊情形"评估有误

101 原告声称，本案共存在3种特殊情形，因此应适用《2006年罚款指南》第37条的例外规则，排除适用罚款数额计算的一般方法。这3种特殊情形分别是：第一，原告的大部分收入都来自销售单一产品——光盘驱动器；第二，接近销售额10%上限的罚款数额对原告而言打击尤其严重，因为他们是唯一在被罚款之后仍决定继续在光盘驱动器市场上经营的企业，所以他们的总营业额才相对较高；第三，原告声称，由于他们在很多方面依赖母公司，他们的财务状况已经岌岌可危，不得不进行重组。

102 The Commission disputes the applicants' arguments.

103 Point 37 of the Guidelines, which envisages the non-application of the general methodology for calculating fines provided for by those guidelines, is worded as follows:

'Although these Guidelines present the general methodology for the setting of fines, the particularities of a given case or the need to achieve deterrence in a particular case may justify departing from such methodology or from the limits specified in point 21.'

104 According to settled case-law, in adopting rules of conduct such as the Guidelines and by announcing by publishing them that they will henceforth apply to the cases to which they relate, the Commission imposes a limit on the exercise of its discretion and cannot depart from those rules on pain of being found, where appropriate, to be in breach of general principles of law, such as equal treatment or the protection of legitimate expectations (judgments of 28 June 2005, Dansk Rørindustri and Others v Commission, C 189/02 P, C 202/02 P, C 205/02 P to C 208/02 P and C 213/02 P, EU:C:2005:408, paragraph 211; of 12 December 2012, Ecka Granulate and non ferrum Metallpulver v Commission, T 400/09, not published, EU:T:2012:675, paragraph 40; and of 8 September 2016, Goldfish and Others v Commission, T 54/14, EU:T:2016:455, paragraph 133).

105 It should be noted at the outset that a reduction in the amount of the fine may be granted under point 37 of the Guidelines only in exceptional circumstances when the particularities of a given case or the need to achieve deterrence in a particular case may justify the Commission departing from the general methodology for the calculation of the amount of the fine provided for in those guidelines.

106 The applicants argue in that regard that the particularities of the present case, to be found in the combination of three circumstances which were already set out during the administrative procedure, justified the Commission departing from that methodology. Moreover, the applicants argue in paragraphs 25 to 27 of the reply that the Commission analysed those criteria separately instead of assessing whether the combination of such factors justified recourse to the exception laid down in point 37 of the Guidelines.

102 欧盟委员会对原告的第一项主张提出异议。

103《2006年罚款指南》第37条预设了可以排除适用指南规定的计算罚款数额的一般方法的例外情形，该条规定的原文如下：

"尽管指南提出了计算罚款数额的一般方法，但如果特定案件存在特殊情形，足以使得欧盟委员会排除适用计算罚款数额的一般方法也具有合法性，则可以排除适用；为了使罚款达到威慑作用，确有必要排除适用第21条规定的罚款上限，也可以排除适用罚款上限。"

104 根据以往判例，欧盟委员会通过《2006年罚款指南》等行为规则，并将其公之于众，宣布今后这些规则将适用于相关案件时，就是对其自由裁量权进行了限制，欧盟委员会不能背离这些自己通过的规则，否则会被认定为违反平等待遇或保护合法期待[①]等一般法律原则。（参见判例：2005年6月28日，Dansk Rørindustri and Others v Commission，C 189/02 P，C 202/02 P，C 205/02 P至C 208/02 P和C 213/02 P，EU：C：2005：408，第211段；参见判例：2012年12月12日，Ecka Granulate and non ferrum Metallpulver v Commission，T 400/09，未公开，EU：T：2012：675，第40段；参见判例：2016年9月8日，Goldfish and Others v Commission，T 54/14，EU：T：2016：455，第133段）

105 首先应当指出，只有当某一案件存在特殊情形，或确有必要使罚款达到威慑性，足以使欧盟委员会排除适用计算罚款数额的一般方法具有合法性，欧盟委员会才可能依据《2006年罚款指南》第37条的例外情形排除适用罚款数额计算的一般方法，从而如原告所愿减少罚款数额。

106 对此，原告认为，本案中存在的3种特殊情形（在欧盟委员会查处卡特尔的行政程序中已经提出过），足以使欧盟委员会排除适用计算罚款数额的一般方法具有合法性。此外，原告主张，其在答复函的第25至27段中已经提出，欧盟委员会单独而未综合考虑其提出的3种特殊情形，使其无法满足《2006年罚款指南》第37条规定的例外情形，这一做法是不妥的。

---

① 保护合法期待原则的意思是，基于行政机构或司法机关已经发布生效的相关规定，当事人对其行为将受到的法律制约有心理预期，也有合法的期待。如果行政机构或司法机关背离了自己通过的规定，则会使得当事人的合法期待落空，违背了保护合法期待的一般法律原则。——译者注

107 It is appropriate to examine, in the first place, each circumstance alleged, and, in the second place, those three circumstances invoked by the applicants together.

(1) The fact that the applicants derive the bulk of their revenue from a single product

108 As regards the first circumstance relied on by the applicants, according to which they derive the bulk of their revenue from sales of a single product, namely ODDs, it should be noted, first of all, that, as the Commission maintains, the single product nature of the applicants' business is not relevant for assessing the legality of the calculation of the amount of the fine.

109 It has been held that the Commission is not obliged to take into account, when assessing the gravity of the infringement, the relationship between the total turnover of an undertaking and the turnover produced by the goods which are the subject matter of the infringement (see, to that effect, judgment of 8 July 2008, Saint-Gobain Gyproc Belgium v Commission, T 50/03, not published, EU: T: 2008: 252, paragraph 93). The Commission is therefore not required to take into account the single product nature of the applicants' business in assessing the gravity of the infringement.

110 Similarly, as regards the scale of the infringement on the market and the share of responsibility borne by each cartel participant, it should be noted that the proportion of turnover derived from the goods in respect of which the infringement was committed is likely to give a fair indication of the scale of the infringement on the relevant market (judgment of 7 June 1983, Musique Diffusion française and Others v Commission, 100/80 to 103/80, EU: C: 1983: 158, paragraph 121; see also, to that effect, judgments of 14 May 1998, Mayr-Melnhof v Commission, T 347/94, EU: T: 1998: 101, paragraph 369, and of 8 July 2008, Saint-Gobain Gyproc Belgium v Commission, T 50/03, not published, EU: T: 2008: 252, paragraph 94) and constitutes an objective criterion which gives a proper measure of the harm which the restrictive practice in question does to normal competition (judgment of 11 March 1999, British Steel v Commission, T 151/94, EU: T: 1999: 52, paragraph 643). Therefore, since the proportion of turnover derived from the goods in respect of which the infringement was committed is likely to give a fair indication of the scale of the infringement on the relevant market, the Commission did not misapply the methodology laid down by the Guidelines which provides for the calculation of the amount of the fine on that basis.

107 因此，对于原告所称的本案存在三种特殊情形，本院先依次逐一分析这三种特殊情形，然后再作全面的综合分析。

（1）原告的大部分收入来自单一产品

108 关于原告主张的"第一种特殊情形"，即原告的大部分收入都来自销售单一产品——光盘驱动器。对于原告提出的这一事实，首先应当指出的是，正如欧盟委员会坚持的观点，业务的单一性与评估罚款数额计算方法的合法性无关。

109 根据以往判例，欧盟委员会在评估卡特尔违法行为的严重性时，没有义务考虑企业总营业额与卡特尔行为标的物所生产的营业额之间的关系。（参见判例：2008年7月8日，Saint-Gobain Gyproc Belgium v Commission，T 50/03，未出版，EU：T：2008：252，第93段）因此，欧盟委员会在评估卡特尔行为的严重性时，不必将原告业务的单一性这一因素纳入考量范围。

110 同样，关于卡特尔行为的市场规模和每个卡特尔成员所承担的责任大小的问题，应当指出，某一卡特尔成员从卡特尔行为涉及的产品中获得的营业额比例很可能直观地显示该卡特尔成员在相关市场占据的规模。（参见判例：1983年6月7日，Musique Diffusion française and Others v Commission，100/80至103/80，EU：C：1983：158，第121段；另见判例：1998年5月14日，Mayr-Melnhof v Commission，T 347/94，EU：T：1998：101，第369段和2008年7月8日，Saint-Gobain Gyproc Belgium v Commission，T 50/03，未出版，EU：T：2008：252，第94段）这是衡量相关卡特尔对正常竞争造成损害的一项客观标准。（参见判例：1999年3月11日，British Steel v Commission，T 151/94，EU：T：1999：52，第643段）因此，由于某一卡特尔成员从卡特尔行为涉及的产品中获得的营业额比例很可能直观地显示该卡特尔成员在相关市场占据的规模大小。欧盟委员会使用《2006年罚款指南》所规定的以营业额为基础的一般罚款计算方式并无不妥。

111 Furthermore, without prejudice to the findings that it is for the Court to make in the context of the examination of the claim for variation of the contested decision, it should be noted, as the Commission observes, that the argument that the applicants derive the bulk of their revenue from a single product is also irrelevant to the assessment of whether the Commission wrongly refused to depart from the general methodology for calculating fines under point 37 of the Guidelines.

112 The applicants' strong focus on the development and supply of ODDs and the lesser degree of diversification of their activity compared to other cartel participants cannot suffice, in themselves, to establish that the Commission breached the principles of equality and proportionality by not applying specific criteria for the calculation of the amount of the fine imposed on the applicants. It follows from the case-law that the proportion of the overall turnover deriving from the sale of products in respect of which the infringement in question was committed is best able to reflect the economic importance of that infringement. Consequently, since the applicants derive a particularly large part, if not almost all, of their overall turnover from products which are the subject of the infringement, the fact that the amount of the fine imposed on the applicants represents a higher percentage of overall turnover by comparison with other cartel participants merely reflects the economic importance of that infringement for the applicants. Such a result is not contrary to the principle of equality or proportionality (see, to that effect and by analogy, judgment of 15 December 2016, Infineon Technologies v Commission, T 758/14, not published, EU: T: 2016: 737, paragraph 269, and Opinion of Advocate General Kokott in Pilkington Group and Others v Commission, C 101/15 P, EU: C: 2016: 258, point 100).

113 Nor is this conclusion called into question by the fact that, in the past, the Commission granted reductions in fines on an individual basis, in order to do justice to the characteristics of the business models of individual cartel participants. The Commission's practice in previous decisions, contrary to what is maintained by the applicants, does not serve as a legal framework for imposing fines in competition matters (see, to that effect, judgment of 7 September 2016, Pilkington Group and Others v Commission, C 101/15 P, EU: C: 2016: 631, paragraph 68).

114 Lastly, the applicants argue, contrary to the foregoing, that they do not contest the amount of their fine because it is higher, by reference to their turnover, than that of other undertakings fined. They submit that, in the present case, they are the only companies which continued to operate on the market.

111 此外，关于原告主张的其大部分收入来自单一产品这一主张，只要不影响欧盟的法院对欧盟委员会决定进行合法性审查而查明的事实部分，则正如欧盟委员会所指出的，这一主张与认定欧盟委员会是否错误地适用了罚款数额计算的一般方法①无关。

112 与其他卡特尔成员相比，原告专注于光盘驱动器的开发和供应以及原告业务的多元化程度较弱。但这一事实本身无法证明欧盟委员会适用与其他卡特尔成员一样的一般方法来计算对原告的罚款数额，违反了平等待遇和比例原则。从以往判例可以看出，某一卡特尔成员就其卡特尔行为所涉产品销售额占其所有产品总销售额的比例，最能反映卡特尔行为在该成员整个业务活动中的经济重要性。因此，由于原告的总销售额中有很大一部分（如果不是几乎全部的话）来自卡特尔产品，与其他卡特尔成员相比，其罚款数额占其总营业额的比例更高，恰恰反映了该卡特尔行为对原告的经济影响是至关重要的。这样的结果与平等待遇或比例原则并无矛盾之处。（参见判例：2016年12月15日，Infineon Technologies v Commission，T 758/14，未出版，EU：T：2016：737，第269段，以及Pilkington Group and Others v Commission案中佐审官General Kokott的意见，C 101/15 P，EU：C：2016：258，第100点）

113 原告认为，欧盟委员会在以前的判例中曾经为了公正对待个别卡特尔成员，因其商业模式特点而给予罚款减免。对此，原告对欧盟委员会在本案中的做法提出质疑。本院认为，欧盟委员会在以往决定中的做法并不能在相关竞争法案件中形成一个如何计算罚款的一种法律上的框架。（参见判例：2016年9月7日，Pilkington Group and Others v Commission，C 101/15 P，EU：C：2016：631，第68段）

114 最后，原告又称，与上述主张相反，他们对罚款数额提出异议不是因为从销售额比例来看他们面临的罚款比其他卡特尔成员的更高，而是因为在本案中他们是唯一被罚款后继续在市场上经营的企业。

① 原告认为，本案存在特殊情形，符合《2006年罚款指南》第37条规定“例外”，所以可以排除适用罚款计算的一般方法（按照卡特尔成员的销售额比例来计算罚款数额）。但是欧盟委员会未能采纳原告的主张，而是适用了罚款计算的一般方法。故原告在本次诉讼程序中请求初审法院认定欧盟委员会适用罚款计算的一般方法是错误的。——译者注

115 However, as the Commission observed in the rejoinder, the fact that the applicants are the only companies still operating on the market, which is a matter relating solely to their business strategy, constitutes a factor which the Commission was not required to take into account when calculating the amount of the fine and which could not require the Commission to apply the exception laid down in point 37 of the Guidelines.

116 In those circumstances, it is necessary to reject the applicants' arguments relating to the single product nature of their business.

(2) Continuation of business activities on the ODD market

117 As regards, the second circumstance, according to which the fine imposed on the applicants, close to the 10% cap, severely affected them given that they are the only companies that were fined that decided to continue to operate on the ODD market as a result of which their overall turnover was relatively high, it must be observed, in the first place, that the basic amount of the fine imposed on them was, contrary to what the applicants claim, approximately 8.45% of their overall turnover for 2014 and that that amount was reduced by 50% under the leniency and partial immunity granted in respect of part of the infringement. It must therefore be observed that the total amount of the fine imposed on the applicants is EUR 37 121 000, namely 4.22% of their overall turnover. Consequently, the applicants' argument that the fine which was imposed on them is close to the 10% cap has no basis in fact.

118 In the second place, as is apparent from paragraph 115 above, the fact that they are the only companies that were fined which decided to continue to operate on the ODD market is a matter relating solely to the applicants' business strategy and cannot call into question the legality of the calculation of the amount of the fine.

119 Consequently, those arguments must also be rejected.

115 然而，正如欧盟委员会在答辩状中所指出的，原告是唯一仍在市场上经营的企业这一事实，仅与其商业战略有关，而不构成欧盟委员会在计算罚款数额时应予考虑的因素，更不能成为要求欧盟委员会适用《2006年罚款指南》第37条规定的例外规则的依据。

116 综上所述，本院驳回原告关于其业务单一可以减免罚款的相关主张。

（2） 原告在光盘驱动器市场上的持续经营活动

117 原告主张的“第二种特殊情形”，即对原告处以接近10%上限的罚款，对他们产生了严重影响，因为他们是唯一在被罚款之后仍决定继续在光盘驱动器市场上经营，这才显示出较高的营业额。关于这一点，与原告的主张相反，原告的罚款基数约占其2014年度总营业额的8.45%，且该数额还因欧盟委员会所给予的宽恕豁免而减少了50%。因此必须指出，对原告的罚款总额为37 121 000欧元，仅占其总营业额的4.22%。所以，原告认为对他们罚款接近10%上限的主张没有事实根据。

118 另外，正如上文第115段所述，原告是唯一被罚款后仍决定继续在光盘驱动器市场上经营的企业，这一事实仅与其商业战略有关，而不能成为质疑欧盟委员会罚款数额计算方法合法性的依据。

119 因此，本院驳回原告的上述主张。

（3） Financial difficulties

120 As regards the third circumstance, the applicants allege, first of all, that they rely on their financial difficulties without claiming to bring a request for inability to pay pursuant to point 35 of the Guidelines. Next, they claim that their financial difficulties stem from the fact that the fine had a negative economic impact on two aspects: in the first place, on the plan to restructure their business and, in the second place, on their continuing to operate on the market. Furthermore, the applicants maintain, contrary to what the Commission contends, that they suffered losses on ODD sales during the third and fourth quarters of 2015 because, following the exit from the market of Toshiba Samsung Storage Technology Corp. and Toshiba Samsung Storage Technology Korea Corp.（together, 'TSST'）, they faced increased costs. Lastly, the applicants submit that the reduced ability of an undertaking to pay may be relevant for the application of point 37 of the Guidelines for the purpose of reducing the amount of the fine, independently of the formal inability to pay procedure under point 35 of those guidelines.

121 It must be pointed out that, according to settled case-law, the Commission is not in principle required, when determining the amount of the fine to be imposed for an infringement of the competition rules, to take into account the loss-making financial situation of an undertaking, since recognition of such an obligation would be tantamount to giving an unjustified competitive advantage to undertakings least well adapted to market conditions（judgments of 28 June 2005, Dansk Rørindustri and Others v Commission, C 189/02 P, C 202/02 P, C 205/02 P to C 208/02 P and C 213/02 P, EU: C: 2005: 408, paragraph 327; of 12 December 2012, Ecka Granulate and non ferrum Metallpulver v Commission, T 400/09, not published, EU: T: 2012: 675, paragraph 94; and of 8 September 2016, Goldfish and Others v Commission, T 54/14, EU: T: 2016: 455, paragraph 135）.

122 For that reason, the mere finding that the applicants are in an adverse or loss-making financial situation, due to their restructuring or their continuity on the market, cannot oblige the Commission to uphold a request seeking a reduction of the amount of the fine under point 37 of the Guidelines.

123 It follows that it is necessary to reject the applicants' arguments relating to their adverse financial situation.

（3） 原告面临财务困难

120 原告主张的“第三种特殊情形”是：首先，原告表示他们面临财务困难，但并不主张其存在《2006年罚款指南》第35条规定的无力支付罚款的法定事由。[①]其次，原告表示他们的财务困难是由于罚款造成的，罚款对两个方面产生了负面的经济影响：一是对他们的业务重组计划产生了负面影响；二是对他们在市场上继续经营产生了负面影响。此外，与欧盟委员会的说法相反，原告坚持认为，在2015年第三季度和第四季度，由于东芝三星存储技术公司和东芝三星存储技术韩国公司（以下统称为TSST）退出市场，生产光盘驱动器的成本增加，他们的光盘驱动器销售额下降。最后，原告认为，企业支付能力的降低可能导致适用《2006年罚款指南》第37条从而减少罚款数额，但与《2006年罚款指南》第35条规定的无力支付罚款的法定事由无关。

121 本院认为，根据以往判例，原则上，在确定卡特尔企业的罚款数额时，欧盟委员会没有义务将企业的不良财务状况纳入考量范围，因为如果要求欧盟委员会承担这种义务则意味着给予最不适应市场状况的企业以不正当的竞争优势（参加判例：2005年6月28日，Dansk Rørindustri and Others v Commission，C 189/02 P，C 202/02 P，C 205/02 P至C 208/02 P和C 213/02 P，EU：C：2005：408，第327段；参见判例：2012年12月12日，Ecka Granulate and non-ferrum Metallpulver v Commission，T 400/09，未出版，EU：T：2012：675，第94段；参见判例：2016年9月8日，Goldfish and Others v Commission，T 54/14，EU：T：2016：455，第135段）。

122 因此，仅认定原告确实面临重组或在市场上持续经营而处于不利或亏损的财务状况，并不能要求欧盟委员会采纳原告关于适用《2006年罚款指南》第37条的规定而减少罚款数额的诉求。

123 综上所述，本院驳回原告关于其处于不良财务状况的相关主张。

---

① 关于无力支付罚款的法定事由，详见上文第76段。——译者注

(4) Combination of the three circumstances

124 The applicants take issue with the Commission for having examined the three particular circumstances separately instead of assessing whether the combination of those factors justified the application of the exception provided for in point 37 of the Guidelines. They claim that the combination of those three circumstances distinguishes them from the other companies that were fined, in particular TSST. They maintain, in essence, that it was necessary to continue their activities on the ODD market in order to avoid shortages of supply and possible price increases. That, in their submission, is why they decided to resolve their financial difficulties by taking themselves through a restructuring plan and acquiring new activities.

125 In the present case, it should be noted that the applicants themselves acknowledged that PLDS continued to operate on the ODD market and that that market was in decline. It should be further noted that the applicants have not demonstrated that their withdrawal from the market would have led to shortages of supply to the detriment of consumers.

126 Although it is true that the purpose of the fine imposed is to have the necessary deterrent effect, the fact remains that, according to the Court, Article 101 TFEU also aims, like other competition rules laid down in the TFEU, to protect not only the interests of the competitors or of consumers, but also the structure of the market and, in so doing, competition as such (see, to that effect, judgment of 6 October 2009, GlaxoSmithKline Services and Others v Commission and Others, C 501/06 P, C 513/06 P, C 515/06 P and C 519/06 P, EU: C: 2009: 610, paragraphs 62 to 64).

127 However, the applicants cannot rely, in the present case, on the alleged supply shortages and possible price increases to the detriment of consumers for the purposes of applying the exception laid down in point 37 of the Guidelines. Those circumstances, which are purely hypothetical, cannot be regarded as particular for the purpose of that provision, and, accordingly, are not capable of justifying, in themselves, a reduction of the amount of the fine. The fines imposed on undertakings by the Commission pursuant to Article 23(2) of Regulation No 1/2003 would be deprived of their deterrent effect if such difficulties were automatically to be taken into account.

（4） 综合考量“3种特殊情形”

124 原告称，欧盟委员会单独分开审查上述3种特殊情形而没有综合考量这3种特殊情形叠加在一起的理由，如果综合考虑了这些因素就应该适用《2006年罚款指南》第37条规定的例外条款。对此，原告表示异议。原告声称，将这3种情形加在一起综合考量就可以使他们有别于其他被罚款的企业，特别是TSST。原告坚持认为，从本质上讲，为了避免相关市场上光盘驱动器供应短缺和可能的价格上涨，有必要在光盘驱动器市场上继续经营，所以原告才决定通过重组计划和获得新业务来解决财务困难。

125 在本案中我们应注意，原告承认，除了原告以外，飞利浦建兴数码公司（建兴电子科技股份有限公司和飞利浦公司共同成立的合资公司）仍继续在光盘驱动器市场上经营，即便如此，这一市场正陷入衰退。需要进一步指出的是，原告未提供证据证明他们退出市场会导致光盘驱动器供应短缺，损害消费者利益。

126 诚然，必要的威慑作用确实是罚款的目的之一。但事实上，《欧盟运行条约》第101条与《欧盟运行条约》的其他竞争规则一样，其目标是保护竞争对手或消费者利益、维护市场结构以及促进市场的有效竞争（参见判例：2009年10月6日，GlaxoSmithKline Services and Others v Commission and Others，C 501/06 P，C 513/06 P，C 515/06 P和C 519/06 P，EU：C：2009：610，第62段至第64段）。

127 然而，在本案中，原告并不能证明由于供应短缺或可能的价格上涨将损害消费者利益为由，主张对其适用《2006年罚款指南》第37条的例外条款计算罚款数额。原告提出的理由纯粹是假设的情况，不能被视为《2006年罚款指南》第37条项下的“特殊情形”。因此这些理由不能证明减少罚款数额的合理性。如果不假思索地将这些所谓的困难因素纳入考量范围，欧盟委员会根据《第1/2003号条例》第23条第2款对企业处以罚款的规定将失去其威慑作用。

128 In any event, it should be noted, as the Commission observes, that, in order to identify the relevant factors raised by the applicants for the purposes of calculating the amount of the fine, they should be evaluated separately and those that are irrelevant for the purposes of that calculation should be excluded, in order to avoid any unjustified advantage which could limit the deterrent effect of the fine.

129 Therefore, it should be noted that, as is apparent from paragraphs 108 to 123 above, the Commission was right to take the view that none of the three alleged circumstances was, in the circumstances of the case, relevant for a reduction of the amount of the fine under the exception laid down in point 37 of the Guidelines. Accordingly, the Commission was entitled to conclude that the combination of those circumstances was not capable of changing its assessment.

130 In those circumstances, the first complaint must be rejected as unfounded.

（b） Second complaint: breach of the principles of equality and proportionality of penalties

131 The applicants claim, first, that the application of the 10% cap in cases involving single-product suppliers gives rise to a risk that the Commission will be prevented from differentiating the fines sufficiently among the cartel participants, calling into question the fairness and proportionality of the fines. The applicants maintain that the fine imposed on TSST ought to have been higher than that which was imposed on them, since, although the basic amounts of those fines were very similar, the applicants benefited from particular circumstances, notably the reduction of their fine by 50% under the leniency granted by the Commission.

132 They claim, second, that the fact that they continued their activities on the ODD market in spite of their financial difficulties ought to have been taken into account by the Commission for the purposes of sufficiently 'personalising' the fines imposed on the companies concerned, thus avoiding a proportionality issue. They contend in that regard that a further reduction of their fine under point 37 of the Guidelines would restore the gap between the amount of their fine and the amount of the fine imposed on TSST in such a way that the reduction granted to them under the Leniency Notice would be appropriately reflected.

133 The Commission disputes those assertions and maintains that the applicants rely on a flawed interpretation of the case-law of the Courts of the European Union.

128 值得注意的是，正如欧盟委员会所指出的，为了审查原告为减少罚款数额而提出的各种相关因素，应当逐一分别对这些因素进行评估，并排除那些与计算罚款数额无关的因素，以避免出现任何可能削弱罚款威慑作用的不当利好。

129 因此，从上文第108段至第123段可以明显看出，欧盟委员会适用法律正确。本案中，原告所称的“3种特殊情形”都与《2006年罚款指南》第37条项下可以减少罚款数额的特殊情形无关。因此，欧盟委员会有权得出结论，综合原告所称的“3种特殊情形”并不能改变其罚款数额计算结果。

130 综上所述，原告的第1项理由缺乏依据，本院予以驳回。

（b） 第2项主张：欧盟委员会违反平等待遇和比例原则

131 原告声称，首先，在涉及单一产品供应商的案例中适用10%的罚款上限会导致欧盟委员会无法有区别地对卡特尔成员处以罚款。①这将引起对欧盟委员会的罚款是否符合平等待遇和比例原则的质疑。原告坚持认为，对TSST所处的罚款应该高于对原告所处的罚款，因为尽管他们的罚款基数非常相近，但原告的罚款数额因欧盟委员会的宽恕豁免而得以减少50%。

132 其次，原告认为，欧盟委员会应当考虑到他们尽管面临财务困难，但仍在光盘驱动器市场上继续营业的事实，使罚款能体现出足够的区分度，从而避免违反比例原则。最后，他们还称，如果根据《2006年罚款指南》第37条的规定进一步减少其罚款数额，将缩小其罚款数额与TSST的罚款数额之间的差距，从而突出其获得的宽恕豁免的作用。①

133 欧盟委员会对原告的这些主张有异议，并认为原告所依据的是对欧盟法院以往判例错误的解释。

---

① 基于卡特尔成员在卡特尔中的作用不同，产生的限制竞争影响也不同，所以根据其轻重程度有区别地处以罚款，这是比例原则的要义。原告在本案中认为欧盟委员会没能体现出足够的区分度，所以指责欧盟委员会违反了比例原则。——译者注

134 In the first place, it should be observed that, as is apparent from Sections 8.3 to 8.5 of the contested decision, all of the adjustments made to reflect the individual gravity of the infringement, the duration of the applicants' participation in the cartel and their role in the cartel were taken into account by the Commission in calculating the amount of the applicants' fine.

135 Admittedly, although it is true that the fine imposed on the applicants is the second highest among the companies which were fined — despite the fact that this amount was reduced by 50% under the Leniency Notice, unlike for the other undertakings that were also fined — the reason why the applicants received that fine is because they had a much higher turnover for a longer period. Since the proportion of the overall turnover deriving from the sale of products in respect of which the infringement was committed is best able to reflect the economic importance of that infringement (see, to that effect, judgment of 23 April 2015, LG Display and LG Display Taiwan v Commission, C 227/14 P, EU: C: 2015: 258, paragraph 55), the fact that the applicants received a larger fine than that of the other cartel participants, even if the amount of the fine was reduced by 50% under the Leniency Notice, merely reflects the economic significance and the duration of their own participation in the infringement at issue (see paragraph 112 above).

136 Furthermore, as is apparent from paragraph 129 above, the Commission was right to find that the circumstances invoked by the applicants cannot constitute particular circumstances or circumstances which are necessary to achieve a specific level of deterrence for the purpose of point 37 of the Guidelines. In addition, it should be noted that, as is apparent from the previous paragraph, the fine imposed on the applicants reflects the economic importance and the duration of their own participation in the infringement and, consequently, a reduction based on the alleged circumstances would only limit its deterrent effect and would be contrary to the applicable rules, thus favouring the applicants.

137 In the second place, it should be noted that the limit of 10% of turnover, provided for in Article 23 (2) of Regulation No 1/2003, seeks to prevent fines being imposed which it is foreseeable that the undertakings, owing to their size, as determined by their total turnover, will not be able to pay. The fact that TSST benefited from that limit when it came to determining the amount of its fine (recital 572 of the contested decision) and that that limit has reduced the gap between the fine imposed on TSST and the fine imposed on the applicants cannot affect the legality of the contested decision in the light of the principles of proportionality and equality. Moreover, the Commission merely applied to the TSST companies the rule stipulated in the applicable competition rules regarding the maximum amount of the fine that can be imposed on the undertakings participating in the infringement.

134 本院认为，首先，应该注意到的是，从欧盟委员会决定第8.3节至第8.5节可以明显看出，欧盟委员会在计算原告罚款数额时，已经充分考量了所有反映原告违法行为严重程度、参与卡特尔的持续时间以及在卡特尔中的作用等因素，并根据这些因素调整了罚款数额。

135 诚然，在被罚款的企业中，对原告的罚款数额是第二高的——尽管与其他同样被罚款的企业不同，该罚款数额是根据宽恕政策已经减少了50%以后的数额——但这是由原告参与卡特尔的时间更长导致产生更高的营业额所造成的。由于卡特尔行为所涉产品产生的总营业额比例最能反映该卡特尔行为的经济重要性。（参见判例：2015年4月23日，LG Display and LG Display Taiwan v Commission，C 227/14 P，EU：C：2015：258，第55段）尽管已经依据宽恕豁免而减少了50%，原告的罚款数额仍较其他卡特尔成员更高的事实，恰恰反映了其卡特尔行为的经济重要性和持续时间（见上文第112段）

136 此外，从上文第129段可以明显看出，欧盟委员会正确地认定了原告所主张的"特殊情形"不能被视为《2006年罚款指南》第37条项下可以适用罚款例外的"特殊情形"。并且，从上一段可以明显看出，对原告的罚款数额反映了其卡特尔行为的经济重要性和其自身参与卡特尔的持续时间。因此，仅根据原告所主张的情形就减少对原告的罚款数额，将限制罚款带来的威慑作用，与所应适用的规则相矛盾，使原告获得不当利好。

137 其次，《第1/2003号条例》第23条第2款规定罚款数额不得超过营业额10%的上限是为了防止卡特尔成员企业由于可预见的规模（由其总营业额确定）因素而无力支付罚款。基于该上限规定，TSST的罚款数额被降低了。但是TSST在被罚款时受益于该上限规定（欧盟委员会决定第572段），以及由此导致缩小了TSST罚款数额与原告罚款数额之间的差距这一事实，并不影响欧盟委员会决定在遵循比例原则和平等待遇原则上的合法性。更何况，欧盟委员会仅是对TSST适用了竞争规则中对卡特尔成员企业可处最高罚款上限的规定而已。

138 In those circumstances, it must be held that the fine imposed on the applicants does not infringe the principles of equality and proportionality of penalties.

139 Consequently, in so far as it is put forward in support of the claim for annulment, the second complaint must be rejected and, consequently, the second plea must be rejected in its entirety.

140 Accordingly, since none of the pleas of the application is capable of resulting in the annulment in part of the contested decision, that claim for annulment must be rejected.

B. The claim for variation of the contested decision

141 As a preliminary point, it should be noted, on the one hand, that the first plea, alleging breach of the principle of sound administration and of the obligation to state reasons cannot, in any event, lead the Court to vary the contested decision. Indeed, even if the Commission wrongly failed to explain why it did not accept the applicants' request to apply point 37 of the Guidelines or failed to pass that request on to the Advisory Committee and the College of Commissioners, the Court's finding of those irregularities could lead, where applicable, only to the annulment of the contested decision, but, under no circumstances, to a reduction in the amount of the fine imposed on the applicants. Consequently, in so far as it is put forward in support of the claim for variation, that plea is ineffective. Moreover, as is apparent from the considerations set out in paragraphs 68 to 96 above, the applicants have not established that the Commission committed a breach of the obligation to state reasons or the principle of good administration.

142 On the other hand, as regards the second plea, it should be observed that, as is apparent from paragraphs 101 to 138 above, the Commission did not commit an error of law or an error of assessment in considering that it was not appropriate, in the present case, to apply point 37 of the Guidelines and to depart from the methodology laid down in those guidelines when calculating the amount of the applicants' fine.

143 Nevertheless, it should be borne in mind that, as regards the review carried out by the European Union judicature in respect of Commission decisions on competition matters, the unlimited jurisdiction authorises the competent court to vary the contested measure, even without annulling it, by taking into account all of the factual circumstances, so as to amend the amount of the fine (judgment of 9 September 2015, Panasonic and MT Picture Display v Commission, T 82/13, EU: T: 2015: 612, paragraph 155).

138 在这种情况下，必须认定对原告所处的罚款并不违反平等待遇和比例原则。

139 因此，原告请求撤销欧盟委员会决定的第2项主张亦应予以驳回。由此，原告的第2项理由应予全部驳回。

140 综上所述，原告提出的所有理由，没有任何一项足以支持原告关于撤销欧盟委员会决定的诉请，故本院驳回原告的该项诉请。

B.请求变更欧盟委员会决定的罚款数额

141 原告的诉请是请求初审法院变更欧盟委员会决定中对原告的罚款数额。首先应该强调的是，一方面，原告为支持其诉请而提出的第一项理由：欧盟委员会违反了良好行政原则和未履行说明理由的义务。从这点来看，在任何情况下都不能导致初审法院变更欧盟委员会决定中对原告的罚款数额。事实上，即使欧盟委员会未能解释其为何不接受原告关于适用《2006年罚款指南》第37条例外条款而减轻罚款，或者未能将该减轻罚款的申请转交给咨询委员会和欧盟委员会的委员们征求意见。即便是初审法院认为欧盟委员会违反了规定，也只能是撤销欧盟委员会的决定，而不会减少对原告的罚款数额。因此，原告为了支持其关于请求初审法院变更罚款数额而提出的理由是一种无效的理由。更何况，从上文第68段至第96段的论证可以明显看出，原告未能进 步证明欧盟委员会未履行说明理由的义务或违反良好行政原则。

142 另一方面，关于原告为支持其诉请提出的第二项理由——欧盟委员会法律适用错误。但是，从上文第101段至第138段可以明显看出，欧盟委员会在本案中未采纳原告关于依据《2006年罚款指南》第37条的例外条款而排除适用计算罚款数额的一般方法，而是适用一般方法计算对原告的罚款数额。欧盟委员会的这一做法不存在法律适用错误。这部分说明尤其重要。

143 必须强调的是，当欧盟司法机关对欧盟委员会关于竞争事项的决定进行合法性审查时，如果认为欧盟委员会的决定无须全部撤销，则司法机关才有权行使罚款数额裁量权，并可以基于案件具体情况变更罚款数额。（参见判例：2015年9月9日，Panasonic and MT Picture Display v Commission，T 82/13，EU：T：2015：612，第155段）

144 In the present case, it is therefore necessary to examine whether the circumstances relied on by the applicants under the second plea may, even in the absence of an error of law or an error of assessment committed by the Commission, justify the Court's reducing the amount of the fine imposed on the applicants by the contested decision.

145 As regards, in the first place, the particular circumstances in support of their request that the Commission reduce the amount of the fine and which are invoked in the context of the first complaint, it should be noted, first of all, as was observed in paragraphs 110 to 112 above, that the proportion of turnover derived from the goods in respect of which the infringement was committed is likely to give a fair indication of the scale of the infringement on the relevant market and its economic importance for the applicants' activities. Consequently, the principles of equality and proportionality do not justify a reduction in the amount of the fine imposed on the applicants, on the ground that, because of the single product nature of their business, the amount of the fine imposed on them represents a higher percentage of their total turnover by comparison with other cartel participants.

146 Next, the applicants' decision to continue to operate on the ODD market does not justify a reduction in the percentage of the overall turnover that ought to serve as a basis for calculating the amount of the fine. Indeed, as has been pointed out in paragraph 118 above, that decision is a matter relating solely to the applicants' business strategy. Moreover, as was observed by the Commission in the rejoinder (paragraph 62), the applicants' market share rose from 25% in 2011 to 39.5% in the fourth quarter of 2015 and they have therefore benefited from the reduced competition. Moreover, nothing justifies, in the light of the principles of proportionality and equality, a reduction of the amount of the fine being applied to companies which remained active on the market to the detriment of those that withdrew from it. Such a practice might, moreover, weaken the deterrent effect of the fines.

147 Lastly, as regards the applicants' financial difficulties, it should be observed that, as the applicants have stated, they do not claim an inability to pay within the meaning of point 35 of the Guidelines. Furthermore, it is not apparent from the documents before the Court that their financial difficulties would, in the present case, constitute a particularity justifying, by way of exception, that that circumstance be taken into account in calculating the amount of the fine imposed on the applicants, even though they do not claim to be in a situation in which they are unable to pay. Moreover, the applicants do not contest that, as the Commission noted in the defence, they were supported by their parent companies and that, even though they expected a reduction in their profits in 2015, their business remained profitable. The applicants have therefore not established that the amount of the fine imposed on them is a source of financial difficulties for them such that, in the light of the principles of equality and proportionality, they are in a special situation which justifies that amount being reduced.

144 在本案中，即使欧盟委员会不存在法律适用上的错误或事实评估错误，本案仍然审查了原告的第2项理由所提出的情形是否足以使初审法院有理由减少欧盟委员会决定中对其罚款的数额。

145 第一，关于上述提及的原告声称欧盟委员会应据以减少其罚款数额的特殊情形是否成立。首先，如上文第110段至第112段所述，某一卡特尔成员企业从卡特尔行为所涉及的产品中获得的营业额的比例很可能直观地显示卡特尔行为在相关市场上的规模及其对原告活动的经济重要性。因此，原告主张基于其业务的单一性，与其他卡特尔成员相比，其所受罚款数额与总营业额之间的比例更高，因此应该适用平等待遇和比例原则减少对其罚款数额，这一理由是不能成立的。

146 其次，原告被罚款后决定继续在光盘驱动器市场上经营的事实，并不能成为降低罚款比例（欧盟委员会决定作出前一营业年度原告总营业额的一定比例作为罚款基数）的理由。事实上，正如上文第118段所指出的，这一决定仅与原告的商业战略有关。更何况，如欧盟委员会在答辩书第62段中所述，原告的市场份额从2011年的25%上升到2015年第四季度的39.5%，可见他们从卡特尔导致的市场竞争力削弱中受益。此外，根据比例原则和平等待遇原则，如果减少在市场上仍然活跃企业的罚款数额，将损害那些退出该市场的企业的利益，这是不合理的。而且这种做法还可能削弱罚款带来的威慑作用。

147 最后，关于原告声称的其面临财务困难。应当指出，如原告所述，他们并不主张存在《2006年罚款指南》第35条规定的无力支付罚款的法定事由。此外，尽管原告不主张存在无力支付罚款的情形，但从提交给本院的资料也不能明显地得出，原告所谓的财务困难在本案中构成一种特殊情形，并且成为计算对其罚款数额时应考量的因素。更何况，正如欧盟委员会在答辩状中指出而原告也并不否认的，他们得到了母公司的支持，而且尽管他们预计2015年利润会减少，但他们的业务仍然是盈利的。因此，原告未能证明罚款是导致他们财务困难的原因，不能根据平等待遇和比例原则减少对其罚款数额。

148 It should be added that, although the applicants submit that the combination of the three circumstances set out in the context of the first complaint must be assessed in order to determine whether there are grounds for a reduction of the amount of their fine, it does not appear that such a combination — given that each of those circumstances, taken by itself, is not capable of justifying such a reduction — constitutes a particularity which is capable of altering the assessment of the Court in that regard.

149 As regards, in the second place, the arguments relating to the insufficient 'personalisation' of penalties owing to the application of the 10% cap on turnover, relied upon in support of the second complaint, it should first of all be recalled that, as has been noted in paragraph 137 above, the mere fact that the application of the 10% cap to TSST had the effect of reducing the gap between the amount of the fine imposed on TSST and the amount of the fine imposed on the applicants cannot, in itself, justify a reduction of the applicants' fine in order to make it fair and proportionate. Indeed, that result is merely the consequence of the substantial differences in turnover between the two companies, which is exactly what the application of the 10% cap allows to take into account.

150 However, the applicants argue, relying on the case-law derived from the judgment of 16 June 2011, Putters v Commission (T 211/08, EU:T:2011:289, paragraph 75), that the Court should exercise its unlimited jurisdiction since, in the present case, the application of the Guidelines does not allow for appropriate differentiation of the fines imposed, in particular, between the applicants and TSST.

151 In the present case, as is apparent from paragraphs 134 to 136 above, the Court cannot apply a different method of calculation to the applicants on the ground that it is appropriate to differentiate sufficiently the amount of their fine from that of the fines imposed on the other undertakings that were fined, as this differentiation is not necessary and would provide an unfair competitive advantage to the applicants by reducing the deterrent effect of their fine. As regards the calculation of the amount of the fine, there cannot, by the application of different methods of calculation, be any discrimination between the undertakings which have participated in an agreement or a concerted practice contrary to Article 101(1) TFEU (see, to that effect, judgment of 19 July 2012, Alliance One International and Standard Commercial Tobacco v Commission and Commission v Alliance One International and Others, C 628/10 P and C 14/11 P, EU:C:2012:479, paragraph 58 and the case-law cited).

148 另外，尽管原告认为必须对其提出的三种“特殊情形”进行综合评估，以确定是否有理由减少其罚款数额。但鉴于每种情形就其本身而言，都不能证明减少罚款数额具有合理性，所以也无法得出综合这3种情形可以让初审法院改变欧盟委员会的决定。

149 第二，关于原告第二项理由所提出的将营业额10%作为罚款上限使得罚款对各卡特尔成员的区分度不足的观点。[①]如上文第137段所述，对TSST适用10%的上限缩小了对TSST的罚款数额与对原告的罚款数额之间的差距，这一事实本身并不能证明降低原告的罚款数额就符合平等待遇原则和比例原则。事实上，这一结果仅是两家公司之间的营业额存在的巨大差异造成的，而这正是应用10%上限时所允许考量的因素。[①]

150 原告又主张，依据欧盟法院于2011年6月16日对“Putters公司诉欧盟委员会案”(T 211/08, EU: T: 2011: 289，第75段)作出的判例所确定的规则，基于本案中《2006年罚款指南》的适用未能对卡特尔成员，尤其是原告与TSST之间的罚款进行区分，所以请求初审法院行使罚款数额裁量权减少对原告的罚款数额。

151 本案中，如上文第134段至第136段所述，初审法院不能以为了更好地对原告的罚款与对其他卡特尔成员企业的罚款作出区分为由，对原告采用不同的罚款计算方法，因为这种区分是没有必要的，并且如果这样做将使得罚款的威慑作用减弱，反而赋予了原告以不公平的竞争优势。在罚款数额的计算上，不能通过采用不同的计算方法来歧视任何一个违反《欧盟运行条约》第101条第1款规定而参与价格协定或协同行动的卡特尔企业。(参见判例：2012年7月19日，Alliance One International and Standard Commercial Tobacco v Commission and Commission v Alliance One International and Others, C 628/10 P和C 14/11 P, EU: C: 2012: 479，第58段和引用的判例)

① 如前文所述，欧盟委员会基于10%罚款上限而减轻了TSST的罚款数额，客观上缩小了原告的罚款数额与TSST罚款数额的差距，原告认为这样做是不对的，使卡特尔成员之间的区分度不足，违反了比例原则，原告称为了遵循比例原则，也应该相应地降低原告的罚款，使得卡特尔成员之间的差距回到基于10%上限而降低TSST罚款之前的水平。——译者注

152 In those circumstances, it must be held that none of the circumstances relied on by the applicants justify the Court exercising its unlimited jurisdiction by reducing the amount of the fine, in particular on the basis of point 37 of the Guidelines.

153 The claim for variation must therefore be rejected and, consequently, the action must be dismissed in its entirety.

Costs

154 Under Article 134(1) of the Rules of Procedure, the unsuccessful party is to be ordered to pay the costs if they have been applied for in the successful party's pleadings. Since the Commission has applied for costs and the applicants have been unsuccessful, the latter must be ordered to bear their own costs and to pay those incurred by the Commission.

On those grounds, THE GENERAL COURT (Fifth Chamber)

Hereby:

1. Dismisses the action;

2. Orders Hitachi-LG Data Storage, Inc. and Hitachi-LG Data Storage Korea, Inc. to bear their own costs and pay the costs incurred by the European Commission.

152 因此，本院认为，原告所主张的任何情形都不足以支持本院行使罚款数额裁量权来重新评估原告的罚款数额，特别是不能根据《2006年罚款指南》第37条的例外规定而减少对原告的罚款数额。

153 综上所述，本院驳回原告关于变更欧盟委员会决定中罚款数额的诉请。由此，原告的所有诉请均予以驳回。

诉讼费用

154 根据《欧盟法院程序规则》第134条第1款的规定，如胜诉方请求由败诉方承担诉讼费用，则应判令败诉方承担胜诉方的诉讼费用。由于欧盟委员会已就此提出请求，而原告也败诉，因此本院判决由原告承担自己的诉讼费用并支付欧盟委员会发生的诉讼费用。

综上所述，本院（第五法庭）判决如下：

1.驳回原告全部诉讼请求；

2.原告日立乐金数据存储有限公司和日立乐金数据存储韩国有限公司自行承担诉讼费用并支付欧盟委员会发生的诉讼费用。

后　记

《欧盟竞争法经典案例》第4辑在今年疫情期间完成了校对、编译工作。禁足在家无处可去，研读欧盟判例也可以排遣每天焦虑的心情。在写后记的今天（4月8日）武汉解封了，这是一个值得纪念的日子。

这些判例都是近年来一边上课一边讨论积累起来的。第4辑收入2016年欧盟法院判决的5个案件和2019年欧盟初审法院审理的1个案件。这些案件涉及欧盟的宽恕政策、罚款豁免的具体标准、罚款基数的计算方法、罚款时效对母公司责任的影响、欧盟与成员国对管控烟草产品价格的法律解释，以及欧盟委员会在查处卡特尔程序中的行政合法性问题。2019年的这个案例是新加的，因为这个案例跟我们之前翻译的几个卡特尔案例不同。为了对比不同之处，我们把它放在这辑里。这个案件涉及欧盟法中一个有意思的词——良好行政原则。该案中原告指出，欧盟委员会没有就他们关于排除适用计算罚款数额一般方法的申请向咨询委员会或欧盟委员会的委员们征求意见，而征求意见是作出罚款决定前的重要程序。原告提出本案存在特殊情形而向欧盟委员会申请减轻罚款数额，欧盟委员会没有将此申请向咨询委员会征求意见，这就违反良好行政原则。所以，初审法院在审理中要证明欧盟委员会在查处卡特尔的行政程序中是否“足够勤勉”。本案中，初审法院在论证欧盟委员会“足够勤勉”时例举了大量的事实，通过程序上的审核、事实上的论证以证明欧盟委员会未违反良好行政原则。初审法院的说理部分使我们对欧盟法的逻辑和法理有了进一步的认识。可见，翻译案例并不是简单地把案例故事告诉大家，而是通过案例体会到法官们对欧盟法的理解，以及他们用什么方法来进行法律逻辑推理，阐述法律思想，体现欧盟法的精神。这是翻译案例带来的另一个收获。

我的研究生朱玥、应嘉毅、胡海龙、郭清宇、李彦龙和游昕雨参加了翻译工作。第一次的翻译初稿几乎无法读下去。我和研究生们一起研读、讨论、修改，经过三次以上的修改，他们大致了解了这些案例的前因后果。有一个学生毕业后去一家国际律所工作，恰好工作内容涉及欧盟竞争法规则。他兴冲冲地告诉我，之前的翻译对他帮助很大，现在他对这些工作可以得心应手了。我听后很高兴，有一种成就感。其实，翻译案例是烧脑的活儿，我们不仅要找到不同语言之间的转化模式，更重要的是我们要领悟不同法律文化所传递的法律思想。我们既要学会不同法律语境下的思维方式，还要在我们的语境下用自己的语言表达出来。我一直感叹，我们的学生除了学习专业外，更应该学好语文。

感谢戴娜同学，她始终有一颗初心。她在法院工作，但她对翻译案例具有一种偏爱和执着，这是难能可贵的。她不仅协助我校对了每一个案例，而且还查阅了很多类似案例进行比较分析。她在工作之余埋头于这些案例校对，我们在一起讨论案例时她总有灵感和火花。

我的好友刘丽君女士始终是我的后盾。她在美国工作了20多年，中英文俱佳。我有任何疑难问题，她都会一一解答。没有她的帮助，我很难坚持编完手头上的三本书。

第4辑的出版还要感谢法律出版社的沈小英女士，她看了我的写作计划后慷慨地说，我们可以出。在她的鼓励下我又重新开始第3辑、第4辑和第5辑的编译工作。感谢张泽华女士，她认真审阅了书稿，对书稿中的细小错误都一一提出修改意见。她对本职工作真的"足够勤勉"了，我们很感动。

第4辑马上要出版了，写了以上这些闲话算是后记吧。囿于我们的学识水平，翻译中的错误在所难免，敬请读者批评指正。

林燕萍

2020年4月8日于上海

图书在版编目(CIP)数据

欧盟竞争法经典案例. 第4辑 : 汉英对照 / 林燕萍编译. -- 北京 : 法律出版社, 2020

ISBN 978-7-5197-4460-1

Ⅰ. ①欧… Ⅱ. ①林… Ⅲ. ①欧洲联盟-反不正当竞争法-案例-汉、英 Ⅳ. ①D950.229

中国版本图书馆CIP数据核字(2020)第067664号

欧盟竞争法经典案例(第4辑)
OUMENG JINGZHENGFA JINGDIAN ANLI(DI-4 JI)

林燕萍 编译

策划编辑 沈小英
责任编辑 沈小英 张泽华
装帧设计 李 瞻

出版 法律出版社
总发行 中国法律图书有限公司
经销 新华书店
印刷 固安华明印业有限公司
责任校对 晁明慧
责任印制 吕亚莉

编辑统筹 法治与经济出版分社
开本 710毫米×1000毫米 1/16
印张 21.25
字数 371千
版本 2020年7月第1版
印次 2020年7月第1次印刷

法律出版社/北京市丰台区莲花池西里7号(100073)
网址/www.lawpress.com.cn
投稿邮箱/info@lawpress.com.cn
举报维权邮箱/jbwq@lawpress.com.cn
销售热线/400-660-8393
咨询电话/010-63939796

中国法律图书有限公司/北京市丰台区莲花池西里7号(100073)
全国各地中法图分、子公司销售电话:
统一销售客服/400-660-8393/6393
第一法律书店/010-83938432/8433 西安分公司/029-85330678 重庆分公司/023-67453036
上海分公司/021-62071639/1636 深圳分公司/0755-83072995

书号:ISBN 978-7-5197-4460-1 **定价**:98.00元
(如有缺页或倒装,中国法律图书有限公司负责退换)